PRAISE FOR
ROD KANE'S
VETERAN'S DAY

"Kane gives an *Apocalypse Now* style account . . . of just how senseless life on the battlefield was, and how life after the war never can be the same . . . [a] howl of pain and frustration with a clarity that burns."
—*Los Angeles Times*

"Provocatively written . . . An inspired piece of work . . . Kane writes about the war and the ensuing two decades of his life in a relentless style that's propelled by manic bursts of dialogue. . . . There also is a great deal of pain in these pages."
—*Washington Post Book World*

"This is the best memoir that I've read since [Robert] Mason's *Chickenhawk*. Undoubtedly Kane gets the joke: The war will kill us if it takes the rest of our lives."

—Larry Heinemann,
author of the 1987
National Book Award winner
Paco's Story

"Rod Kane writes well enough to put sweat on your palms."

—*Newsweek*

(more . . .)

VETERAN'S DAY

A Combat Odyssey

ROD KANE

POCKET BOOKS

New York   London   Toronto   Sydney   Tokyo   Singapore

POCKET BOOKS, a division of Simon & Schuster Inc.
1230 Avenue of the Americas, New York, NY 10020

ISBN: 0-671-72523-8

First Pocket Books printing January 1991

10 9 8 7 6 5 4 3 2 1

To fathers and brothers,
uncles and sons,
nephews and cousins,
men with no one.

Prologue

I AM A BOOMER. I DIDN'T KNOW IT AT THE TIME, BUT THEN, none of the others did either. Everyone starts out on square one.

Boomers came about as a result of the end of World War II, when our moms and dads could sleep with each other again. Some dads never saw us. A few moms never did either. We are the spoils of war.

We are the baby boom, protected from the enemy by the atomic boom and its mushroom cloud. We are bundled in bunting, cuddly-cute in our carriages, as if to say, "Yes, Virginia, there is life after war, just look at all these little boomers."

We little boomers take our seats in the peanut gallery. "Stand straight. Sit down. Stay in line, for god's sake, there are so many of you." We boomers begin to stray from square one.

The baby boom arrived in time to hear the sonic boom. Hear it rattle the storm windows. See it shake the swing. Watch it roll the TV picture, interrupting the commercial boom, but not the war in Korea.

Uncle Paul was a paratrooper in Korea. When he came back, he couldn't tie his shoes. He always had a cigarette in his mouth. He died soon after I met him.

I was raised to be a soldier of Christ. I saluted the flag every morning in school. The Memorial Day parade was always proud and gay. Nana would say, "Everyone is out of step but my boys." The man on TV would say, "This week the Camel Cigarette Company is sending one hundred cartons of cigarettes to the Veterans Administration Hospital in Nashville, Tennessee."

"Dad, did Uncle Paul smoke Camel cigarettes?"

"Uncle Paul is dead."

"I know, but did he smoke Camels?"

"No, he smoked Hit Parades."

"Oh."

There is a pause for a moment as the little boomer sorts out his little boomer thoughts about his great boomer future.

"Dad?"

Quiet.

"Dad?"

"What, son?"

"If I get to be a soldier of Christ and I go to war, can I smoke cigarettes?"

"We went to war so you won't have to go to war, son."

"Oh. Does that mean that when I grow up I can't smoke cigarettes because there isn't a war?"

"You can smoke cigarettes anywhere but in church or school."

"Oh boy! I hope when I become a soldier of Christ I get wounded so I can be sent to a Vetrin's Ministration hospital and smoke free cigarettes!"

The boomers grow up as taxes go up. The mushroom cloud that is supposed to protect us sends everyone scurrying into fallout shelters as the big sirens wail, "This is a test. This is only a test. In the event of a real emergency. . . ." We hide under our desks at school.

Saturday morning television is something to look forward to all week long. There is mild discomfort on that morning because Dad barfed up most of his beer after watching the Friday night fights. Mom said she would be damned if she was going to clean it up.

"Okay, Mom, I'll clean it up, but first . . . how come the Cisco Kid talks funny?"

"Who?"

"The Cisco Kid and Pancho. They're on TV. They talk funny."

"Oh. You mean the Mexicans who live in the south."

"Are they like the Confederates?"

"No, they're Catholics, like us."

The first boomer year of 1946 was followed by banner boomer years and I was "blessed" with three brothers and a sister. The older two followed me everywhere. We became half of any football team in the neighborhood. They both wanted to be soldiers of Christ and smoke cigarettes too.

"Ah, could I have a pack of Camels, please?"

"They aren't for you, are they?"

"Naw, they're for my Uncle Paul."

"Okay, twenty-five cents."

We boomers swelled the hallways at school and I became a lieutenant on the Safety Patrol. Then I got kicked off for fighting.

We represent ourselves at church as dapper boomer brothers. I line up outside the confessional every Saturday evening to shed my weekly sins so I can be counted in Christ's ranks as we file to the Communion rail on Sunday morning. I come to realize that quite a few boomers don't believe in what we believe. Some boomers don't even want to be soldiers of Christ. I wonder if the Mexicans want to be soldiers of Christ. I hope the Cisco Kid is on our side.

Disneyland is the home for us Mouseketeer boomers. When we outgrow our ears we move to Philadelphia to

3

be close to "American Bandstand." Girl boomers start to grow out as boy boomers get a tingling sensation.

"Roddie, are you still in the bathroom?"

"I'm not doin' nothin'."

Boy boomers realize there are girl boomers. Girl boomers realize that boy boomers are usually a day late and a dollar short. That doesn't stop boy boomers from bragging about everything, from "copping feels" to "blue balls."

High school is where the boomer business gets serious. We have our own money to spend because we mow lawns, deliver newspapers or baby-sit. We tune in to the radio man and he tells us how to spend our money. We go to record hops. We cut our fingers on pop tops.

All of a sudden we are the class of '64. Time flies even if you aren't having fun. Time drags when you are recuperating from a beer bust hangover. By now every boomer has had to plan which square to move to next. A few would just as soon go back to square one. A few others would be happy hanging around the high school square. There are college squares. Town squares. City squares, and hang-around-the-house squares. There are farm squares, family business squares and "I'm gonna have lots of babies" squares. Finally, there's the "I'm going in the army" square.

With a dim view of the world, outside of pop tops and record hops, this boomer doesn't see too many squares open to him. So with his Camel cigarettes, memories of Uncle Paul and draft obligations, he heads down to his local army recruiter.

"Hi. I'm Sergeant Hartmann."

"Yes, sir. I'm Rod Kane, Uncle Paul's nephew. I hear I'm going to be drafted if I don't get off the street corners, so I came by to see what you got."

"Well, Mr. Kane, we have various plans. Did you say you were being drafted?"

"No. I'm not eighteen yet. But, just in case I do get drafted, or have to get out of here . . ."

"You aren't in any kind of trouble, are you?"

"Well, I'm not going to graduate with the rest of my class. There isn't much room left at home. Mom says there's too many mouths to feed. I've been working since I was fourteen . . . anyways, what you got?"

"I see. Sounds familiar. Here. Fill this out now, before you leave. I need to see your birth certificate. Do you have it with you?"

"No, sir, but I can get it."

"Complete that, in your own hand. Come back to see me in a week, with your birth certificate."

"I'd like to be in the infantry, like my Uncle Paul. He was a paratrooper."

A week later:

"Okay, Mr. Kane. The police clearance form you filled out came up clean. You didn't need to put down that you were a lieutenant on the Safety Patrol, so I crossed that out. It doesn't hurt that you don't have any experience. Now, I hope this is your birth certificate."

"Yes, sir."

"You don't have to call me sir. You can just call me Sergeant Hartmann."

"Yes, Sergeant Hartmann."

"So, let's see. Born June 25, 1946. The first year of the baby boom. Eighteen in another three weeks. So. What do you want? Infantry?"

"Well, I've had a week to think about it, maybe I could do something like save people, like medics."

"Yes, that's no problem."

"And still be a paratrooper?"

"Depends."

"On what?"

"Well, you'll be at draft age soon."

"Yes, well, I'll serve my two years."

"And you can volunteer for the draft before you're drafted."

"I can?"

"But there's one hitch."

"Huh?"

"I can't guarantee you medic's school on two years of active duty."

"Oh."

"Look, Kane. Here's what we got. You get drafted, you serve two years as what and where we tell you. Volunteer the draft, I still cannot guarantee you anything. You do and say as we please. Then, after you get out, you have to serve two years' active reserve, meeting every month, two-week summer camp, and then two years' inactive reserve to fulfill your six-year obligation."

"Oh."

"Now, if you volunteer for three years, I can guarantee you medic's school and, provided you pass the necessary tests, then you can complete jump training. Be a medic and a paratrooper like your Uncle . . . ?"

"Paul."

"Paul. You can also get priority on the assignments overseas. If you like . . ."

"Europe?"

" . . . one of our most popular assignments. After your three years of active duty are completed, you have three years of inactive reserve to complete your obligation. No summer camps or monthly meetings as the draftees have."

"Yeah. I'd like to get it all done at once."

"We can do it any way you like."

"Sounds like three years . . ."

"Remember what President Kennedy said."

"Huh?"

"Ask not what your country can do for you. Ask what you can do for your country."

"Oh, yeah. We canceled our senior play the day he was shot."

"It was a crime!"

"I was backstage. I'll never forget it."

6

"Come back in when you're eighteen and we'll draw up a three-year contract."

"Yeah. Ah, does that mean I have to go in in June?"

"No. You have up to ninety days to go in after you sign up."

"So I could have the summer to fool around in."

"Sure, sure. Oh, and if you have some free time between now and your birthday, how would you like to go to Syracuse to take some tests and get your induction physical? I can get you out of school for the day. Free meals. Hotel overnight."

"Really?"

"Yep."

"Sure, I guess."

"I'll send the information to your home address. Give me a call when you get it."

"Yes, sir."

"I'm proud of you, son!"

"Thank you, sir. I mean Sergeant Hermann."

"Hartmann. And remember, 'Ask not what your country can do for you . . .' "

" ' . . . but what I can do for my country.' Yes, sir, I will. Thank you."

Part One

A YEAR TO THE DAY AFTER I AM INDUCTED INTO THE army, we land in South Viet Nam. All of a sudden, because of something that happened in a place called the Gulf of Tonkin, we have to go to Southeast Asia to keep the dominoes from toppling.

I had no problem with medic's school. Jump school was fun. I was assigned to the same unit Uncle Paul served with in Korea, the 185th Airborne Infantry. We were shooting blanks at each other in West Georgia one minute and loading onto a boat headed to the Orient the next. There was time to change our unit name to 1st Brigade (Airborne), First Cavalry Division, but we only had thirty days' sailing time to review the book on jungle and rice paddy warfare in a country the size of Florida. Everyone was green at the gills from the boat ride, but even greener to combat.

When we finally arrive, we land like marines, charging off land-assault boats onto a white sandy beach. We meet resistance in the form of a dozen little children standing on the dunes, demanding candy, money and cigarettes. They offer us boom-boom in the guise of their virgin mothers and sisters.

We are immediately picked up by helicopters and flown inland to a valley in the central highlands. We are let off in a large, flat area called "the golf course" which nestles up against a mountain named Hong Kong. Nothing sets us apart from the enemy but three rolls of barbed wire. We sleep on the ground, wrapped in our ponchos and poncho liners. On the first morning wake-up "in-country," I stick my hand in my pack. A scorpion crawls out between my fingers. I am unstung. I am lucky.

We can't shoot until we are shot at, though they have issued us live ammunition. When we are on perimeter guard we are allowed a "mad minute" at dusk and dawn to clear our weapons by shooting across the barbed wire.

Besides perimeter guard every night, we have "gook guard" every day, which is when we watch over the local Vietnamese hired to clear away the brush and the jungle outside the barbed wire. It is the only contact we have with these strange, frail people, and associating with them doesn't offer any answers as to why we are here other than we are here.

As I said, none of us has seen any combat except for Henderson, our line platoon sergeant. The guys I'm responsible for come in all shapes and sizes, all creeds and colors. We have in common that we are paratroopers and proud of it. The guys, some of them, are aching to get shot at so they can shoot back. I'm in no hurry as it's all pretty interesting without getting shot at. That is not going to be the case, though, as we are scheduled to go out on our first air assault tomorrow morning, to a place called Happy Valley. Which is why I'm going to cut out and go to sleep on the ground and hope I dream of cheap boom-boom, rather than dream of fucking up.

The jungle is as thick as a florist's display window. The humidity is something like a shower room after

August football practice. Drip, drip, drip, the bamboo drinks.

We came up on the village in Happy Valley so quickly in the assault choppers that we scared the Viet Cong right out of their black PJs. A few of them fired a couple of shots at us as the choppers flew off. Then everything was quiet. The local population disappeared down tunnels or into the jungles. We threw grenades down the tunnels.

"Fire in the hole."

Then we pass through the group of thatched huts, the village. There is no electricity or indoor plumbing, but cooking pots simmer on their fires.

We step back into the rice paddy fields that surround the community and we sweep across the open area as the late morning sun burns through us.

This is where I come about my first casualty. Pratt, a machine gunner, is hit by the heat. The combination of gun and sun knocks him to his knees: heat exhaustion. I turn the machine gun over to his assistant, Eddie Malewicz. The rest of the platoon plops down in the rice paddy muck as I look for some shade where I can put Pratt.

I'm standing in the middle of a dried-up water cistern. The cistern is huge, twice the size of a stateside swimming pool. It stands at a depth of about ten feet and is meant to hold a ton of water to irrigate the rice paddies below. The walls are five feet high—packed with mud—with another five feet of shrubs atop three of the sides. The fourth wall of the cistern is the jungle's tree line.

The heat has become so intense that anything beyond arm's length shimmers. I step toward the jungle shade. The closer I get to it the less it looks like a place to put Pratt. The foliage is more of a wall the less it shimmers. I try to see into its depths. There is too much of it. I take giant steps back to the middle of the cistern. I turn back around and face the jungle. With a good running start and two good steps up the mud wall, I can grab the ground vines and . . . "Don't go in there!" comes the shout in my head. It stops me dead in my tracks. I don't know why, but I realize I may be too close to the jungle to see its trees. Yet the jungle seems to see me. It towers over me. I step back, away from an omen. I can't move as fast as I want, so I stop. Trying not to telegraph alarm, I take casual stock of the rest of the cistern. I get turned away from the jungle wall and see the way I got in here. I start toward it and freeze. My hand flexes over the .45 caliber pistol on my hip. The hand freezes. I check my feet—they are stuck to the mud floor like bare skin sticks to frozen metal. In the midst of the steam-boil of this heat pit, I am frozen. Frozen in the heat.

I realize what is wrong with the jungle behind me. It is frozen, too. Everything has stopped. As I can't move, neither does anything else move. No bird chirps. No snake slithers. No vine twines. Frozen in its nature, the jungle has stopped. Nothing grows. Nothing feeds. Nothing crawls. Nothing reproduces. Everything waits. Life is frozen in anticipation.

In the freeze I hear it. I feel it first. I'm not sure, but it breaks through the ice. It is the feeling of being watched. Eyes back in the jungle, watching. I feel eyes. Hear them move, blink, behind me. In this mad silence, eyes rule. I stand and shiver in sweat.

I feel it as the eyes move through my helmet, drill into the back of my head. It is as if the eyes are searching for the spot on me wherein they can shatter my life. They move to the nape of my neck. I bristle under the gaze as neck hairs stand taut to the threat. The eyes balance at the top of my spine: a spine that is as frozen as an icy ladder, each vertebra a slippery rung in the searing heat. The eyes step down the spine cautiously. As they descend, the spinal column becomes a spinal canal. Ice floes thaw. Sweat flows, soaking my fatigue shirt like a sponge.

I'm a freeze frame in someone's view. I try to shout, but it freezes in my throat. I search with my ears for the shot to ring out that will break the moment I'm stuck in. Fire me up, goddamit, so I can thaw!

Dum.

At last, a sound. Distant. Vague, but it distracts.

Dum.

A hollow, empty sound, like the drip from a faucet into a drain cover.

Dump.

Dump. Dump.

Time to go home and fix that leaky faucet.

Sploch.

I'm thawing out as the sound gets closer.

Sploch.

I'm coming out from under enemy eyes.

Sploch.

A bead of sweat drops between my eyes and falls off the end of my nose. I follow it.

Sploch, sploch, sploch.

A puddle has formed on my canteen top. I jerk my head back up, breaking out of the freeze frame. I snap to. Sprint for the cistern wall. Got to get back to the others.

"Give it your best shot now, motherfucker . . . or . . . forever . . . hold . . . your . . . peace."

Eddie Malewicz was standing next to me when Brandt's squad got hit. I ran ahead, toward the screams for Doc. Eddie took one in the neck. I didn't know because I was wrapping up Tracks. The rest of the guys pulled back, leaving six of us to fend for ourselves.

Trapped in the open, we have no shelter from the rocket spray of our own gunships, but their arrival is enough of a distraction for us to sprint, one at a time, to an island of shrubs and cover. Eddie still lies in the open. Gibbons crawls out and slips a rope around him. Lerch and I pull Eddie back in. He is so heavy and his eyes are still open. He could be asleep, but there is a big hole in his neck, no blood in his body—and I was standing right next to him. I close his eyes, offer absolution, and pull the leeches off him. I don't know why.

We go back in the next day by way of a creek bed. Things haven't changed much since Custer went hunting Indians. We get hit from the high ground on both sides."Spread out!" I have to dive into the creek to avoid the hand grenades coming from the right. I come up for air. Gunner is standing there, dripping blood and screaming something at me about just killing a kid who was throwing grenades. The grenade barrage has stopped. I go to the creek edge and peer over it. A child lies splayed over a bag of grenades.

"Why wasn't the little fucker home watchin' cartoons?"

I try to settle Gunner down. I tell him it was okay. It was the kid or us. He won't listen. The AK-47s start popping from the left and a .30 or.50 cal opens up ahead. I lead Gunner back out of the creek to a clearing. Safety? We stumble on Grits, who is dead with a hunk of lead in his head. I kneel and quickly offer absolution. Then direct Gunner to carry Grits back across the creek shallows toward safety. Gunner quits sobbing, picks the man up and heads to the rear.

More guys come pouring out of that creek gauntlet. Ortiz drags Coins, who is dripping his own intestines. Ortiz took one in the right side of the face. It came out of the left side of his neck. One walks, the other talks.

"Doc, they caught us."

I do the best I can and send them on.

Another shredded soul comes staggering toward me. It's Knucks. He falls and rolls, rolls, rolls as snipers open from behind us. I reach for more bandages. None. Tourniquets? Gone. I grab an aid pack from the body of Otis. He's long gone. I offer a hurried absolution as I take my shirt off. I rip it up and pull the belt from my pants. Bandages and tourniquets. When Knucks can roll no more, he lies still long enough to realize he's alive. I go to his side to look for wounds. Many. He heaves himself up. I push him back down.

"Got to get out of here, Doc."

"Let me stop the bleeders first."

I begin to wrap up the worst of the punctures. A commotion starts behind us that culminates in me being crushed on top of him. I roll over on my back, ready for hand-to-hand. It's one of ours, Stennis. He's demanding that I save him.

"Get me outta here, Doc."

Knucks gets up and slowly staggers off. Stennis begins to flail about, stepping on dead and wounded. He kicks and rants at the death at hand. The snipers stop. I guess even they are surprised. Stennis screams at the sins of man that have brought on this moment. I grab for a weapon on the ground. He comes back to me, in beseeching hysteria, begging to be saved.

"God Almighty has cursed this moment, Doc."

I make sure the weapon is loaded. He doesn't wait for me to save him, rather, he whirls and runs back toward the creek chaos. I raise the weapon. I get him in the sights. He drops to his knees on inspiration, turns and scurries back past me on all fours, heading toward the rear. I follow him through the sights. When he disappears, I shoulder the weapon and gather up the wounded. And the dead. Slowly we filter out of danger. Welcome to the war.

Dear Jane:

Hi! How're ya doing? Fine, I hope. I'm fine too, I guess. I mean, I'm okay, if you know what I mean. I'm in great shape because we walk a lot. Listen, I've been thinking of ya lately. We don't get much chance to write, but, you know, I thought I'd drop you a note. So . . .

Well, anyway, ah, I guess I'd like to say, when I

hear saxophones, a sound that takes me home, I think of you.

Sincerely,
Doc

P. S. That's what they call me now.

I had to get that letter off because I might run out of . . . time or something. Life has taken a different turn. I do want someone back in the States to know that I wish. I want. I should. I'm afraid I'm going to die a virgin.

First thing I learned when we got back to base camp was that I was KIA (killed in action). I told our company clerk that it happened right before my very eyes. All kidding aside, we are a bit stunned because more men did not return than did. You can tell by the number of duffel bags piled like a mound of dead bodies in front of battalion headquarters.

The word is that a couple of us are going to get medals for what we did. I'm not real comfortable with gloating over heroics at the expense of so many dead and wounded. Anyway, I don't see what is so heroic about wanting to call time-out. That was one of the first things I thought of doing when all hell broke loose. Call time-out. The difference between green troops and combat veterans is the same difference as thinking you can call time-out and knowing you can't.

While I'm at it, and seeing as I have nothing to lose, I'd like to know why, when Cong finally split and let us have that valley, newsmen and camera crews pop up everywhere and I'm still scrounging for bandages and tourniquets.

Also, we have yet to be issued any jungle fatigues or jungle boots. We come back to base camp and everyone is wearing jungle fatigues and jungle boots. And they're trying to get in front of the cameras.

This one's for you to digest, Mom. Because we are the first here in-country, there are no eating facilities set up. We have been eating a steady diet of C-rations, they are like K-rations were to World War II. So, I'm opening up a can of B-3 white bread when one of the guys says that the date it was made is on the bottom of the can: 1948. Baby boomer bread. The only thing here that is younger than me. Have you ever enjoyed bread two years younger than you? I also got a courtesy pack of Hit Parade cigarettes. Uncle Paul could have used them in Korea.

Speaking of age, am I going to make it to twenty? You know what was one of my thoughts after everything had settled and I could think? Was I *old* enough to give absolution? Should I *give* absolution? Is there *time* for absolution? What *is* absolution? Who *needs* it? I'm confused. I'm at a loss. I can still see it, like a movie. He's standing next to me one minute. The next time I see him, he's dead, leeches crawling up his leg.

"Hey, Doc."

He didn't have any blood left in him. So why not say a prayer and let the leeches be?

"Hey, Doc, what are you staring at?"

Or pick them off until the evac choppers get here.

"Doc, what are you staring at?"

A poke on the shoulder brings me face to face with Kelly.

"Whoa. Hey, Kelly. What?"

"What are you staring at, Doc?"

"Oh, nothing. Just thinking. Thinkin', that's all."

"I'm going into town, into An Khe. I'm lookin' to get laid. You want to get laid, Doc?"

I start to think about that, then stop.

"Absolutely."

"C'mon. Let's go."

I don't know how long we've been out this time. Lifetimes, someone said, but that only means what happened yesterday. What happens today, anyway? Not knowing what will happen is the only defense against getting sniped, booby-trapped or ambushed.

It's getting so we really never know who we're looking for, or how many. Ten Cong? A North Vietnamese division? If some of the guys realized what, how many, who was out there, they'd probably want to sit down at the nearest peace table. As they say in the movies, "It ain't no picnic."

So it's hot, 111 degrees in the shade. We've done eight "kliks" today, chasing the remnants of a Cong battalion that ambushed the poor suckers who replaced us here. These suckers who bought it—a company of one hundred forty plus—after the ambush they numbered thirty-five. One hundred five killed or wounded. We're back here to seek revenge. Why wasn't it us?

We cross, knee deep, a leech-soaked rice paddy. There's a news camera crew watching us from the shade of the tree line. The guys start to ham it up. Find Cong. Catch Cong. Kill Cong. Fuck it, let's get in the shade. No camera crew is ever around when the shit hits the fan.

Once in the shade, we move to the village. We swept through it last week, the B-52s have just finished sweeping it again. It doesn't need cleaning anymore. So it smolders.

Closer in I see I'll have to designate a volunteer gravedigging squad. We spread out to pick up the pieces—human, animal, jungle. Some of the guys pull out their cameras.

"Hey, Doc! Doc! Over here!"

The call sends me scurrying to the fringes of the former village. There stands Two-Tone on the edge of a B-52 crater, pointing down into its bottom.

"Check that out, Doc."

Unbelievable! I cannot believe this. There's a woman lying at the bottom of the bomb crater! A real woman! A real white woman, with round eyes. Not bloody. Not sprawled in grotesque death. She looks as though she's in the middle of a comfortable sleep, naked, smooth, soft, her auburn hair lying languid on her bare ivory shoulders. So lovely! Really! I mean it! Two-Tone is right here to prove it!

She looks like all my lovers, if I'd ever had any lovers. Still, all I had ever imagined, peeked at in all those books, wanted in all those dreams, is right here. It's been so long since I've seen a real woman!

"Doc, this shit stinks."

Two-Tone brings me abruptly back to reality.

"What?"

"This shit stinks. Hey, Doc? You think we been in the sun too long?" Two-Tone looks from the woman, lying in sweet repose, to me, then over his shoulder, to see where the others are.

"Why?"

" 'Cause, if we ain't sunstroked, if we okay. Then that round-eyed white woman down there is in the wrong place."

He says that as he gazes back down into the hole. His tongue wets a cracked lip.

"Wrong place?" I gaze back down at her. She's not in the wrong place—I'm in the wrong place. She's at the bottom of a B-52 bomb crater—I'm at the top. I should be down there. . . .

"Don't do that, Doc."

I feel the tug at my sleeve, realize Two-Tone's pulling me back to the top of the crater.

"This ain't good, Doc. You can't go down there and touch her. It ain't good for us. It'll split us up, all of us."

"What do you mean?"

"I mean, you white boys see that, they'll all go rushin' down there and dig in that bitch. Touch her, dream, want, remember. Us bloods, we stand here at the top, feelin' the same need, but knowin' that it don't mix, 'specially at the bottom of a bomb crater.''

I look around now, to see if any of the others have noticed. None.

"You mean, we get along fine if there ain't any women around?''

"Have we ever, Doc? I mean, if you crackers go down there, hang on that bitch, revive her, fuck her—fuck her even if she's dead—well, there's gonna be a nigger up here that'll see his chance to get rid of one and all. And if one of us sees it, we all see it.''

As he spoke, he swung his M-79 off his shoulder. The M-79 is like a portable mortar with a single-barrel load like a shotgun. It has a stock so it can be fired from the shoulder. The barrel is about as wide as a bathroom drainpipe. The shell it fires is four times the size of a shotgun shell. It explodes with a kill radius of five yards. It mutilates. The fired shell must travel about twenty-nine feet from where it was fired before it arms itself. Sophisticated. We're thirty feet from the bottom of the crater.

"What're you doing, Two-Tone?''

"Takin' care of some illusions.''

With that remark, Two-Tone spot-fires into the bottom of the dream.

Chunk.

"Wait!''

No sooner than the first round . . .

Crack!

. . . hit my woman, then this spade reloads, locks . . .

Chunk.

"Christ, Two-Tone!''

Crack!

Chunk.

Crack!

I knock the stock from his shoulder. He lets the .79 fall to the ground. It slides into the crater.

"Why, Two-Tone?''

"The dream is a nightmare," he says as his cracked lip bleeds.

Of course, the firing brings everyone running.

"What y'all got?"

"Did ya git sumpin', Tone?"

"Anythin' left?"

Two-Tone and I stand gazing down at what is left of the woman. She is bloody now, bent in grotesque death. The lieutenant comes to the edge of the crater.

"What is it, a goat?"

"What?"

"Is it a goat?"

"Yeah, it was a goat."

Well, I didn't say anything. Two-Tone turned away, leaving his M-79 in the crater. The others gazed, shrugged, mumbled, took pictures, then turned back to collecting souvenirs. I retrieved Tone's .79 and carried it the rest of the day. When we settled for the night I offered it back to him. He thanked me and took it back. I thanked him. We're on the same side.

The day ended uneventfully. I went right to sleep at dusk. Henderson woke me at 3:00 A.M. for radio watch.

Radio watch, night watch, is the most serene time anyone can find in this war. It vies with accepting death, or being sent home, for the only sane wartime moments. Everyone sleeps. Yes, sometimes even Cong. So you have a few hours by yourself. To think. Think, and dream, and want.

I lie back against the radio and think of the woman in the crater.

She was there!

No, she is so many thousands of miles away.

But close enough to burst in a barrage of black rage.

Where is my "round eye"?

(My hands unbuckle my pants. I grope for myself.)

Who sent us to this fucking hole? For what? Speeches? Commitments?

(I feel warm and hard.)

Why are we so bent on hatred and I have yet to love?

Am I a hawk? Am I a dove?

(My knees bend as I choke arousal.)

I never see a paycheck, while millions of dollars pass through assless pants each day. Do they have lovers?

Is this way of life forever?

Are there still families?

Will anyone be waiting?

Can anyone hear me?

Oh, God! It feels so good.

(My loins are warm. My belly wet. I need someone to hold me.)

Dear Doc:

I've only received one letter from you and it didn't even have a stamp on it. I still don't know what you are doing over there. Are you safe? Are you in the fighting?

I look for you on the TV news every night, but it just shows terrible stuff. I am worried about you.

I took my SATs last week. I had to study really hard but Mom says that it is only the beginning if I want to go to college. We took pictures for the yearbook and I looked absolutely horrible. Bill and Candy broke up. She and I caught Fran Allerdyce makin' out with Mr. Close in the chem lab.

Do you remember the song "It's My Party" by Lesley Gore? Well, I know how she feels.

I was elected Homecoming Queen. I didn't want to go, but everyone said I would just hurt myself by staying home and not having any fun. So I went with Jody Jones. He's working as a cashier at Victory Market and waiting to be drafted. He's the only one still around from your class. I guess I'm pretty lonely. I'm sorry. I won't write again unless I hear from you. Take care of yourself, Doctor.

XOXOXOX
Love & Kisses,
Jane

Well, I'm about as far away from the Victory Market, my Homecoming Queen and Lesley Gore as anyone can get. I can't seem to find it within me to write a letter. She sounds so young. The saxophones are fading.

> *It's my party and I'll cry if I want to,*
> *Cry if I want to, cry if I want to.*
> *You would cry too, if it happened to you.*

Can you imagine singing that to yourself as you saw through a bamboo stake embedded in the chest of one of your people? Poor Grub, first day on point and he trips a wire that whips out a stake hidden in the shrubs. Now he's sitting on his knees burping blood bubbles. I don't want to pull the stake out because it has cauterized the wound. But the fucking thing is four to five feet long and I don't know how he'll fit into the chopper. It looks awful strange, folks. The only consolation I have is in knowing that this will flip the people at the MASH unit right out of their gourds.

That was a couple of weeks ago. "Grub and the Stake" is how we refer to it. I believe he made it, at least he was fighting to breathe and he hadn't pissed or shit in his pants. The last three steps out of mankind . . . piss your pants, shit your pants, die. So far I've just pissed in mine.

Enough of this scatological summary. We're in the tail end of the monsoon season. It's been going on for two months. Two-Tone says we should have started building an ark as soon as we got here. Instead, we built the Sugar Shack for Lee.

Being whittled down from full strength by Happy Valley, the wet creek ambush, booby traps, Ia Drang Valley, and Bong Song, we number, at the most, nineteen. So, we got a daytime job and we retire at night to the Sugar Shack and Lee. See, we've always got rookies coming in, FNGs we call them: fucking new guys. We're doing day patrols around An Khe to break them in. A respite, in the sense that we can loosen our boots at night, but how does one break anyone in to the World of Live Ammunition? It takes its toll.

Like the day Kelly was walking point. He was our pro, and he'd been through everything Two-Tone and I had been through. He was the best of the best. And proved it once again on a jungle trail. Somehow he smelled out some fresh-cut bamboo and shavings off the trail. That was the clue.

Swaggering as he walks farther down the path, all of a sudden he drops to one knee. The pros freeze. The kids bump into each other like cars on a struck train. Henderson moves up.

"What is it, Kelly?"

"Shhh!"

Kelly raises an arm for quiet; it's like sometimes you can see better when it's quiet.

"C'mere, Doc, Two-Tone, up!"

Henderson waves us forward. A meeting of the Board of Directors.

"Look. Check this out," Kelly says, as the three of us peer over his shoulder. He passes an index finger about knee high across the trail, then straight up through vines on the right.

"I can't see a fucking thing!"

"Shut up, Doc!" Henderson seems to see better when it's quiet, too.

"Yeah, yeah, I see it," says Two-Tone, and the three

26

of them stand on the trail, nodding. I stand shaking my head and squinting.

"Look!" Kelly points to something even I can see. A large piece of bamboo suspended high in the foliage. It is about two feet long and its ends are packed with dried mud.

"What the fuck is it?" one of the new kids exclaims as he walks up to us.

"Don't step there!"

Twang!

What it was was full of bees or wasps. The kid trips the wire on the path, breaking the tension. The bamboo drops. The mud packing breaks open. These fucking things come swarming out of their captivity, mad as hornets. That's just what Cong wanted.

You see, Cong planted punji stakes off to the left of the trail, about hip high. Three guys, including the poor fucker who tripped the trap, were impaled at nut level. Kelly died of bee stings. Two-Tone said it was probably the most ingenious trap we were ever going to come upon. I hope so.

(Dammit, I am going to miss Kelly. God, damn this fucking war, will you please?)

Well, back to the Shack. The Sugar Shack is where we go after a hard day on the job. The job being a patrol along Highway 19, the land artery of the central highlands. It connects Qui Nhon to Pleiku, passing through us at An Khe. The Red Ball Express is the truck convoy that makes the daily trek from seacoast to highland.

The choppers pick us up early every morning from a landing zone at the edge of An Khe and drop us somewhere on or near the highway. We wander around, bumping into things. Things bump into us. The choppers come and get us.

One evening, when we flew back into our little camp, there was this Vietnamese chick waiting for us with a mess tin of iced Coke. She was Lee, and the Coke tasted good, even in the rain. Two-Tone took to her

27

right away. He gave her a poncho as cover from the weather. She showed up at the end of every day with our refreshment.

Somehow, Lee and Tone set up an Afro-Oriental sort of communication. He interpreted to us that she was a young Catholic girl saving her money so she could join some convent in the States. Two-Tone advanced her some money. Lee started showing up with iced beer. One of the guys tried to put the moves on her. Tone had me send the guy to the dentist. At Tone's suggestion, we built Lee a shelter from the rain, and we christened it the Sugar Shack. The sun came back out as soon as we finished it.

Lee quit selling Coke, raised the price of beer, and started taking in laundry. Two-Tone started reeking from profit. We had the Sugar Shack to look forward to at the end of each day. We pooled our bucks and got one of those radio cassette players the Japs were importing. We got mentioned on Hanoi Hannah. Someone in the States sent us a real ball-breaker called "Homeward Bound" by Simon and Garfunkel. I didn't think it was meant to rub, but when you live like we have to, you end up humming "It's My Party."

It's hard to note interruptions, but no sooner had I started to lament over a stupid song about partying than, guess what? The shit hit the fan.

Christ! What a way to live. Everything is so "here today, gone tomorrow." Bloody. Destructive. If I had realized it was going to be like this. . . . Everything so foreign. Out of place. This war stuff has been going on for centuries. Do people really believe they're civilized?

Don't answer that. I'll quit complaining and start explaining. It is still a bit fuzzy, but we were at the end of another hot, humid day along the highway. The Red Ball had rolled through with a full complement of toilet paper, condoms, and *Playboy* magazines for Pleiku. We were waiting for the choppers.

Everyone was sweaty and feeling shitty, standing around Two-Tone as he rapped out the latest of his worldly observations. He could be quite funny and it helped bring the group together. We try to have a good time.

I was off to the side, writing. The guys were laughing at Two-Tone. The choppers were droning toward us, I could hear them above the banter. So could someone else . . .

I can't remember if the helicopters landed and blew up or blew up in the air. Both, probably, because the rocket trails and tracers crisscrossed every which way. I lost my pen, as some men lost their lives. And. And . . . I could not get to anyone. No one could move, because they were dead, or burning, or fucked up, or pissing in their pants and about to shit in them. Whenever anyone did move, more shots came from everywhere, and someone didn't move anymore. More troops were brought up by choppers as it got toward nightfall. They were ambushed east of us amid more explosions and screams. Troops came by highway from the west, which was stupid. They exploded while we were bait all night long among moans and screams of people being picked off because no one knew who was who by the parachute flares confusing everything while we killed each other as someone moaned Momma, Momma, Momma, Momma, Momma.

I lay there on my back all night long. I was watching a show. I kept my .45 on my chest, my aid bag under my head. I didn't move anything but eyes, ears, and nose. Not even bowels. The only time I saved my own life.

Two-Tone crawled under Diminco and Palmer, who had bought it instantly, and played out the night as a dead man.

At first light, the Air Force napalmed the piss out of the jungle, which burned away the foliage, the cover. It exposed the North Vietnamese who had tied themselves into the trees. They were burnt dead, weapons dangling from charred limbs. It was like living in autumn with Halloween creatures watching from the trees. Smelled terrible.

I'm not settling well with this at all again. It's so easy to remember the laughing, explosions, screaming, dying, darkness, flares, fire, dawn, autumn, burnt trees harboring burnt bodies tied to tree trunks . . . I really don't think writing another war story is what I can do. God! When Two-Tone crawled out from under those two guys he was turned bad. Changed. Wait. Wait a bit here while I get this god-forsaken smell of burnt human flesh out of my mind.

Sometimes this brings me so close to chaos that I have to stop to define what the fuck I'm doing, talking death, dying and destruction. It looks so morbid on paper, but the replay on my mind's eye is even worse. It goes over and over and over.

Anyway . . . the human condition can sure endure. Jungle climate, nine months, ambush, crater women, death, two-month monsoon seasons, booby traps, oozing wounds, sixty "daze" of rain, a dozen guys, give or take a few, Two-Tone, rookies, me, mud, Lee, beer.

Lee and the Sugar Shack turned out to be something less than we needed, at least for Two-Tone. I guess he'll never really come back from the dead. I know I haven't, but Two-Tone was really affected. They shipped him and me back to base camp, unscratched. Indeed. This kept us out of touch with the Sugar Shack. Kept Two-Tone out of touch with Lee.

We stayed in base doing menial jobs, and visited Lee when we could sneak over the wire. She didn't really welcome us back, though she knew we had survived the massacre on Highway 19. She acted real involved with the business, but wouldn't let Two-Tone see the receipt book. She didn't let him follow her into the back room— her bedroom—either. Laundry prices had skyrocketed, as had beer prices. Tone was getting a minimum return on his investment. Lee was in demand, even as she withstood Two-Tone's hasty advances and managed his hasty withdrawals. She trotted her buns in our faces, business as usual, then slept close to no one while we all slept alone. So did Two-Tone.

The frustration with Lee came to a climax, no pun intended, the night she shut the bar down early. We had been crawling thirsty after a sweaty, shitty, red clay–encrusted day of digging a defensive perimeter around the officers' area. We sneaked over the wire early. By dark we had drunk too much—so fast that we couldn't make it back to the wire.

Lee got fed up because we had to stay. She kept whining in Vietnamese and pointing to her crotch. She cut us off. That put Two-Tone on edge because he figured it was his beer. He paid for it.

"No way," said Lee. She shut the bar down completely and moved to the back room, her bedroom.

Two-Tone wanted more. She was closed. He did not care. Charging into the back room, her bedroom, he put his boot in someone's ass.

"It's not very big," Lee whispered in my ear before she died, but Two-Tone's boot pushed someone up into her vaginal wall. It erupted. She bled to death.

We serve our own beer now. Everyone is horny. Two-Tone is doing three to five years in the stockade for womanslaughter.

Everyone is gone but me.

That's not true. I'm just feeling sorry for myself. Actually, I wanted to see what it looked like on paper. Everyone is gone but me. Ugh! I don't like it. I've been trying to write home, toward home, with home in mind. I can't. I've lost home. Fuck home.

Folks, I can't get it out of my mind. I lay there all night and didn't get to anyone on that highway. I failed in my responsibility. I didn't crawl, roll, spin, bandage, tie off, absolve anyone. Goddammit, I let everyone down.

I'm still alive, but who could say I couldn't have brought a couple back with me?

I froze. I stopped.

"Hey, Kane."

I stuttered. I stuck.

"Hey, Kane. You in there?"

(High-pitched voice from inside tent.) "No. Kane's not here. He's been sent back to the States. He has bullhead syphilis of the chin. Or is it the wong. I'm not sure."

"C'mon, man, I know that's you in there. Come out here, I got something to show you."

"Come on in."

"Whoa, no, man. I ain't comin' in there. Come on out here. It'll be worth it to ya."

Shit. Well, at least he interrupted the pity party. The guy really is a chicken shit. Horn. They put him in charge of the grave-digging squad. Nobody wanted him in the line units. So now there's sordid talk of what Horn does to the dead.

"All right. What?"

I step out of the tent.

He goes into a shifty little pace at my appearance.

"Hey, Kane, how ya doin'?"

"What you got?"

"Look, Kane. Look!"

He offers me a hand, palm upturned. In it sit three lumps of . . . of?

"What the fuck is it, Horn? Brown goat turd?"

"Gold!"

"Gold?"

"Gold!"

I peer closer. Finger one of the lumps. It is heavier than it looks.

"Where the fuck did you get this?"

"I was on the grave-digging detail over off Highway 19. Hey, it's as easy as pie. Just like a prospector.

Kick'em in the head until the teeth come out. The stuff just pops out.''

I look into his elated face, then back to the gold. How the fuck do I handle this one?

"Oh! I get it. You're like a gold kicker rather than a gold digger.''

"Yeah. Nifty, huh?''

"Great idea. They'll love it back in the States.''

"Yeah. Well. What do ya say? You want to buy 'em?''

I look deep into his face. He doesn't flinch an inch. He's serious.

"Horn, why would I want to buy them? They probably won't fit.''

I turn away.

"No, man, you don't understand. You don't wear 'em. You melt 'em down.''

I turn back.

"Horn. I'm afraid you and I don't see eye to eye. I think it's because I stand about five feet eleven inches taller than you.''

"Huh?''

What a worm! I put some distance between us. I've got to get off both his case and mine. Puttin' down, puttin' down. Why am I surprised by Horn's enterprise? Since man found a way to get gold out of the ground and into the mouth, he's found a way to get it out of the mouth and into the pocket.

Okay, things are weird. I mean so weird I'm speechless. You wish, huh? Well, I quit writing home. What's the use? What can I tell 'em?

Dear Mom:

Kelly died of bee stings. I helped Gunner kill a kid who should have been home watching cartoons. We had a massacre out on Highway 19. Horn came on to a gold mine. So, don't worry, Mom, I'm doin' okay.

While I'm battling with this bitterness I get a letter. No, not my Mom, she doesn't get much chance to write, what with the other kids and all. Anyway . . .

Doc Kane:

Shit.
I got a lot of time now so I'm going to try what you seem to be pretty good at. Tell me what you think.

10:00 A.M.

by Gene Clark

Can't say it's justified
Admit it could be worse
sealed inside this tunnel
Branded as a curse
Felons and fallen fellows
Take heed of this misery
The sheep bleat under the wolf's heat
while we compete for the prison meat
Locked in tight
Can't sleep at night
Horns howl in anger
Lights swing in search
Sittin' here chained to a pig-iron perch.

What do ya think of that, Doc? Pretty good, huh? From here they're supposed to transfer me to Leavenworth. Guess they figure this will be over in a couple of years. It's a hell of a way to get home, but a better shot than you got.

I received $2,000 in cash from a couple of officers over at Division Admin. for the Sugar Shack. Already sent it to my grandmom. When I/we get back to the States, I'll show you a good time if you come to Chicago.

Good luck, Doc. I hope you make it and we can get together.

In blood, brother,
Tone Clark

Gene Clark, that's Two-Tone's slave name.

I am amazed that so many people are making money on this little skirmish. I ain't been paid since I was declared KIA in Happy Valley. Still, I'll only make about $2,900 for the whole tour . . . lots of memories though. I'm glad I'm not Two-Tone. I'll take my chances out here in the real world. Anyway, I'm gabbing around like this because I don't want to make up my mind.

Remember in the wet creek ambush I almost fired on one of our own troops because he went bonkers? Stennis was his name. Well, they sent him back to us. We just sent him back again. Dead.

Robert O. was just finishing another notch in the stock of his M-79 when Henderson came back and told him to cross it out. He'd scored, yes, but one of ours.

Stennis went out over the perimeter wire to take a lunar poop.

Stennis bought it.

Stennis never had a chance.

So I'm lying here mulling over the phraseology of my letter to the big boys. Let's have a go at it. Been a long time since I wrote a good letter.

General Westmoreland:

Sir. First let me express my concern for your health. The last time I saw you, your arm was in a sling. I presume you were shot, though word out here has it you broke it playing tennis in Saigon. Either way, hang in there.

Then again, sir, some other sort of scuttlebutt is

circulating about what you did with one of my evacuees. The kid who went hysterical on us, started trampling everyone. He ran. We didn't mind.

So you go ahead and confront him at the field hospital. He's shaking. You shake him more. He quivers. The doctors and nurses are aghast. Your aides snap to attention. The reporters start writing. The kid comes back to us. He's dead now.

General, I'm writing to point out to you one serious flaw in your action. As a combat medic, I handle casualties on the front lines. I live with these guys. I am proud to be a paratrooper. I also feel good when I hear you speak of your pride in us. Thank you.

But, General, sir. It's about this kid. The one who "ran." Or, for that matter, people like him. I mean, with my experience in combat I know I have a series of trauma cases who are all fairly immobilized or in shock or incapable of taking care of themselves. Here comes this kid. Berserko. Hysterical. Stepping on everyone. Giving away our position.

General Westmoreland, sir. The kid broke down under fire. People break down. The shit hits the fan. It's an insane time. Someone breaks down. Goes off. Becomes hysterical. Flips out. We do not need any more hysteria than we've already got!

General, do you realize what it is like to have to deal with someone like that in the middle of a firefight?

Keep the next one, sir, out of our way. We have a war to fight and the kid got in the way. He's not in the way anymore. He did it once. He did it twice.

No more.

Get the next one to sterilize O.R. instruments. Keep them out of our fucking hair. This is a war we are fighting, sir, not some initiation rite for membership into the Knights of Columbus.

Please. Thank you.

Sincerely,
Doc Kane

I got that letter back. It looked like it traveled all the way to the White House. Westy took it personally. LBJ too. I wish a lot more people would take it personally. That would hurry this war up a bit.

So with the appearance of the letter comes this order that I need a break, a rest. I'm supposed to go on I & I. That is the Intercourse and Intoxication aspect of R & R, Rest and Relaxation. The only thing that bothers me is going alone. Why Rest and Relax alone? What about the guys? The group, go together. I always end up alone.

• • •

He slowed, awaiting my arrival. He stopped in Catholic Relief Keds, baggy shorts and a once-white T-shirt. Appropriately dressed for any sandbox, his nose leveled at my belt buckle.

"Two hundred p.," he exclaimed.

"Where?" I challenged.

"You come, we go," he replied, and scurried down the dim back street, one of many in this town of Vung Tau.

This is the R & R center of South Viet Nam, for both sides, someone said. This coastline city has the tropical weather that was so well portrayed in *South Pacific*. Romantic. The urban setting is more "Westernese," with these southeast Asians aping everything American— eggs to egos. It becomes hard to realize that these folks are fearful of losing their individual freedoms to a communist horde.

I come here to have fun, like the centuries-old warrior's reward—after the fight comes the wine, women, and song. The beer is warm. The women are whores. I'm singing "I Can't Get No Satisfaction" along with the Rolling Stones. Within the last nine months I've fought and fucked for the first time. Now it seems like the fuck is the fight and I can't sleep at night. A double scotch on the rocks on the veranda of the Grand Hotel is no more pleasurable than the fruit cocktail portion of

C-rations in the jungle. So, following this little critter ain't much different from tracking Cong. Will this be the search that destroys me?

Like a Little Leaguer kicking up his heels, the little pimp scampers ahead, waving and chattering at me to follow. I become more fearful as we venture deeper into No-American's Land. A thought prompts a burst of fear in me. I run to catch him, to grab him to keep him from dragging me any deeper into foreign lust. This night life is killing me!

The little fella just runs out of sight. I slow. I wonder where his enthusiasm comes from. I stop. He couldn't be making any money on 200 p.

I'm being set up. Ambush?

Hell, I'll just turn around and get the fuck outta here. I can hide in a bar or a church. I turn back.

"U. U. Hey, U, 200 p."

I hear someone chasing me and I turn involuntarily. My little nemesis is running right at me.

"Aw, shit."

"Hey, U, 200 p." He halts, waves to me to follow. I hesitate. I weaken. I follow him mutely.

"Hope the bargain disappears before we get there," I mutter to myself as I attempt to stay within the lighted limits of the back streets. My courier darts in and out of the shadows. I am mesmerized, out of my own control.

"Hey U. Hey U." He shouts from the base of a wrought-iron stairway. It follows up the side of an old-French-built tenement. As I get to the base of the stairs, weak from lack of conscience, the little one bounds up them, taking two at a time. At the top, three Vietnamese men are leaning luxuriously against the ornate rail. They are dressed in the latest Western fashion. They could be discussing anything, from the stock market to death tolls.

The little guy dances around the waists of the men, explaining. The three glance down at him, then peer down the stairs at me. One man nods to the kid then glides back into the rhythm of the conversation.

The boy motions for me to go away—which really means "come here" to the Vietnamese. Everything is ass backwards. Come instead of go. Death instead of life. Fuck instead of love. Maybe this 200 p. comes built with a sideways "you know what," as the myth goes.

I scramble up the stairs, in fear that if I don't move, this pip-squeak will make a fool of me. Actually, I'm afraid it's too late for that.

"Two-hundred p. Two hundred p." He holds his hand out. I look unassuredly at the men as I grope for the watermarked bills. The men chat among themselves, giving me no notice. I fold the two dollars' worth of piasters, unsure as to who will get them. The little one snatches them from my hand, quickly thumbing them for authenticity.

Satisfied, he slides them into the hand of his guardian. Without seeming to notice, the fellow slips the bills into his pocket, continuing in the cadence of conversation.

Short Stuff scampers along the balcony, then stops at a door about halfway down, and disappears. I'm stuck to my spot. The three men are taking no more notice. All's fair in love and war. The kid reappears, gives me that "come as you go" motion, and I become unstuck. I move toward him. He grins, points to the entrance and runs off the other way at a Cub Scout trot.

Oh, fuck. Well, 200 p—might as well see.

I push through the door and into a tidy, sweet-smelling room. Large, but partitioned off like most houses of such repute. I step into a strange serenity. There's no sound. I feel alone.

"Thank God. No one's here. So that little . . ."

"Hey U. Hey U." From the first cubicle comes the sound of a light feminine voice. I move to her as a hummingbird to a flower. She lies before me, a beautiful, unblemished woman, under layers of silken shroud.

"Oh, what a sight." I smile, heart bounding.

"U. U. Boom, boom number one."

She leans up on one elbow, letting flow her beautiful black hair. She smiles, and her teeth gleam in the soft candlelight. Incense.

"U. Come."

She reaches for my sleeve, bringing me down to her. She places an assuring hand on my shoulder. I lie down alongside her, placing my hand on her belly.

"Oh, my god, 200 p!"

She is bloated with child.

• • •

"Hey, Doc, you gonna be tendin' bar at the club tonight?"

"No, I have to stay straight tonight. I'm on call here at the aid station."

"Oh no you don't, Doc. You don't have to stay straight. You can be fucked up and still take care of us."

"No, I can't."

"Yes, you can."

"Well, I don't want to."

"Okay, fuck you, Doc. Don't get loaded with us. Sit by yourself and beat your meat."

"I'll give it some thought."

"Okay, Doc. See ya around."

"Right."

"Hey, wait a minute, Doc. While you're sittin' on your ass, could you do me a favor?"

"Maybe."

"Could you write my mom a letter?"

"Okay."

"Really, Doc. I mean it."

"Okay, I will."

Dear Mom:

Hi, it's me. I'm okay. Things are okay here. It's been rainin' a lot but I'm stayin' dry, honest.

I'm gettin' your letters pretty regular. Sorry to

hear about Mrs. Russel fallin' and breakin' her hip.
Why didn't Gene shovel her sidewalk? You made
me do it all the time.

The guys are doin' all right. Doc's still with us.
He's writin' this letter for me. You always said
my handwritin' was pretty bad.

We lost Lieutenant Anderson, some other guys
too, though I didn't get to know them. Anyways,
Doc evacuated them. I wish he'd evacuated me!
Just kiddin', Mom.

Don't worry.

Well, I ain't got much more to say. Say Hi! to
everyone for me. I got 102 more days left over
here.

Love,
Mike

Polishing off the letter, I reach for an outdated magazine. I settle into some C-ration pound cake and warm
water. Cold water is still a luxury.

I came back from R & R AWOL but ALIVE. I cele-
brated my birthday while gone. I'm not a teenager anymore. I got back just in time to return to Henderson's
platoon. The Doc who had replaced me caught some
shrapnel, another rumble in the jungle. We came back
into base camp this morning. There's such a shortage of
medics that I have the night watch at the battalion aid
station. It will be a welcome rest.

I usually tend bar when we come in out of the field.
Nothing elegant. They get drunk. I get drunk. We all
numb up, pass out and forget what we just went through.
There is no sense to Viet Nam when one is sober.

The club is going full blast out in the distance. The
guys are serving their own drinks, I'm sure. I move
closer to the light of a candle to try and catch up on
three-month-old stateside news. There are some comforts in Viet Nam. Oh, what a relief not to have to get
drunk!

The shouting, laughing, glass-breaking, does not produce one casualty. I don't even get a torn toenail, active ulcer, or instant clap. I begin to get tired, unassisted. I blow out the candle. I don't want the warm glow to advertise a shoulder to cry on. This boy is exhausted.

"Doc. Hey, Doc, wake up."

Someone is shaking me into that shade of gray just before dawn.

"Huh?"

"Wake up, Doc. It's me, First Sergeant Thompson. A Company. I got a dead man in my company area."

"Who?"

"I don't know who, but there's a dead man in one of my tents. You better come down and take a look."

"Ah, shit," I groan, getting to my feet. "Where is he, Sarge, A Company?"

"Yes. You better call the doctor, too, Doc. I'll meet you back at the company area."

He hurries off and I bend over my boots, hopping around on one foot as I try to get each boot on. They don't want to go. I don't want to go. We fight on the same side—against each other.

"Yes, what is it?"

"Good morning, sir. This is Kane, down at the aid station. Sorry to wake you, sir, but First Sergeant Thompson from A Company just stopped by. He says he has a dead man in one of his tents. He wants you to check him out."

"Have the dead man meet me at the aid station in half an hour."

"I'll tell him, sir."

"Good."

That motherfucker is the most useless piece of shit in the whole fucking battalion. Our real Doc, who went on R & R, was replaced by this dude. Doctor Duck, we call him, because he tries to duck every responsibility that comes near him. I think he's a real-estate broker, because that's all he ever talks about.

Balancing a folded stretcher on my shoulder, I throw my first-aid bag over the other shoulder and head down to the troop area. Probably another suicide. Christ, I hope he isn't messy.

"Over here, Doc."

First Sergeant Thompson brings me out of my chagrin. I walk to where he stands at the tent entrance, hands on hips, his brow furrowed in concern.

"Where's the doctor?"

"He'll be at the aid station."

"Okay." He whirls, jerking back the tent flap. We enter into darkness. Shadows and whispers in the tent hint at a wake.

"Down at the other end, Doc."

"Right. Could someone turn up the tent flaps so I can see?"

"Sure. Hey, you men, Doc's here. Give him some room and roll up those tent flaps so he can see who this fella is."

As the dawn's early light brightens the interior I make my way to the back bunk.

"Is he dead, Doc?"

"I don't know. I'm not there yet!"

It's Mike. He is, at the least, sleeping heavily.

"Where's the Doc? Where's the Doc?"

Someone outside the tent sounds for me. I look up from Mike as a semihysterical trooper interrupts the somber atmosphere by bursting through the other entrance of the tent.

"Doc! Doc! Where are ya? Where are ya? We got a dead man!"

The trooper comes rushing down the aisle and trips over his own consternation. I twist out of the way of his fall. The folded stretcher on my shoulder swings smack up the side of someone's head. I may have to call in some help.

• • •

Mike is for sure dead. I don't know how. He may have flat given in. He lies on his side. Curled in a fetal position, thumb in mouth. Eighteen years old. I'm interrupted while giving absolution . . .

"Doc, we got a dead man over in B Company."

The trooper who tripped rises to his feet.

"He's laying half off a bunk and his eyes is wide open."

"Go back and close his eyes. I'll be there in five."

"Close his eyes? Close his eyes! I'm not a Doc. How do you close some dead guy's eyes?"

"Stick your fingers . . . no. No. Go back and wait outside the tent. I'll be there soon."

"What's the matter with this guy?"

"He's dead."

"Wow! Really? His eyes are closed."

"Go back to B Company."

The fellow I accidentally hit with the stretcher is being helped to his feet.

"Doc. Carver gots a gash on his haid."

"Let's see."

I inspect. He'll need stitches.

"Hey, man, I didn't mean to hit you."

"Sawright."

"You're going to need to see the doctor."

I pull a field dressing out of my bag, rip off the foil, and apply the direct pressure bandage to the wound.

"Hold that."

He does. I tie it tight.

"Go to the aid station. Wait for the doctor. Tell him you are not the dead man. Show him your head. Wait. You, go with him! Tell the doctor you're not dead either, but I have one, possibly two down here who are."

"Okay."

I turn back to Mike. Quietly I question, "Oh, Michael. Little fucking Mike. What happened? How are we going to mail that letter? Why should we?"

"What'll we do with him, Doc?"

The question brings me back around.

"Send him back to the States."

I open the stretcher.

"Okay, you guys, load him up."

Those in the group do so as I fill out the casualty card.

"Who is he, Doc?"

"Mike O'Donnell, B Company. One of my boys."

"What's he doin' in A Company?"

"Came here to die, I reckon."

The abrupt nature of that remark allows me some silence so I can finish the paperwork that goes with the dead. Mike. Fucking Mike. Why?

"Should we take him to the aid station, Doc?"

"Yeah."

I tuck the tag in Mike's pocket. "Tell the doctor this one is dead, get another stretcher, and meet me at B Company."

They trudge off with Mike. I watch. I'll send that letter. What the hell.

I walk over to B Company, buried in thought. Why do I even care anymore? I get to know folks, even kids, and they die. Why care? Why care?

If I don't care about life, I'm as good as dead. I don't know why I try to figure death out. Actually, I do know why. Because I'm still alive to do that. When I'm dead I'll have all the time in the world to figure life out.

"Doc! Hey, Doc! Over here."

I react to the shout, head toward it. The semihysterical trooper stands by a tent, cradling one arm in the other.

"Doc, hey, Doc, when I tripped over that dead guy I fucked up my wrist. Remember?"

"You didn't trip over a dead man. Anyway, let me see."

He offers me a swollen right wrist.

"Turn it."

"I can't."

45

"Try."

"I can't."

"I'll do it."

"No! No! Wait! I'll try . . . yeeeow!"

"Okay." Go up to the aid station, tell the doctor you're not the other dead man. Show him the wrist. Where's the dead one?"

"In there. Thanks, Doc."

"You're welcome."

I step into the tent, and into a circle of spectators watching a dead man. I bend closer in hopes of recognizing the face. If only the dead knew how intently they are watched.

"Who closed his eyes?" I ask. No answer. I peer closer at the contorted soul. He is on his back, bent way over the side of the bunk. It appears he is being tipped. One hand is slid down in his pants, arm cocked at the elbow. He was grabbing for his handle at the last to pull himself up. The other hand, arm, is slung over his head. A verse prompts me to mumble . . .

> I'm a little teapot,
> short and stout,
> this is my handle
> this is my spout.

"Who is this guy?"

"Don't know. This is Little Mike's bunk."

My knees buckle under the weight of Mike O'Donnell's fate on a different bunk.

"Yeah, and we can't find Mike anywhere."

I straighten and state, "I just sent him up to the aid station. He's dead."

"Really, Doc?

"Yeah. He was on a bunk over in A Company. Someone go get First Sergeant Thompson for me."

"Sure, Doc." The aura of death settles over the tent. I try to take a closer look.

"Roll up the tent flaps for me, please."

The added light displays a corpse, not a teapot. A thick saliva has dried around his nose and mouth and runs in streaks up the face, welling in the eyes and ears. Drowned, puked himself to death.

"I'm a little teapot . . ."

I try to say a prayer over him, but the stench drives me back. I'll let Doctor Duck figure this one out. The stretcher and bearers walk through the door.

"Here's your stretcher, Doc."

"Open it up. Load him on."

"His arm is stuck out, Doc."

"Don't try to move it, you'll break it off! Rigor's set in."

"He smells like he bin drinkin'."

"You want to see me, Doc?"

Thompson confronts me gravely.

"Yes, First Sergeant. Do you recognize this man?"

I point to the corpse on the stretcher. He peers at it.

"Goddam, it's Dawson. New man. He just came in, two days ago. He has a wife and three children."

There's a commotion outside the tent. I can't help but hear, "Where's the Doc? Where's the Doc?"

What the fuck is going on around here?

"He's in here."

"I'm in here."

Another hysteric enters another tent.

"Doc. The real Doc says you should come up to the mess tent. Cookie dumped hot water all over his front, on his balls and everything."

"The real Doc says?"

"Yeah. I went up to the aid station for help and the real Doc said he was too busy trying to figure out who was dead and who was alive."

"Let's go."

I start out of the tent, and then turn back.

"First Sergeant, would you please escort this poor drowned soul to the aid station for me?"

"Can do, Doc."

"Tell the doctor that the gentleman is for sure dead, whoever he is, and so on."

"I got it."

"Thank you. This sure is a fucked-up morning, isn't it?"

"Sure is."

I walk to the mess tent begrudgingly. I hate burns. More than any other victim, the burner is the bitch. Screaming, as fluids ooze through shredded skin. Raw, raw, raw. . . .

"In here, Doc."

"Here's Doc!"

"Thank God, Doc, you're here. That fuckin' Doc at the aid station wouldn't come over . . ."

"Right, where's Cookie?"

"Over by the stoves."

Blam!

An explosion sends me instinctively to the ground. I try to gather my senses. Not close. Mortars? Friendly fire?

Blam!

Blam!

Grenades.

"Mortars?"

"Incoming?"

"We're under attack."

They don't know what they're talking about. It's grenades. Not close. I low-crawl over to the stove area, to Cookie. He's quiet, thank God. All the spectators around him are acting like victims, flat out on the ground, immobile. There's only one difference. He's helpless. They're not.

"What was it?"

"Mortars!"

"Rockets!"

"Charlie!"

"It was grenades. Our grenades. They aren't so close. Someone go into the officers' mess to the cooler. Get me some ice."

"I ain't movin'."

"I ain't either."

"Ah, fuck you guys."

I jump up and run into the officers' mess. I anticipate another explosion, a blinding flash, piercing shrapnel. I open the cooler door and grab as many bags of ice as I can. I drink warm water and they get bagged ice. How 'bout this war!

Still no explosions. I run back to the kitchen as screams for Doc! Doc! Doc! come from down the hill. Of course! Like I've got twelve fucking hands! I drop the ice next to Cookie.

"Get the fuck up, everyone. Wrap your shirts around this ice. Pack it around him. Someone get a stretcher. Move his boiled balls up to the aid station. You others get more stretchers and come find me down in the troop area."

"Where were those explosions, Doc?"

"That's what I'm going to find out."

I run down the hill, following the flow of the crowd. As I push through, I come upon two dazed souls. Each has pockmarks of blood on his bare chest, arms, head, as would happen from a grenade burst. I push the crowd back.

"Get the fuck out of the way. Give them room. Get me bandages, all of you. Get your aid packs. Get me tourniquets."

Put them to work, keep them busy, out of the way.

"What happened, Doc?"

"They were playing spitball."

My cynicism is becoming as much a wound as any I have treated. I direct the two walking wounded into the tent.

"Both of you, sit! Now, who else got it?"

"Washington is back there, on the floor."

"Are either of you bleeding bad from anywhere?"

"No."

"How 'bout you?"

"I'm okay."

"Sit. Watch each other while I check on Washington. Be right back."

Grenade shrapnel has left the tent walls porous to sunrise. I thread my way through an eerie darkness.

Thunk.

"Ouch!"

I split my shin on a fucking bunk bed!

Hobbled.

"Washington!" I command, looking for someone to blame for the pain.

"Washington?"

Silence. Darkness.

"Where is he, guys?"

" 'Bout halfway down, I think."

"Washington!"

I limp back and forth in the middle of the tent. Silence. I light a match. He lies below me, on his back. Sweet repose.

"Washington."

I push the bunks out of the way. Use another match to light a found candle. I bring it down and pass it over him. The candle flickers, giving him too many dimensions. He's anywhere between life and death.

"One of you guys have a flashlight?"

"I do."

"Gimme, please."

There is a color of skin, a subdivision of the darkest of the major races, that matches the color of blood. This Washington is that color, a blood-tone. I can't find a wound anywhere.

"Here, Doc, here's the flashlight."

The beam slices the darkness. I take it.

"Thanks. How are you doing?"

"Okay."

"Dizzy? Nauseated? Feel wet, soaked anywhere?"

"Just pissed my pants."

"That's normal. Keep an eye on your buddy."

I turn back to Washington. Outside, the alarm is spreading, too many people screaming too many orders to so few. I hear rifle bolts slam shut on rounds of ammunition. Everyone is getting ready. For what?

"Washington?"

In the newfound light, I nudge his shoulder. His head sets funny. I lift it. Brain, like mud slush, spreads out under him. I don't have to look any further. I get dizzy from the sight of the wound. I lean away, choking back the stomach bile. I'll never get used to it. This whole fucking business makes me fucking sick.

Blam!

Blam!

I don't even feint to duck. Fuck it! Even in this dimness, this shroud, I can envision the blast, the blams.

"What was that, Doc?"

"SOS. Same old shit."

I become engrossed in the business of offering absolution.

"I hope you go to Washington, heaven, because it has been hell here."

What the fuck am I saying . . .

" . . . hope you go to heaven, Washington, because it has been hell here."

Christ. I can't relent even for a minute and I'm fucking up. Take stock. Be Doc. I bounce up and buckle under the cracked knee. I hop to where my two wounded sit.

"How you guys doing?"

"Okay."

"Okay."

I try to get the record straight. Three dead—suicide, drunken drowning, and bled brain; five wounded—lacerated head, wrist sprained, scalded balls, and two shrapnel punctures. And all I can say to describe it is "same old shit."

"Doc?"

"Yeah?"

"Never mind. You better go, huh?"

"Are you all right?"

"Yes, we're okay, Doc."

"I'll send someone to wrap you up."

"We can take care of each other, Doc."

"I know."

I limp out of the tent. Most of the crowd has disappeared in the direction of the last explosions. A few voyeurs are still standing around.

"What's going on around here today, Doc?"

"Haven't you heard? We're celebrating Veteran's Day."

"Hey! Is it, Doc?"

"Veteran's Day! Hey, is it? That's us. We're veterans."

"Right. If we get out of here alive. Did someone get those bandages I asked for?"

"Yeah. Here, Doc."

"No, you keep 'em. Go in there and bandage up your buddies. You! You help him. Then walk them up to the aid station. You other two wait here for the stretchers that are coming down from the mess tent. Take one. There's a dead Washington in there, by the candle. He goes home, by way of the aid station. Send the other stretchers after me."

I move off gingerly in the direction of the last explosions. I begin to feel the strength return to my knee.

"You want the tourniquets, Doc?"

"Huh?"

I turn back to the question. One of the guys dangles tourniquets in my face. Octopus tentacles.

"Yeah. Yeah, give 'em to me."

I grab the tourniquets, turn back, and begin a fractured trot toward what may be in store. Where the fuck are the other guys? Alvarez. Farmer. I'm not the only fucking Doc in this battalion. Christ! What the fuck is going on? I jump a trench. The knee responds. I flex it while looking back into the trench. It's a haven for stagnant water, beer cans, and *Playboy* magazines. I want to stop. Fish. Drink beer. Get excited over the girls. Instead, I head for the crowd, a sizeable group milling around in front of the club. Half of the battalion, even in their underwear, are armed to the teeth. I push my way through.

"Out of the way. Medic. Step aside. Doc comin' through. Comin' through. Out of the way. Doc here."

They fold back before me, mumbling among themselves like restless natives. As I get a better view, I see a couple of my cohorts are already administering to the situation. I step out of the crowd.

Crack!

I'm yanked to the ground as a familiar sound zips past my ear. It is not a bumblebee. I feel as if my shoulder has been pulled out of its socket. Everyone hits the ground, screams, shouts, chaos. Out of the corner of my eye I see a spectator crumble. I've seen such an instance before, too late for him.

A command voice takes over.

"Cease fire! Cease fire! Cease fire!"

No one fires. Everyone is too deep in the dirt. I reach for the sharp pain in my shoulder. I look at it, follow it down my arm to my hand. I'm still holding the tourniquets, but one of them has somehow wrapped itself around the trigger mechanisms of an M-16. The rifle lies on the ground, the veritable smoking gun. I let go of the tourniquets, go to the aid of the fallen trooper. He's alive and conscious.

"Hey."

"Yeah."

"How're you doing?"

"I'm hit."

"Where?"

53

"Back. Shoulder, I think."

I reach for my own shoulder as I look at his. There is no comparison. He doesn't have a shoulder. I feel better for me. I feel worse for him. Fucking tourniquets. Fucking guns. Fucking war. FUCKING WAR! Fuck me.

I bend over him with a compress bandage in hand. He shows no sign of pain as I apply pressure to stop the bleeding. Wonderful drug, shock is.

"What is it, Kane?"

"Hey, Alvarez, where the fuck have you been?"

"Sleepin'."

"Great! It's been me, three dead, six wounded, and Doctor Duck, the real-estate broker."

"Sorry."

"So am I. What's over there?"

"It can wait."

"Good."

I shout over my shoulder, "All right, shooting gallery is shut down. Hands off your guns. Everyone get me a stretcher."

The command voice takes over. "All right, men, you heard what the Doc said. Back to your tents or get a stretcher."

"What about chow?" someone demands.

"Chow is going to be late this morning. Cookie burned his balls. Now everyone back to your areas. If I see any swinging dicks standing here by the time I count to ten, you burn shitters for a week. One. Five. Ten."

The crowd evaporates. The bleeding stops. I'm numb. "Watch this guy, Al. I want to check the other one out."

"Okay."

I move over to where Doc Farmer is half bent over what had once been a human being. It has been split open down the center, nose to knees. It's all meat, guts, bone-mutilated, crushed, an anatomy lesson. No, a slaughterhouse. The only discernable identity is combat boots and close-cut blond hair.

"Who is it, Farmer?"

"Oh! Hi, Kane. Someone said it was someone named Ring."

"Grenades?"

"The two pins are right here." He lifts his foot, exposing the cotter pins that hold grenades together.

"He must be the one who just fragged B Company."

"Yeah, well, he was headed toward the club."

"Why? The party's over."

"Not really. We were still drinkin', five or six of us. I was in there when he blew up."

"He was planning to get himself some more?"

"Probably."

"Strange."

"Here're the stretchers, Docs."

"Unfold one, put it down next to him. Take the other one over there to Doc Alvarez, help him."

The stretcher sits parallel to Ring. I grab the ankles, Farmer grabs under the shoulders. As we lift, the legs begin to tear away from the torso.

"Hurry! I don't need two legs in my hands."

We drop the carnage on the stretcher.

"Whew, that was close."

"Really."

"Grizzly work."

"It started before dawn."

"Saddle up!"

That shout comes from the battalion headquarters tent. Farmer and I look up in disbelief.

"Saddle up, everyone."

"Oh, no!"

"Thank God."

The area erupts like an army of ants. Troopers, already alert, come pouring out of their tents, scurrying every which way, looking to be led.

"Saddle up. Saddle up. Drop your cocks and grab your socks. On your feet and into the heat."

"Shit! I'm still fucking drunk."

Doc Farmer kicks the corpse as he squeezes his temples with his fingers.

"Thank fucking God." I'm not going to hide my relief.

"Saddle up, Docs. The Seventh Cav was ambushed by the 325th Division. We got to go bail them out."

I turn away from Farmer and the corpse, heading toward my tent.

"Where you goin', Kane?"

I turn, answer. "I'm going back out in the field, where it's safe."

I begin to limp toward my tent. I realize what I just said. I slow down. What is going on? All year. The last month. Since this morning. Seeps deep. Very deep. I stop. I realize this may go on forever, at least until I die. I bow my head. Tears well up. I choke them back. They try to surface. I can't hold on to all this. I can't do it anymore. I can't do it. I can't. I can't.

Yes I can.

I blink back the tears. I have to remember to mail that letter to Mike's mom.

• • •

Well I ain't dead yet and I'm going back to the States tomorrow. In one piece. The way it's supposed to be. Like in the movies. Everyone believes it will happen to them. It happens to me. I'm lucky.

Alvarez is lucky too. He's the only other medic who made the whole tour with me. Twenty-four of us started on the line, two are left. He comes stateside in two days, knock on wood. Only one man is left from my original line platoon, Henderson. He says he is going to stay on "until the motherfucker is over."

The rest have gone ahead . . . or am I leaving them behind? I roll over on my side in reaction to that thought. I almost fall off the top bunk. I always seem to stop at the edge. Anyway, I'm in a Quonset hut on the edge of Pleiku Airfield. It is the night before the next day of the rest of my life. Rain crashes like automatic-weapons fire against the furrowed tin roof just inches above me. I lie here as dry as a smug bone. First time I've avoided a soaking rain or sweat in this lifetime.

Have I told anyone? I'm going back to the States! Tomorrow! Flying back! It took a month to get us here by boat. It will only take twenty-three hours to get back. Of the ninety or so of us housed here along the airstrip, I know not a soul. All the souls from this hut are down at the local Sugar Shack trying to forget their last night in this country. I'm lying here because this is one I want to remember. Remember going back to the States.

Wish some of the guys could have made it. Fuck it. Never mind. Bums me out. Makes it lonely, empty. Real empty. Hope we don't get mortared tonight. Wonder what it's going to be like back in the States. Don't need no rocket attacks tonight, Cong. No sappers either. Stay at home tonight, guys, it's raining. Yeah. Call in sick, say "Kane's leaving tomorrow and out of respect we ain't going to hit Pleiku Airfield tonight. Let's wait. He'll put up too much of a fight."

Yeah. I ain't moving and I ain't taking any shit. From no one. For nothing. Not until I hear that plane come screaming down the runway. Staying right in this spot until I hear that last call for Arlington Hall, then I'll roll off this motherfucker and hit the ground running out the door across the open field toward the landing zone carrying everyone in particular as the load master waves for me from the bottom of the open plane ramp as it picks up speed, speed, speed, and the AK-47s start popping from the tree line. I don't think we're going to make it because Eddie's awful heavy, still I've got to try to dive for the ramp as the load master stretches himself toward us in a screaming beseech at the screaming brakes that can't hold back the power of the screaming jet turbines that are going to evacuate. . . .

Crash!

. . . scrape the heels of my hands on the concrete

runway to brake my fall down the steps of the Air Force
C-141 Starlifter.

Stunned.

I roll over on my back, facing into the heat of a
blazing sun. Is it Pleiku? Ia Drang? Happy Valley? Bong
Song? Kontum City? Travis Air Force Base. Wet? Dry.
Mud? Concrete. Central highlands? Central California.
Have I made it? Is this the States? I've never been to
California.

I made a fervent vow to kiss the first ground I
stepped on in the States so I roll over on my stomach,
nose to the concrete runway. Not very inspirational.
Not . . . can't . . . feel dazed. No sense. Got to slow
down.

I push myself up, picking up the little Air Viet Nam
bag I bought in An Khe. I retrieve the Montagnard
crossbow and Uncle Ho Uniroyal sandals. My booty. I
wonder if there is reefer for sale in this country. Well, it
doesn't really matter, I'd rather have an ice-cold beer.
Yeah. Now that will inspire me, an ice-cold beer. I
squint at the gold hills surrounding the airstrip. Where
do I get a beer around here? It's sort of unfamiliar. No
green. No jungle. Just the Golden West, I guess. I've
actually lived long enough to see it. I've made it. I can
relax.

The quick make it back after the dead.

"Let's go, soldier."

I turn from my reverie to the imposing figure of an
Air Force load master. Something about him looks
familiar.

"What's your problem, soldier? Want to go back?"
He says this with the right amount of taunting.

"Maybe," I retort.

"Well, make up your mind real soon because this
bird you flew in on is loading up to go back."

I look over his shoulder at the plane, a one-way ticket
back to survivalization. I squint back at him.

"How 'bout a raincheck on that?"

He smiles and turns away. I turn mine, which is toward the sign that says U.S. Customs. The others from the plane have formed four lines under the sign. I approach the line and become somewhat apprehensive. Everyone is standing too close together. I don't know if I'm ready to stand in line. I ain't got time. I got to catch up on living and loving.

I look over the area. Where are the marching bands? I don't see any flags waving. I stand in the dry heat as the others filter through the checkpoint. The line thins as everyone steps back into the U.S.A. My turn comes. I plop my booty down in front of the customs officer. Feels like an invasion of my privacy, someone poking around in my personals. I peer around at California as he sizes up the Uncle Ho sandals. There are no ecstatic young girls on their tippy toes on the other side of the fence, trying to get their first look at me.

"You have anything to declare?"

"My life. I'd like it back."

I wonder how R. O. is going to smuggle his necklace of ears through customs. I remember hearing him talking about that with grave concern a couple of nights ago. Well, I passed my test. Doc Kane passes through customs—no ears, no dope, no gonorrhea. Now what do I do? Grab the first available woman around the waist, kiss her passionately, say "Let's go raise a family, baby"?

I hadn't notified anyone that I was going to make it back. There are no guarantees. I hadn't written to my family since before I went on R & R. Now I'm on a crowded bus, rolling up a northern California interstate, headed east, where I started this damn journey. In thirty days I have to report to Fort Bragg in North Carolina. So between here and there I start with a visit to the immediate family in Sacramento, then buy a car and drive cross-country, stop to see old friends in Utica. God, that will do it. That will complete the circle. Start to finish, that does it. I'm back. I'm alive, in one piece, in the States. Family. Is there such a thing? My family. I wonder . . . ? God, I'm tired . . . I'm real tired . . . I'm real fucking tired . . .

"Sacramento, Sacramento everyone. All off for Sacramento."

I snap awake to unfamiliar surroundings, panic momentarily, then relax as I realize it's just people getting off a bus. I hate feeling trapped. I grab my spoils and clamber down into the terminal. I walk into the main lobby, still a little groggy. Should I call home and tell them I made it? I wonder where I put the new number? I put the spoils down and search through the stiff khaki uniform pockets. Civilized clothes are so uncomfortable. I'm not even sure of the address. Wonder what it will be like to use a phone? I should get a cold one first. Then make the call, get directions, watch those jugs jiggle out of the corner of my eye. Oh my God! Look at those knockers! She doesn't even have a bra on! I can't believe it! Legs! Ass! Where have you been all my life? Look at what I lived for!

I follow the round-eyed woman out into the street where I see more round-eyed women and more breasts and more commotion and crowds and confusion.

"Taxi?"

More short shorts. More wiggles. More walks.

"Taxi?"

I turn to that question as a cabbie waves me to him. I wonder what it will be like to ride in a car again. I walk over to him.

"Where you need to go?"

"Ice-cold beer."

"C'mon."

As soon as the cabbie found out I was back from the Nam he started in on "how the fucking anti-war demonstrators are fucking up the war. And we ain't even got it started yet."

At about this time I realize I have bowels and a

bladder that are about to burst. I look out the window to see if there's a clump of trees where I can dump a load, then I remember that I'm supposed to be toilet trained.

"Anyways, you guys aren't kicking enough ass over there. You oughta had that thing wrapped up in a year."

Maybe I'll just drop my drawers and shit right here on his back seat. I look around for something I could wipe my ass with. I don't see anything that would work as good as leaves.

"Mind if I take a shit on your back seat, man?"

"You better get out right here, young fella. You can get a cold one here," he says as he pulls up in front of a tavern. He changed his tune quick enough.

"How much I owe you?"

"Seventeen dollars."

I pull out a twenty and throw it on the front seat. I climb out of the cab like leaving an amusement ride. There is still no comparison to clipping rice paddy hedges in an assault chopper.

As I enter the tavern, I'm momentarily struck still by the air conditioning. My eyes adjust to the dimness but I shiver uncontrollably in the coolness. I start to leave, then I remember that it is just as foreign out in the heat and concrete, cars and streets. I stop shivering and walk over to the bar, focusing on the barkeep, who is leaning against the cash register talking to a trio of Happy Hour patrons.

"Howdy." I beckon from the end of the bar. "I'd like a nice cold draft please. I need to use your . . . ah . . . shi . . . er . . . toil . . . ah . . . bathroom is?"

The barkeep unfolds his arms and points toward the back of the room.

"The head's in the back, on the left."

I move at his direction as the patrons turn and grin at me. They must be happy to see me. Bet they don't realize I saved the lives of more than forty people.

I don't have to be graphic about being reunited with

the toilet. I must confess to having trouble with this uniform, these pants, the zipper.

"Ouch!"

Got to remember to start wearing underwear again. I walk back out to the bar, grimacing from my near-miss with the zipper. I go past everyone and look for my beer. Where is it? The bartender saunters over to me, his tongue toying with a toothpick.

"Going off to war, young fella?"

I look into his eyes. Not another wiseacre motherfucker! I look past him at the trappings of his bar. American flag, American Legion booster. Veterans of Foreign Wars auxiliary . . .

"No, I just got back from one."

He chuckles, as if enjoying a joke.

I reiterate, "I'd like an ice-cold draft, please."

He grins even wider, looking closer at me, then over his shoulder at the others. One of them doesn't grin. The barkeep turns back to me.

"Sure, kid, you got any I.D.? Got to be twenty-one to buy alcohol in the state of California."

A realization crashes down around my head and shoulders as I reach for my brand-new wallet. I try to recall how old I am. I'm not nineteen anymore. I take out my military I.D., saying, "Yeah, well, I just got back from the Nam."

"Sure, sure you did. Did you bring any I.D. back with you?"

I slide the identification across the bar. He snaps it up as he pulls glasses out of his shirt pocket. He spits the toothpick on the floor and peers through the magnification at the end of his nose.

"Nope. Sorry. Not old enough." He pulls the glasses away and flips the card back to me. He says, firmly, "Your card says you just turned twenty last month. You're gonna have to wait almost a year 'fore you can drink in this state, young fella."

"But . . ."

"You can't stay here."

"But . . ."

"Sorry, son, it's the law. You have to be twenty-one to be served alcohol. I could lose my license if I served you. Now you'll have to leave."

I guess it was kind of stupid for us to make plans, over there. We planned to meet somewhere back here. Have a reunion, relax together with some cold ones. Except for me, I'm not old enough. I have to wait outside.

"You were going to say something?" she slurs, snapping me back from bitter bewilderment.

"Nah. Fuck it. It ain't nothin," I growl. I forgot she was there. Here.

"Do you want anything else besides Coors and Camels?" she asks.

"Get yourself whatever you want. You got enough money, don't you?"

I reach into my pocket for more greenbacks. This money seems so foreign. I feel like I could cut my hand on it, it's so new. It has an edge, like elephant grass. How many dollars to a piaster?

"Are you listening? I said I have enough money. You seem to be somewhere else. You're not going to leave me, are you?"

I turn and reassure her. "No. No. I'm not going to leave. I ain't going anywhere."

She slides off the front seat and wobbles into the liquor store, leaving the car door open. She had followed me out of that Tavern-for-Grownups and caught me before I could find out how to get back to Viet Nam. She offered to take me to a liquor store and buy me what I wanted if I would share it with her. It's the best offer I've had since I can remember.

So I swallowed a pint of Seagram's. It helped me lose some of my edge. Now I'm driving her Cadillac and we're back at the liquor store to try the beer. Am I lucky.

Am I lucky? Well, part of me is feeling some relief. Still . . . something . . . I haven't been back . . . shit. I grind a cigarette out in the ashtray. Happy enough to be alive, I guess. I hit the wonder bar on the radio. Try to find a familiar song. The only thing familiar is the language. At least it's in English. This bleary-eyed round eye I'm with, she's got to be wearing all that makeup to make up for the years. What am I bitching about? I'm driving her Cadillac. I forgot about all this. That this was all . . . all . . . available? Forgot. Foreign. Like all sorts of things I never knew.

Now take that rice paddy out there. It's ahead of me. Across the road from where I'm parked. Now *that* is something I know about—rice paddies. They aren't as big in Viet Nam, though. I could drive this car across that levee. Huge rice paddies and levees. Christ! Where the fuck did all that come from? Like it's a new, improved rice paddy. A rice paddy that would take all year to sprint across. There's no way we could get across that sucker without getting nailed from the tree line.

"I got two sixes of Coors."

I leap in the seat.

"I forgot how many you wanted. Do you want me to take one back?"

She swings on the car door. For some reason I'm glad to see her.

"Hey, sweetheart, where are we?"

"Whaddaya mean? We're at the liquor store!"

"No, honey. I mean, like, what's those rice paddies doing out there, across the road?"

"Yeah, that's because we're in the delta. The Sacramento delta."

"Really!" I look back out over the huge dikes. "I don't think I could have made it across that motherfucker."

"Do you want me to take one of these sixes back?"

"Huh? No. Fuck it. C'mon, get in before you hurt yourself. We'll drink it."

She throws the beer and smokes between us, then plops onto the seat, closing the door. "I can't believe you aren't old enough to buy your own beer! How old did you say you were?"

"Twenty."

She tries to judge me in her drunkenness. "Wha's your name again?"

"Doc. Just call me Doc."

"Doc. You know I have a son tha's older than you. He just got married so he wouldn't get drafted. Can you believe that, Doc?"

I guess I could believe that, but my mind is on these rice paddies in front of me. Huge fuckers! I can see it happening again as I run across a dike toward Brandt's squad. I start the Cadillac and shift into reverse. Cousins reaches for me and pulls me down. "Get down, Doc, they'll get you. Get down!" I ignore the situation and set to working on Tracks's arm, which has been shattered by a bullet. From somewhere behind me, the rear speakers I guess, I hear Henderson's shout. "Eddie's dead. We're pulling back." I look over my shoulder as I press the accelerator to the floor and the Cadillac reverses, spinning wheels in the gravel. Brandt's pink face turns white. He stammers and stutters next to me. Choppers, gunships, come chopping up and hover behind us. I brake and shift the Caddy into drive. Without looking, I pull out onto the highway on screeching tires and head into a setting sun.

The gunships let loose with their rockets. The smoking trails pass too close over our heads, smashing into the tree line. I pick up Tracks's M-16, flick the safety to rock and roll, and empty a mag into the tree line. The speedometer rockets up to eighty. A blast from the past comes onto the radio, "Soldier Boy" by the Shirelles. Tracks grabs me by the arm with his good arm.

"Don't leave me, Doc. Don't leave me here!"

She grabs me by the other arm, "Slow down and we'll find a motel, Doc. Hey, Doc, slow down and we'll get a room. We'll party!"

I am too confused. So many things should make sense, yet not enough does.

"We gotta get outta here, Doc."

I made it back alive, but I have to leave because I'm not old enough to drink.

"Who goes first? We can't stay out here on this dike. You go, Doc. You first."

I'm lost, stunned, tired.

"No, I'll go last in case any of you are hit. I can pick you up."

Christ, how much longer will we last? How soon will we get it? When will it be over? I am so tired. Dead tired.

"Hey, we gotta get Eddie's body."

Part Two

ALVAREZ MAKES THE TURN WIDE, CATCHING ME OFF guard. I start to fall out of the car. Two-Tone grabs and pulls me back in. We resettle on top of the rear seat of the convertible. Henderson rides shotgun. The street is lined with silent, sullen spectators who halfheartedly wave flags at half mast.

We turn down a suburban side street, on the way to where my family now lives. The spectators disappear. The sky casts a vacant gray. The trees are bare. A slight breeze turns the fallen leaves, gathered in clusters along with Styrofoam cups and clumps of hair.

"This looks like it, Kane," Alvarez says. He stops the car in front of a brick ranch rambler. I look in disbelief. I wouldn't know if I was home, even if it had KANE painted on the mailbox. Did they get any of my letters? Do they realize I'm still alive?

I slide over the side of the car. Two-Tone hands me the Air Viet Nam bag, Montagnard crossbow and Uncle Ho sandals. I put them down. We trade a strong grip. I step to the driver's side, shake hands with Alvarez. I reach across and do the same with Henderson. He beams. "We are the coolest motherfuckers in all of Viet Nam."

"Come and see me and my family down in the Bay Area when you get time," Alvarez says. I step away from the car, nod and smile. Al steps on the gas. Two-Tone falls back on the trunk, pulls himself upright, shouting, "See you when I get out of jail, Doc."

I wave, shout after the car. "Thanks, guys, I couldn't have made it without you." It comes out as a whisper.

The dead leaves somersault on their tips across the landscape, scraping the sidewalks. The wind is a tombstone territory wind.

I face the house.

The shades are drawn. It appears lifeless. I step off the sidewalk. It feels so foreign under my feet. I walk on the grass parallel to the house, trying to figure the boundary. A fence blocks my view of the side of the house, the backyard.

It's too quiet. Nothing moves without the wind. I pace across the front lawn to the other boundary, the driveway. More fence encloses the rest of the backyard.

I return to the front walkway, pick up my gear, and begin a dubious saunter toward the house. Stop. Drop to a knee. Look under the shrubs that stand on either side of the entrance. Looks okay. Move closer.

I set the gear down beside the stoop. Step back, survey around the door. This is where the trap will be if it's anywhere. I listen, trying to hear the danger through the silence. I smell for danger signs. It's too quiet.

I step back to my bag. Bend to unzip it without taking my eyes off the house. I feel the white phosphorus grenade and take it out. Squeezing the handle of the grenade, I pull out the pin, looping its ring around a finger. I step up to the entrance, opening the screen door slowly with an ear for a snap or a pop. Nothing. I knock on the front door. The knock pushes the door open. I shy away, shielding my face. Nothing. I step close, examining the entrance for wires, for any hint of a booby trap.

"OOOHHH!" comes from inside the house.

Ping!

The handle flies off. I don't take any chances. Toss the grenade in the house. I step to the side of the door. Crouch quickly, using the brick facade as cover.

Blam!

The explosion and burning of the phosphorus create a cloud of smoke that fills the interior. What if it's the wrong house? There ought to be some reaction, some movement. I swear I heard something. I push the door open with my foot, smoke billows out.

Anxiously, I slide inside and to the left of the entrance. Even in the cloud of smoke, I recognize the crucifix on the wall. It's encircled with fronds from Palm Sunday. I look further, see Mom's knit afghan hanging over a chair. Yep, it's the right place. I'm home. I stand in relief.

"Hi, Rod."

I whirl, at the ready. My brother Gene lies on the couch.

Did the grenade burn him?

"Gene! Did it get you?"

"Naw. Fast sleeping." Saying that, he sighs and rolls deeper into a blanket and back to sleep. I shrug, look around the room. It's still too smoky to recognize any more of my past. I step back out the front entrance, wedging the doors open for ventilation.

I walk around the side of the house, look in the garage for cars. None. A gate leads through the fence into the backyard. I check around it for traps then step through. A sprinkler distributes water unevenly over the back lawn. A puddle of water sits at the low point in the yard. I step around it.

A faint but familiar sound seeps through the quiet. I step over near a tree. The sound is a distant whip, whip, whip. I drop to a knee behind the tree. The sound becomes a more distinct chop, chop, chop. I curse the lack of foliage and step out from behind the tree. It should be friendly, but who knows, from the reception I've had so far.

Chop, chop, chop, chop. The chopper comes into view. It's a Huey-D troop carrier. The rotor's wind stirs up the dead leaves as it sets down in the yard. What the fuck is going on?

I shield my eyes from the dust as I try to identify the pilot of the aircraft. Though the flight helmet and sunglasses obscure his identity, the pilot grins just as my father would. He gives me the thumbs-up sign.

Children leap from the side of the carrier. They're my youngest brother and sister. Christopher is dressed in a once-white T-shirt, baggy shorts and Catholic Relief Keds. He has a book bag hanging from his shoulder. Marie is dressed in the prettiest pink. They shout and wave at me.

"Waddy! Waddy! Are you my brover Waddy who is in Biet Nam?" Marie yells as the chopper lifts off the ground.

"Rod. Rod. You're back! You're back!" Chris shouts gleefully. He reaches into his book bag and pulls out a Chi Comm grenade. I tense up. He grins as he skips closer, unscrewing the top of the handle. I reach for my .45. It's not there.

"Rod. Rod. Let's play catch. Let's play catch," he says. He pulls the cord out of the handle.

I think I should just go right at him. He'll overthrow me. I'll get him at the throat and tear.

"Catch, Rod!" He stops, grins, flips the grenade at me. I watch, stunned. It loops lazily toward me.

"No, no, you little fucker. You should be inside watching cartoons."

I step back, the grenade follows me. I dive toward the water.

Splash!

I try to get under as far as I can. I close off my senses to the pain of the explosion. Nothing. I stay under water.

Still no concussion. I will stay under for as long as my breath will allow.

Gasp!

Have to take my chances.

Gasp!

I come up for air.

Gasp!

No blast. I roll out of the water.

I sit up.

Everything is a different color. There is a different light. The grass is a lush green. The trees are full of leaves. I'm shocked. I shake water from my head, trying to clear it. Dawn filters up as the sun rises from the east. I look about, see the blanket in a lump under the tree where I had been sleeping. There is no Chi Comm grenade. Where are brother Chris, sister Marie?

Goddammit!

I crawl back to the blanket, use a corner of it to wipe my face. I grab a cigarette, light it, and inhale. The smoky dawn turns into early daylight.

I can't sleep in the house. I lie silent in the tiny room until all is quiet and dark. Then I shoulder a blanket, grab my smokes, and step out into the backyard, curl up under the tree and get some Zs. I wake up for radio watch as usual, staying awake even though there is nothing to report and no radio to report with. I don't doze off until I've convinced myself I'm back in the States. Right now I'd better get back into the house before someone gets up and catches me out here.

I pull the blanket over me to cover the chill. The floorboards squeak in the hallway. I shift over on the sofa, closer to the ashtray and reach for another cigarette. The floorboards squeak again. The old man is up. I light the Camel. Wait. He steps into view.

Pow! Got you, Dad. You're dead.

He turns as if he heard me.

"Can't sleep?" he asks.

"I'll be all right, jet lag still, I think."

He uses my answer as an invitation to come into the living room. He sits on the sofa, on the other side of the ashtray. He lights a cigarette, then runs both hands through his hair. I'd like to be alone.

I turn my attention to the blank TV screen replaying last night's eleven o'clock news. LBJ comes on, saying, "We need 350,000 more troops . . ." Then the news flashes to gunships, rocket ships, spraying a tree line outside Saigon. So near. So far away.

"You have to forget it, Roddie." He exhales smoke.

Something should be explained—I didn't get along with my father before I left for the war. There was a lot of beating, drinking, hating.

"You have to forget it, son."

I turn to him. I can't remember when he last called me "son." Just when I need some room, this man decides he's going to play my father.

"Fuck it, Dad." I bend over to the ashtray, stamp out the cigarette, reach for another. Light it. It strikes me.

Forget it! Is that what he said? "Forget it, son." He went through World War II, Uncle Paul went through Korea. Did they forget about it? Is that why we're in Viet Nam, because the horror and terror of World War II and Korea were forgotten?

"You ought to watch out with that language, son. Around your mother and brothers and sister."

Should I listen to him treat me like a child?

"And, please, don't use that word motherfucker around your mother."

I did what? I'm supposed to listen to every word I say? I mean, it's not like motherfucker is the most offensive word I've heard in the last couple of years. Sergeant Bingham used to end each of his recon classes with the words, "Just remember, you motherfuckers are expendable."

We would laugh, feeling some pride in the insult. Then we landed in Viet Nam, went out on our first operation. The shit hit the fan. We learned which word is more offensive.

"Dad."

"Yes, son."

"From now on, instead of calling someone a mother-fucker, I'll call him expendable."

* * *

Today

Tone,

It sure is all fucked up.

I'm back. Alive. With all my appendages, except I think I left some of my soul over there. Does that make me any less an honorary soul brother?

How are you, buddy? It was a good feeling, finally stepping on U.S.A. ground. Then I was kicked out of a bar for not being old enough to drink. Since then I've been kicked out of everywhere but a voting booth. There's time yet for that.

When I got tired of Mom buying beer for me, I left California in a Cadillac Coupe DeVille. It's used, but, what the hell, this is all new to me. I drove east, stopped in Chicago to see your "grams" and Dino's girlfriend. Didn't get very far into that town. I was told to turn around. Some of your relatives were burning the place down. They couldn't wait for you to get out of jail, could they, Tone?

Anyway, it seems like everywhere I turn, someone is fighting someone.

So I went back to upstate New York, where I had started this odyssey. It was all so foreign. So small. So unrecognizable. Some of the first things I was asked: "Did you kill anyone?"

"How many of your friends died?"

"Did you kill any babies?"

Goddam, who the hell do these people think they are? Are they above all the shit they sent us through? I didn't answer any questions. I just left town.

75

So, I'm writing this from North Carolina, where they sent me to serve out my last year. I'm with the Eighty-second Airborne Division. I'm supposed to be an ambulance driver. Ugh! Spit-shine boots, starched fatigues and a weekly haircut is our routine. The bush it ain't! The Eighty-second runs everything by the book. We pack up combat-ready every day. I get drunk every night. We take riot control practice every day. I get drunk every night. We are on strategic alert for everything that happens in the world. I get drunk every night.

The only fun around here is going into the local town, Fayetteville, to do our drinking. We call the place Fayette Nam, and the people Fayette Cong. Adds a little touch of excitement . . . which reminds me, gotta split, I'll finish this later . . .

"So, how come they made you airborne guys part of the horse cavalry?"

"It's the twentieth century, kid, we gotta adapt."

"Does the horse really jump with you?"

"Yep."

"How do you get 'em in the plane?"

"We walk them up the back ramp, just like you would into a horse trailer."

"Can you turn them around inside the plane?"

"No problem when you're flying a C-130. Just walk them around inside the plane like you would in a small exercise yard. Now, I don't know but that you may have to back them in when you're jumping out of something like a C-119 or a Caribou transport. It would be pretty hard for airborne cavalry to jump out of a C-119. Probably have to use Chincoteague ponies."

Hudson and I reach the top of the stairs, turn left and pass through the double doors into the barracks area. Almost everyone from the company is here, half out of their fatigues, as we are half into the night. Another Mickey Mouse inspection down at the motor pool has everyone running late and a bit edgy. I head toward my locker. Hudson follows me, like a dog.

"Hey, Payton, c'mere man and listen. Kane's telling about what it's like being airborne and in the horse cavalry in Viet Nam. Right, Kane?"

"That's right."

The invitation draws Payton and a couple of other new recruits.

"What do ya mean, Hudson?" Payton questions in his usual drool.

"It's the twentieth century, man. We gotta adapt. In a war like Viet Nam, ya gotta blend the old with the new. Right, Kane? Tell Payton. Tell him how you made the jumps with the horses."

"So after you load them up, you take off, see? And do the usual flying around to confuse the enemy and your own officers."

"Do the horses get sick?"

"Nah. They weed the queasy ones out in horse jump school."

"Really?" the recruits ask in unison.

"Kane, are you bullshitting the new guys again?" The accusation comes from a corner of the barracks.

"Hell, no, Keyes. You know I don't have to bullshit. Anyways, you guys have heard of horse jumping, haven't you?"

Payton volunteers, "Yeah. I think I have. Ain't it in the Olympics?"

"A well-respected sport."

"C'mon, Kane. C'mon. What next?"

"So we fly around for a while, then they drop the back ramp of the C-130."

"Are you sure the horses don't barf or something?"

"What do you do if they shit in the plane?"

"What if they pee? I always got to pee when they open the doors."

"These horses go through some rigorous training before they can associate with us paratroopers."

"What next? What next?"

"Okay, so the ramp is down. The jump master alerts everybody, 'Get ready.' "

"Just like we do."

"Then, instead of saying 'Stand up,' he says, 'Mount up.' "

"Ah, you're kidding, he does not . . ."

"Shut up, Williams! Kane was there. Tell 'em, Kane."

"So we mount up. Then, he directs us, 'Back up,' and we back the horses all the way to the cockpit."

"Kane, you're sick," comes another accusation from another part of the barracks.

"Who wears the 'chute, Kane? You or the horse?"

"You do. I do. Whoever goes through the seventy-two-hour Horse and Rider Associated Assimilation Jump School. That's where we learn exercises like 'Cowboy Squats.' Got to do one hundred a day. To get the ol' legs in shape for hanging onto the horses when the 'chutes open. Horses can't wear 'chutes 'cause they open them at the wrong time. It's been proven. Anyways, don't try to sidetrack me. So, the jump master shouts out his next command, 'Hook up,' and we hook the static lines to the jump cable. Then he sounds off with, 'Check equipment,' and all the rest of the commands, while we sit high in the saddle, waiting for the red light to turn green. The horses know what's going on. They're chomping at the bit and neighing and ayeing and maybe one of them tinkles a little bit; after all, they're only horses. So everyone is ready as the wind whips through the open fuselage. The plane bucks and the tracers can be seen coming at us like fiery hornets and the horses are trying to maintain their balance as we hold on to the reins with one hand and the static line with the other. 'Stand back from the door,' the jump master yells. We back the horses as far as we can against the cockpit doors."

I pause to light a cigarette. The recruits fidget.

"Suddenly, the red light turns green and the jump master starts using his riding crop and yelling, 'Go! Go!

Go! Go! Go! Go!' We whip our ponies into a lather and run right off the back of the plane.''

"I whip my pony into a lather every night in the latrine. You guys are sleeping." Payton grins, drooling.

"Shut up, Payton!" Hudson snaps. "Kane, are you bullshitting us?"

"Kane, you're so full of shit."

"Thanks for reminding me, Williams," I say, stepping out of the circle. "I'm going out tonight and I damn sure don't want to be full of shit." I head toward the double doors and the latrine, leaving the story, the recruits, and the horses in midair.

"Do the horses land on their feet? Did ya squash your balls?" Hudson asks, exasperated.

I turn back. "Hudson, you're getting a little too far ahead of yourself, buddy."

"What do ya mean?"

"It don't matter how the horses land or how you land. You better hope that parachute opens first."

I leave the room with the men in guffaws and dropped jaws. Keyes comes out to the barracks' center, hands on hips. He admonishes the recruits.

"I can't believe you guys listened to him."

"I can't believe I did either," Cotter admits.

"He sure took you for a ride, Hudson."

"Fuck you, Payton. He took *us* for a ride."

Keyes cuts in. "You guys want to hear some more horseshit? The lieutenant has left an order that we all have to stay here tonight because of Kane."

A unison of "whats?" and obscene declarations fill the barracks.

"What do you mean, Keyes?" Cotter pipes above the rest.

"Lieutenant Glass says we are all restricted to quarters to watch Kane 'cause he's gotten so many Article 15s that he has to be watched."

"'Cause he's had that car wreck, too."

"You mean we got to pay for Kane's fuckups?"

"That's unconstitutional."

"That's unfair. They can't detain us for something someone else does."

"They can't, but they are. Orders are Kane is restricted to quarters and we are restricted to watch him, to make sure he doesn't get in trouble."

Cotter begins pacing back and forth in the center aisle. "He can't do that. They can't do that. Who's in charge of quarters tonight?"

"Alvarez."

"Shit, he's Kane's friend. Maybe, dammit, this is not fair. I got a date tonight."

"Who you got a date with tonight, Cotter? One of the jumping horses?"

"Fuck you, Keyes."

I push through the double doors to a room full of silence. Cotter glares at me as I walk past him and head for my locker. I feel him follow. I hope he doesn't try anything stupid.

I stop at my bunk and empty my pockets. Keeping the keys, I go to the locker and unlock it. Cotter peers at me from over the far end of the bunk.

"Where you going, Kane?" he asks.

"Out."

"You can't go out, you're restricted to quarters. We all been restricted to quarters to watch you." He whirls and stalks off to his own locker.

I strip off the fatigue shirt I borrowed from someone. Only had to rip off the stripes and name tag. Just call me U.S. Army. I pull the madras button-down shirt from a hook. Put the fatigue shirt in its place. God, it's nice to put on real clothes. I pull off the fatigue pants and throw them on the locker floor, put on the shirt and, with a change of heart, pick the fatigue pants up and hang them on a hook. I take down Levis and slip into the cool cotton comfort.

A trooper stops abruptly at my bunk. I look up.

"Hey, Ramirez. What's up? Where've you been? I haven't seen you all day."

"I worked dispensary today," Ramirez says. "Where you going, boy? You're restricted to the barracks area. We all gotta stay in the barracks and keep you out of trouble."

"That's just what I got finished telling him," Cotter whines, walking by the bunk. Christ, he'll hound me all night long if I stay here. I turn to Ramirez.

"I'm going out, Ramirez. If you are supposed to watch me then you better get your ass in gear, because I'm leaving ASAP."

"All right!" Ramirez whirls and claps his hands, alerting everyone in the barracks. "Listen up, everyone, extra duty time. We are charged with the responsibility of keeping Kane out of trouble. We got to watch him. He's leaving, which means we got to leave to watch him. Where you going, Kane?"

"Drop Zone Club."

"We got to watch him go to the Drop Zone Club. Our uniform will be civilian clothes. We will follow orders and watch Kane party."

"I will need help."

"He will need help."

"Duty calls!"

"Get your asses in gear. We're getting out of here."

"Who's buying?"

"We'll pool our money and buy pitchers of beer."

"Hey Kane!" Cotter steps to my bunk again, half into civilian clothes. "You can't go to the Drop Zone Club. You've been busted all the way down to E-1. They don't let privates in."

"And some folks wonder why I drink."

"Hey, we can't all split," Hudson proclaims, coming to my bunk. "We're supposed to be on alert for that Arab-Israeli war."

Ramirez shouts from his cubicle, "We are on Kane alert first, right Kane?"

"Don't tell Bernstein that, he's really into the Israeli thing. I suppose if something starts in Israel, they'll find enough of us to go to it."

"Yeah," Ramirez says. "When they shipped us to Chicago for the race riots, they didn't have much trouble finding us."

"Except for Kane. We couldn't find Kane."

"They didn't look hard enough."

"Hey, Patterson." Ramirez rouses the man in the bunk next to me.

"Patterson, wake up. Wake up, man. We gotta watch Kane, and he's leaving."

"Huh? Wha? Watch?"

"Really, Patterson, we're on Kane alert and this Jewish thing. C'mon. Can't sleep. Got to get on the job. Watch Kane."

"Don' wanna." Patterson struggles to stay asleep.

"Leave him alone, Ramirez," I say as I straighten my appearance. "I'll report him in the morning for not watching me."

Cotter comes back to my bunk in civvies. "Hey, Kane. Did Viet Nam fuck you up like this?"

"Cotter, nothing fucks me up except for whiskey and women." I retrieve my wallet, coins and keys from the bunk, step past him into the center aisle. Almost everyone is in civilian clothes. I guess they *are* going to watch me.

"Kane. I hope you don't mind, but I'm just going to watch you leave. I'd rather read or jerk off."

"Not at all, Keyes. It's going to be the same old boring shit. Drink, drunk, most drunk. Everyone ready?"

"C'mon, everyone," Ramirez orders, as he straightens himself out. "Got to do our duty."

"How can you leave when you're restricted?" Cotter asks me one more time.

"By way of those double doors, I guess."

"Hey, Kane? How are we going to get by the Charge of Quarters?"

"Walk."

"Charge of Quarters is Alvarez, his buddy," Cotter laments. "You guys are really going to get in trouble."

"What are they going to do, Cotter, send me back to Viet Nam?" I ask, heading for the door.

"Yeah," Ramirez asks. "What are they gonna do? Send us to Israel?"

"Send us back to the Dominican Republic?"

"Send us back to the race riots?"

"Don't get too far ahead of us, Kane."

Hic!

There really is no way to tell which yard is whose, even if I hadn't had a bunch of beers. Trailer parks are like that. Ooops! There goes a pink flamingo. Where the hell am I? Where is it? There. That's the one.

I pull up alongside the trailer in the Cobra GT, trying to make as little noise as possible.

Rumble. Rumble. Rumble.

Crunch! Ooops, there goes a plastic wading pool. I stop. Wait for lights to come on in the trailer park, responding to the commotion. It has to be after 1:00 A.M. because that's when the bar shut down. I douse the high beams, flick the car stereo off and shut the engine down.

Hic!

She said he'd be gone a week. Maybe I'll get shot. I shouldn't be messing around with someone's old lady.

I jerk the door open and the interior light flashes on, giving away my position.

Christ!

I drop to the ground, under the car door. I lean against it until it clicks shut. The light goes out.

Hic!

I lean back against the machine, absently reach for a cigarette. I light the Camel, giving away my position. I cup the glow of the cinder in my hand, Nam style. My position, I guess, is that I am about to invade a fellow

G.I.'s house trailer because his wife says she is hot to trot for me. With him away on bivouac, I guess I could just knock on the door. Nah. It wouldn't be any fun if I did it that way.

Hic!

I get up and walk slowly around the tin trailer. Can't reach the bedroom window from the ground, the trailer's set too high. Could throw pebbles at the window. Use a step ladder? Rappeling rope? Christ, I'm turning this into a major operation. I stop back at the car, and lean against the fender.

Where's that window go to, up there? I squint in the dark. I could just climb up the back of the car, lean over from the roof, slide that window to the side and drop in like a letter in a mail slot. Special delivery, mama.

Hic!

I flick the cigarette into the darkness. It cuts like a tracer across the night. They couldn't hit me over there. Nobody is going to hit me back here.

I stand straight and stretch, getting the circulation going. I walk around to the back of the car, step on the bumper. The car dips under my weight. I step on the trunk lid, wary of buckling the softer spots of the car body. With one foot balancing below the back window, I step up on the car roof. Not bad for being half drunk. Now I have things in a better perspective.

Hic!

Should have parked a little closer to the trailer. Gonna have to lean a bit. I rest my left hand on the trailer roof. It's going to be a stretch. I reach with my free hand, ready to force the window sideways. Ooops! It slides without any trouble. I almost fall from overexerting.

Hic!

Now. How to enter? Better to go headfirst. It will split my Levis if I have to stretch a leg.

I lean. I lean further, grazing my shoulders on the window's sides. I get my top half through the window, half in or half out? The interior of the trailer smells stuffy and humid. I stop for a moment. Should have eaten something. Could get sick.

I float my hands out in the darkness, searching for leverage.

Ooops!

Too top-heavy. No handholds. Gonna get sick. Foot, no, don't go!

I start to fall into the trailer as one foot leaves the car roof. I stretch my arm—squish—into something that could be . . . can't keep my balance . . .

Hic!

Spaghetti.

Hic!

Blaugh!

Hic!

Crash!

I tumble into the kitchen sink. My weight carries me head over heels onto the floor. A light flicks on, blinding me momentarily. As I blink, I can't help but see the barrel of a Colt .45 held at my head.

"Hi, Ann . . . I hope!"

"Goddammit, Rod. Why don't you just damn drop in and have some leftover spaghetti?"

"Am I late for dinner?"

"By at least a day and you're a dollar short to boot. You better hope your little nose dive didn't wake up the kids."

She keeps the pistol trained at my head. I try to adjust my eyes to the light. I can't tell how sincere she is with that gun.

"How the hell did you get out here anyway? Sid said you wrecked your Caddy last week."

"Week before last. I borrowed Ramirez's Cobra GT."

"Well, he's a damn fool for lending it to you. How much have you had to drink tonight?"

"Hell, not much lately. What time is it?"

"It's 1:45 A.M."

"Yeah, I haven't had a drink since forty-five minutes ago."

"Had anything to eat?"

My stomach churns, but that could be because she won't take the gun away from my head.

"Yeah, I had . . . some beer nuts . . . and beef jerky."

"Just what I thought. Get up out of the middle of that spaghetti. Damn, you are about the craziest Yankee I ever met."

I try to get up under the glare of the gun.

Hic!

"Got to get rid of these hiccups." I grab the sink's edge and hoist myself up.

"Looks like, from the front of you, you got rid of the beer nuts and beef jerky." She uses the pistol to point out directions. "Now, use some of those paper towels and that sponge to clean yourself off."

"Put that pistol away, will you?"

"Dammit, I ought to use it."

"Well, use it, then put it away." I wipe off my shirt then toss the sponge into the sink. I don't think I'm cut out to be a motherfucker.

"Here, you missed some." She steps up close, smelling of sleep and silk. I sway as she brushes me off, I try to breathe in as much of the woman as possible. What a smell, what a great smell!

"Now, you and me can't be . . . wait a minute." She leaves me in the kitchen and steps into the back bedroom.

Hic!

She returns. "Okay, they're still sleeping." She steps over and fingers my shirt collar, brushing my cheek with her lips. "You and I can't be meeting like this. If you weren't so goddamned cute, I wouldn't be messing with you at all. Why don't you sit and rest a minute then move on for tonight? Call me in the morning."

She turns me out of the kitchen. I head for the front door.

"Do you want to sit?"

My jaw gets military tight. What the fuck did I do this for? So stupid.

"No. No. I'm going to move on. Return the car. Reveille is at 5:30 anyway."

I turn to kiss her on the lips. She quickly turns away. Our future is predicted by a peck on the cheek.

"Thanks for not shooting me, Ann."

"You're welcome, wild man."

I step into the night.

Pulling out of the dirt road, the Cobra GT tires spurt sand then make a shrill sound spinning on the blacktop road. I ram the shifter into second gear, accelerating to a reckless speed.

Hic!

The curve just pops into view as I jam the shifter into third. I'm not ready to negotiate the turn and a large sand patch that covers part of the road. I hit the sand patch. The car starts to slide sideways. The speed seems to increase. Everything becomes weightless, out of control.

Christ! I just went through this a couple of weeks ago. Damn it! How long does it take for things to happen once you lose control?

The car continues to slide sideways. The tires catch on the hard road surface. My speed changes abruptly. The steering wheel spins out of my grasp. So does the wheel of fortune. I'm trying to turn back time so I don't have to go through another fucking car wreck. I can't afford it. Ramirez is going to be pissed. I ought to take one more swallow out of that bottle of scotch before it breaks in the crash. I should have written Mom. I need to return those fatigues I borrowed from Alvarez. I didn't tell you about Alvarez, did I? Well, I haven't got time. I'm glad I didn't get it on with Sid's wife. I'm more expendable than I am a motherfucker. I wish I had finished that letter to Two-Tone . . .

Schreech!

Blumph! Blam! Crash! Ooof!
Blumph! Blam! Crash! Shit.
Blumph! Blam! Crash! Christ!

I had a lot of time to go through quite a few things before the shit hit the fan. I mean, it wasn't like the length of time we took to go through things when the shit hit the fan in Viet Nam, but what do you expect for stateside excitement?

Dust. Glass. Gas. Engine oil. All settling down around me. I'm upside down. I think.

The radio is playing "Everyone's Gone to the Moon." Got to get out of here. Scotch bottle's not broken. I'm stunned. How many more of these can I survive? Gas is starting to leak. The engine is still running. Got to get out. The back window is broken open. Slide out that way. Get the scotch. Hey, I'm on someone's front porch. Maybe they have a spare bedroom, a couch. I'm tired. I could use some sleep. Maybe I'll just lay out right here. Damn, I'm tired. Is it over yet?

• • •

Today

Tone,

Try again.

Sorry I didn't get back to you sooner. I got side-tracked. I'm in the hospital as of this writing because I can't seem to keep my cars between the ditches. Remember how we used to dream about making it through the Nam so we could come home and die in a good old-fashioned car wreck? Well, I did one for me and one for you. You're welcome, I knew you'd appreciate it.

I fractured some vertebrae in my neck and while I'm in here tests are being done because I show signs of still having worms. Anyways, the accident got me out of going back to Chicago to quell another race riot. Damn, Tone, every summer the ghettos burn. It's like we have to fight everywhere I go. Where there's riots in the cities, we get to fight the people we fought alongside of in Nam. It makes me sick. I've decided that I'm not going to fight anyone anymore unless it's to defend myself. I ain't fighting blacks, or Spanish, or Indians, or Polish, or Danish, or squeamish, or Amish. Maybe Irish though.

You know what I mean, buddy?

I'm very angry with myself for not being more alert that night. I might have kept you from going over the edge. Fuck it. It seems like we are all in one sort of jail or another. I still booze pretty heavily, but a good part of that is to knock me out so I can say I've had some sleep. I mean, the nightmare of Happy Valley, Ia Drang, booby traps. The whole ball of wax still has me bugged. Are we ever going to have any peace?

I'm starting to ramble so I'm going to split. I'll be getting out soon. Enclosed is my family's address in California. Is your gram's address still good in Chicago? That's how I'll continue to keep in touch with you. I know you're not going to be in there forever. I hope you still smoke Winstons 'cause that's what you're getting.

Sincerely,
Doc

P.S. Alvarez says hi. He's stationed here with me. Would you believe he still carries a rosary in his pocket? The man is great. He still has faith. I lost my faith about the same time I lost my virginity. Don't tell anybody.

P.P.S. Fuck 'em if they can't take a joke.

"Okay, send him in," the voice booms from the next room. I instinctively look at my fingernails as if preoccupied and unaware that I'm being sought. The orderly rushes out, almost tripping over my outstretched legs.

"Ooops, there you are, Kane. The First Sergeant will see you now."

I get up, cool and nonchalant. I look at the orderly as aloofly as possible. I wish I had a fart in me to insult this procedure.

"Kane. Where the hell are ya? I haven't got all day. Get your ass in here so I can get sick to my stomach and get it over with."

I casually step into his office. Shit. Sergeant Brown and Sergeant Ellis are with him, witnesses. Well, at least there will be no fisticuffs.

"Kane, goddammit, you are fucking up," his voice booms, "and something tells me you're doing it on purpose."

"Whatever, First Sergeant."

"What do you mean, 'Whatever First Sergeant'? You've missed reveille three times, been charged with reckless driving, public intoxication, took the whole barracks on a wild goose chase, spent five days in jail in Myrtle Beach. You've been busted back to private three times, restricted, served extra duty. Now the Colonel wants to have you court-martialed. Whatever do you have to say for all this?"

Honest to God, I've given it some thought. I am not making a rash decision. It's more like a well-thought-out rash decision. I'm tired. I'm exhausted. I don't have the patience. I don't have the respect. I'm burned . . .

"Kane, I want an answer!"

"Fuck it."

His face blooms red. "What did you say?"

"Fuck it."

"What did you say? You can't say that to me."

"Fuck it, First Sergeant."

"Kane. I have witnesses here, you understand, who could testify about your attitude. Your behavior."

"Fuck it, Sergeant Ellis. Fuck it, Sergeant Brown."

"Kane, with that kind of attitude you will get court-martialed."

"Fuck it."

"Well, goddammit, no. I won't stand for this disrespect. You can't do this in my army. You can't carry that kind of attitude around in any man's army. To say the least, Private Kane, I will have you barred from re-enlisting."

Now that catches me off guard. I mean, I don't care if they kick me out, and this guy is going to threaten me with not being able to get back in. I'm confused.

"I beg your pardon, First Sergeant. What did you say?"

"I said, Private Kane, that at least I can have you barred from re-enlisting."

"How can I help, First Sergeant?"

* * *

"That tie looks good, Roddie."

"Yeah, I guess. Do you have the keys?"

"On the table. Be careful driving."

"Okay, see ya." I grab the keys and walk to the door, trying to adjust my shoulders into the sport coat.

"Hey, wait a minute, Roddie?" she calls. "Have you eaten anything? Roddie?"

I almost turn around and say "fuck it," but realize where I am. I can't say "fuck it" to my mother.

"I'm okay," I admit over my shoulder and step out of the house. I pull off the sport coat and throw it through the open window on the passenger side of the car. I scurry around to the driver's side and climb in. After some fumbling, I find the right key for the ignition. I haven't been drunk in a month so even the simplest tasks are hard to perform. I'm not complaining. I'm alive.

I drive down the freeway and through the city traffic in fairly easy fashion. Sacramento is a town I don't know, but it's where the family is and California is the "in" place to be in 1967. I have three years to catch up on and a lifetime of emergency medical experience to share.

There's a parking spot right in front of the Professional and Technical Employment Office. It's my lucky day. I parallel park in two crisp turns of the wheel. Getting out, I put enough change in the parking meter to maintain full tenure on the spot. I walk into the employment building. I walk back out of the building to the car. I grab the sport jacket, roll up the windows and lock the car. I forgot, in America everything and everyone is locked up tight and rolled out of sight.

Back in the building, I figure out which arrows in the lobby are intended for me. I move in that direction. When I find the room, I'm confronted with a sign: TAKE A NUMBER. BE SEATED. It's the right place. I take the number 13 and gloat. Someone's got to be number 13, might as well be me. I made it back. I'm lucky.

I take a seat. Jump out of it, running my hands through all my pockets. It looks like I just sat down on a nest of bitch ants, but I'm only looking for my employment form. The rest of the people in the waiting room don't know that. Everyone around me shies away. I find the 171 form in the document pocket of my sport coat. Sit back down, looking around. These folks better be nice to me. If one of them needs a medic, he's going to wish he hadn't shied away.

"Number 13."

I stand. The others, waiting, continue to eyeball my movements. What the hell, haven't they ever seen anyone make it out of a war?

"Number 13?" the loudspeaker questions.

I walk over to the desk. A receptionist takes my number.

"Mr. Nakashima will see you, thirteen." She points. "He's over there." I look in that direction. A tall, thin Oriental man is standing there. He motions to me. I step toward him. He's an American, right?

"Good morning, Mr. Kane. I'm Mr. Nakashima." He offers his hand.

"Doc . . . er . . . Mr. Kane, Mr. Nakashima." We bow. I don't believe I've ever shaken the hand of an Oriental.

"Sit, please, Mr. Kane." We both do. He continues, "Do you have your 171 form with you?"

I hand it over. He nods to the ashtray as he takes it. "Smoke if you like, Mr. Kane, while I take a moment to review this."

I pull out a Camel, light up and draw out the smoke. My mind wanders to the neon light overhead. I wonder if people can get neon tans working here. Take off your shirt while at work and get a neon tan. Two-Tone used to mock me. "How come you crackers always be putting down blacks then rush out under the sun to get your lily-white asses brown?"

"You're just out of the military, Mr. Kane?"

"Yes, sir." I sit up abruptly in my chair.

"Viet Nam, also."

"Yes, sir."

He pauses, thoughtfully. "We haven't seen too many returning from over there yet. You claim to have medical experience?"

"Yes, sir. I was a medic with the infantry in Viet Nam. My last year, I drove a field ambulance, stateside bul . . . ah, in North Carolina."

"I see. High school GED."

"Yes, sir." I shift uncomfortably. "I left high school after the twelfth grade. I missed graduation by a couple of units. Didn't want to stay around to finish. I took the GED test in my last year of service . . . again, in North Carolina." God, what a hangover I had the day I took that test. It almost made me wish I had finished high school.

"Yes. I see." Mr. Nakashima flips the 171 form over. "How old are you, Mr. Kane?"

"I just turned twenty-one."

"Twenty-one. You were in Viet Nam awfully young, weren't you?"

I shrug. "I don't know. I guess. It doesn't make much difference after a while."

He doesn't seem to hear my last remark. He folds up the 171 form and puts it in an envelope.

"Mr. Kane, you are a resident of the state of California, aren't you?"

"Yes, sir."

"Mr. Kane, did you know you could go to school, to college, here without a high school diploma?"

I don't know what to say to that. I had never thought of going back to school. I have a job, a duty. I save lives. I administer emergency medical care. I did it in the war, under fire. I can do it as a civilian. I do good work, I was rated 100-percent proficient in my job by the military.

"Mr. Kane, the purpose of the Professional and Technical Employment Bureau of the state of California is to find jobs for people who have completed training at professional and technical levels. These people have certifications from accredited institutions. Do you have a certificate from an accredited school?"

"I went to medical corpsmen's school at Fort Sam Houston."

"I'm sorry, that's not the accreditation we recognize. You have nothing outside the Army school?"

"Just my experience."

"The people we find jobs for usually have completed some type of education."

Maybe I don't know how things work out here in civilization as you all know it.

"You ought to think about going back to school, Mr. Kane. You're young . . . you could get an education, fit back in . . . forget the war . . ."

The interview ends in the middle of so many desks under neon suns in the bowels of bureaucracy. We stand, stretch hands across a desk, shake mechanically. No bow. The show must go on. I turn. Walk out of the paperwork maze without bumping into too many things. By following the tail ends of arrows, I find my way back to the main lobby and outside.

Crossing the street without paying any attention to traffic, I take off the sport coat. I step onto the grassy mall, spread the coat out, slip my shoes off and sit. I light a cigarette. Exhale. I'm lucky to be alive. I sit on that mall and chain smoke. I'm lucky to be alive. Chain smoke more cigarettes, get up, walk to the car, take the parking ticket from under the windshield wiper. I'm lucky. Get in the car, head out of the city. No complaints. I'm alive.

Within a week, I'm filing medical records at a local hospital. That's all I qualify for. I can't help but feel out of place, out of the flow everyone else seems to be in. I can't help but be shocked that the system has nothing set up to take advantage of my experience.

Doc Kane,

The longer I'm in here, the whiter I sound on paper. That's what getting an education behind bars gets me, but it does help with scrutinizing military and civilian law books in the prison library. I have found the key to fit the loophole that is going to get me released! It seems I had some rights of entry in the backroom of the Sugar Shack. I will have to accept a bad conduct discharge but better bad paper on the street than blank paper in here. So it looks like I might see you out there if we can find a place where a black brother and a white dude can meet in peace. Send all future correspondence to my gram's address. All power to the people.

Realistically,
Eugene "The Tone" Clark

Rrrrripppp!

I pitch forward, taking a couple of quick steps to regain my balance. I turn and glare at the tear as if it were a booby trap. How can I disarm that? The whole gymnasium floor is covered in ripples of cloth, put down to protect the veneer floor from the scuffling feet of registering students.

"Are you all right?" she asks, coming to my side. I turn and feign a smile.

"Only two kinds of people make it through class registration, the quick and the dead."

"What?"

"Nothing. Did you get that class you wanted?"

"Oh, yes." She smiles. "I got both classes. How did you do?"

"I got the remedial class I needed. Got a couple of freshman 1A classes."

"How many are you going to take?"

"Seven."

"Seven and work full time in medical records? You can't do it. It'll burn you out."

"Naw. It won't. I gotta catch up anyway. I've been out of action for so long."

"Still . . ."

"Hey, I appreciate you giving me a lift over here. Do you have to go back to work?"

"No. I took administrative leave. Do you have to work?"

"Naw. I still have weekend shift, so I have today and tomorrow off. Are you finished with registering?"

"Yes."

"Let's go for a drive somewhere. Do you mind?"

"Not at all."

"I have some Mexican smoke. We can get stoned and talk nasty about the other folks at work."

She giggles. "Good idea. I know a nice place out by Folsom Lake."

"Let's go." We turn, sliding on the cloth-covered floor, and head out the door.

"Did you have a medical background when they hired you for medical records?"

"No, Mr. Brest hired me because of my tits."

We laugh together. These California girls are nervy.

"It is my right to profess that the oppression of third and fourth world peoples is manifested in the struggle of the Vietnamese people against the imperialistic tactics of capitalism."

Huh?

"Now, you don't have to agree with me but I do believe I will prove that point before this semester is completed. The books on my reading list are meant to portray the changes going on in this society as well as in others."

I gaze down at her handout, at the reading list printed on it.

Soul on Ice by Eldridge Cleaver.

The Feminine Mystique by Betty Friedan.

The Wretched of the Earth by Frantz Fanon.

"Now I know that some of you are questioning what kind of reading list this is for a class like Anthropology I. Well, in my estimation, these books best state what anthropology is today."

She pauses and looks over the class. A hand shoots up. She ignores it.

"My office hours and office phone number are up in the right- and left-hand corners of the handout."

The hand waves, causing the jewelry attached to jingle and jangle.

"Yes? What is it there, young woman? I'm sorry. Has your hand been up for long?"

"Mrs. Shanahan, I have a conflict between this class and Psych Op Ed IIIA. Could I just attend . . . I mean I'll do the readings and writings you want, but could I just attend classes for the tests? I mean, you'd be able to tell if I've done the assigned work by my test scores."

"Maybe so, but I have four pop quizzes scheduled for 20 percent of your semester grade. I'm not divulging when I'm going to give them."

"Maybe I could do extra essays or something. Do you need baby-sitting? Psych Op Ed is my major . . ."

"Okay, okay. Hold off. See me after class."

Seventeen hands shoot into the air.

"No. Please. No more questions until after class. Please. This is a short class today, wait until after I've excused the rest. By the way, are there any veterans, especially Viet Nam veterans, in this class?"

Ooops, I start in my chair. I thought I was in kindergarten for a moment. I cover my surprise by nonchalantly lifting my right hand and forearm from the desktop. I'm so cool. Folks turn and look. I'm giving away my position. Off to the right, a brown arm exposes itself, halfheartedly.

"Is that arm raised?" she asks, looking in my direction. I nod.

"Okay. Just two this time. Good. Okay, gentlemen, both of you, I've been instructed by the dean of academic affairs to advise you that the viewpoints put forth in this classroom are not necessarily the viewpoints of the college itself. May I ask you?" she points to the brown arm, "what branch of the service were you in?"

"Air Force," he admits.

"Were you out here at McClellan?" she asks.

"Yes."

"Ever overseas?"

"No."

"And you, mister?" She turns in my direction, standing on her tiptoes to get a clear look. "What branch of service are you from?"

I sit higher in my chair.

"Army Airborne."

She steps down the aisle, cautiously. She looks at me with all sorts of affected concern. "Were you overseas? Viet Nam?"

"Yes."

"Were you in combat?"

"Yes."

Everyone in the class turns to look.

"Were you on the front lines?"

"There were no front lines."

"An adventure nonetheless," she says abruptly, turns and walks back to her desk.

"Did you kill anyone?" someone whispers.

I'm not sure I hear properly. I turn to the left and right, searching the available faces. Each set of eyes I encounter looks away. I turn my attention back to the front.

"Did any of your friends die?"

Behind me, the whisper is behind me. I turn around slowly. I'm confronted by these huge green eyes.

"What did you say?"

"Nothing." Green eyes gulps. She is very fair, very pretty, very well dressed and not very deceptive.

"Excuse me there, Mr. Army Airborne, whoever you are," the teacher calls out. "I don't compete with others in my classroom. Is there something you'd like to share with the rest of the class?"

I turn back to the instructor, my face red. Everyone turns and looks at me. I think it is time for a rash move.

"Ah, yeah, maybe it would be a good idea to answer some questions about Viet Nam. To kind of get things put into perspective." I look around the classroom, angry but in control.

"I tried to kill Vietnamese anytime we were under attack, but I did so to protect my wounded, my dead." I look at faces. Some look away. Some don't.

"I lost most of my friends." My throat gets tight.

"I don't think we should be there, but what I think

99

doesn't make any difference. We are there. I would not go back to Viet Nam because I'm not quite sure I would come back alive. I did not kill prisoners or torture them. I was put in the position of having to kill a . . . never mind. That's all I have to share."

The class is silent. A few students stare at me. I feel a prickly sensation at the back of my neck.

"Well, that was quite a declaration, young man," the instructor says as she steps around to the front of her desk. She pauses, wringing her hands. "I think we can end our first class on that note. All of you people who need to talk to me, please come forward."

The class breaks up, with most of the students heading out the door. I feel somewhat uncomfortable with my outburst but I don't feel any regret. I turn out of my seat as people clear the aisle. Green eyes sits staring at me.

"Are you a hawk or a dove?" she asks.

I pause for a moment, then look at her. "I'm an owl."

"An owl is a bird of prey."

I stand, look down at her. "Yeah, but we owls give it some thought before killing."

I start down the aisle. She turns out in her seat, blocking my way. "Guess what bird I am."

"Tweety bird." I step over her legs and walk out of the classroom. She jumps up and follows me. "Do you like vegetarians? What's your sign? I'm a Virgo. Where are your other classes?"

I quicken my pace, head toward the parking lot, slowing as I realize she has given up following me. Goddam, I'm exhausted. Working full time. Going to school full time. Drinking full time. Damn! How did those guys from World War II and Korea do it?

•   •   •

We are lined up at the cable railing, dressed in full combat gear, kicking at each other's heels. Our static lines are hooked to the top cable. We balance while the boat heaves and rolls in the pitch of the choppy sea. The jump master unhooks the chain, opening the rail. He turns to us, shouts, "I want to be the first son of a bitch to welcome you sorry bastards to South Viet Nam." He looks over the side of the boat, turns back to us, "Get ready."

We shuffle into a tighter line. My face burrows into the static line crisscrossing the parachute in front of me. Someone keeps bumping into my parachute.

"Stand in the door."

Two-Tone steps into the opening in the railing. He looks down, then out over the horizon. The red light turns green.

"Go!"

The jump master tries to slap him on the ass but Tone is already over the edge. The rest of us start whooping and hollering, shuffling and bunching up on the way off the boat.

"Go! Go! Go! Go! Go!"

The bobbing and weaving helmets become fewer and fewer.

"Go! Go! Go! Go! Go!"

The jump master reaches for my sleeve. The boat dips into a swell, the wind roaring, as we're covered with ocean spray.

"Go. Go. Go."

"Whoosh!"

Rrrrippp . . .

Pop!

Yank.

Ooff!

Stop!

Swing, suddenly, in the opening shock as the parachute catches air, my legs spread-eagled as I twirl, twisting under wound-up risers, almost losing my stomach, only to swing silently over magnificent lush green jungle. I stop spinning under a tropical sun, and resettle firmly in the risers' seat. Sometimes, you can sit on a testicle and squirm all the way down.

As we drift slowly to the ground, the first shots ring out. Next problem. This was all sport until we were ordered to load on that boat.

Bizzt! That sound at my ear has me search the ground. The gunshots are coming randomly as the large clearing becomes more of a landing zone.

A quick piercing scream brings other shouts. Someone has gotten his weapon loose enough to fire a burst. I crane and twist, looking below me.

"Oh, God!"

They are hard to see at first because we dangle right above them. We drop slowly. They wait for us. Stakes staked to stick. Points pointing to peck. Spikes spaced to split. Christ! They look to be eight or nine feet tall. Well-weathered poles of wood whittled to a pointed expectation wait while we float down to fulfill someone's scheme, oscillating lightly in the wind. I jerk my head in all directions looking for a bare spot, slower, lower, as the screams of pierced paratroopers echo to distract as one of us is impregnated at the right hip, parachute falling over him—a curtain falling on the final act.

Brrip! Brrip! Blam!

Our only defense. Shoot them over. Blow them up. I lock my legs together and wonder if I could climb up these risers, hand over hand like Jack on the beanstalk. I'll face the giant rather than fall on those goddam things pointing at me, calling, "Hey you, Doc Kane. Come on down. Hey, Doc, have a seat. Doc Kane. Doc. Hey, Doc . . ."

. . . I tear all the sheets and blankets from the bed in an attempt to escape the burning sensation in my bowels, falling to the floor, feeling with all fours, the searing pain splitting as I crawl past the bathroom door, crossing the cold tile floor, burping bourbon bile at the toilet bowl as a barrage of loose stool spews, gas cramps, the stomach retches, sweat, cough, hic, cough, help, hic, help, hic, help.

•   •   •

"He said come back to work Monday with a haircut and clean shaven or lose your job."

"Yes. I see. I don't have your file at my disposal, Mr. Kane. Fill me in on a couple of things."

I miss the last comment as someone pushes against me. Pay phones are always in the way.

"What?"

"You've been with the union how long?"

"Over a year, maybe two."

"Where do you work?"

"I started in medical records. I work in the emergency room now, graveyard shift."

"So you've been promoted."

"No. I had experience from Nam."

"That's not important. You've been promoted."

"Yes." I bristle. "The doctors I work with in ER are tripping over their hair, walking around with cottage cheese in their beards. I grow a moustache. My hair touches my shirt collar, I get fired."

"Wait a sec." I hear him make muted sounds away from the phone. I look out over the student cafeteria. Everyone is trying to get coffee before their first class. It's early for them. It's late for me.

"We'll stand by you, son. Trim the moustache above your lip. Wash your hair before you go to work Monday. Wear a clean shirt and tie. Don't worry, your union is going to stand by you. I have another call waiting. Shall I put you on hold?"

"Naw, fuck it."

Click.

I turn away from the phone. Head toward the cafeteria. A playpen for most of these kids. I get a couple of donuts and a big coffee, search for an empty table, out of the way. Sit by myself.

Christ, what a night. One DOA, two auto wrecks. I'm sick of all the blood, guts, violence, pain and agony. What a week. My brother Gene just left for Nam. He was drafted but got a good Army training school. He'll be a pharmacist over there in a MASH unit. I think he'll be okay.

"Hi. We're gonna sit here."

I give a discouraging look at the two young girls dressed in paisley dresses. They grin and sit anyway.

What's so fucking funny? I turn away.

I talked to Dad yesterday. He's telling me he's getting the Air Force to send him to Nam too. He's in the civil service. Now they're getting into the war act. Well, at least he's sober.

"Hey, we're gonna sit here, okay?" Two young long-haired boys pull out chairs and sit at the table between me and the girls.

Nowhere to run. Nowhere to hide. Fucking Bonnie won't take birth control pills. She says we shouldn't sleep together until we're married. So I wait.

"What you guys talkin' 'bout?" one of the boys addresses the girls.

"Mick Jagger. He broke up with Marianne Faithfull, again."

I started watching the news again. I had quit after the Tet offensive. Made me sick.

"Yeah, that's what I heard. She wasn't giving him enough head."

"That's not true. It was the other way around. She got fed up because he wouldn't go down on her."

"I ain't never had a bad piece of ass."

I started watching again when I heard they were broadcasting weekly death tolls, Cronkite and the others. It's become quite a joke.

"Naw, it was her fault. She wasn't putting out enough for Mick."

"Not true. He was on the road so long. She said she wasn't going to sit at home."

"I never turn anything down."

Last week the toll was three hundred and something. If that keeps up, along with the bombing of North Viet Nam, there won't be anyone left to kill. We'll be able to walk right into North Viet Nam.

"She broke it off! She said she was tired of going down on him and he wouldn't go down on her."

"I'd go down on her."

"You'd go down on anyone."

I can't believe that it still goes on. On and on and on. Fuck it. I ain't going to class. I'll go over to the bookstore and stand in the fucking line. Get those books. Go home. Get loaded. Try to sleep.

*   *   *

My thumb finds the good parts. It gets hung up on the ones with the glossy edges. Flip. Oooh. Flip. That's okay. Flip. Mmmmm. Flip. So what. Flip. Oh. Flip, turn the head sideways for the foldout. Yep. That's her allright. Knew her in high school. Who'd a thunk it? A scag like that. Honestly, I only buy the magazine because I'm looking for an old girlfriend. She's the plain but pretty type. You know, the girl next door . . .

After making sure I got what I paid for, I go back to the beginning of the magazine. To read it. Honest. I read it too. Letters to the editor. *Playboy* Advisor, *Playboy* Philosophy, What Sort of Man Reads *Playboy*, *Playboy* Ribald Classics . . .

Boing!

It hits me.

What am I doing reading *Playboy?* I mean, look at what sort of man reads *Playboy*. Let me flip to the right page.

There. Every month, Hugh Hefner gives us a page depicting the sort of man who reads *Playboy*. There he is. Standing in a train station somewhere in Successful Land. It's early autumn. The train station and tram walk are painted oyster white with a cedar shake roof. Green shutters accent the windows and red benches adorn the walkway. A black steam locomotive pulls into the station amongst colorful shades of fallen leaves. Maple. Oak. Birch.

The man who reads *Playboy* is checking his Omega watch on an arm draped with a London Fog raincoat. It won't rain in the *Playboy* world but our man does wonder why the train is late. *Playboy* men are hard to keep up with.

He is dressed in a Wha Cha Mah Callit, a three-piece suit made to order on his last trip to Hong Kong. He complements the suit with a *Playboy* pink shirt, red and black diagonal-striped tie and *Playboy* insignia cuff links and diamond tie tack. He wears black nylon stretch socks under black laced cordovans. If I told you what he has on underneath the suit, like what kind of underwear he has on, what would you think of me? Ooops, I forgot the Samsonite leather-bound attaché case. He has a blonde-haired playmate on his arm. She has clothes on.

I will be honest with you. I want you to rely on my word. I know I may not have given you a good picture of what I'm like, but I guarantee you this, I don't look or act like the sort of guy who reads *Playboy*. I could be having some sort of identity crisis over this, but I'm not. There may be an identity crisis somewhere else though, like up in Chicago, in Mr. Hefner's *Playboy* mansion. He thinks he knows the sort of man who reads *Playboy*. He doesn't. I know the sort of man who reads *Playboy*. Are you ready, Hugh? Everybody. Picture this . . .

You'll find him in Viet Nam, about nineteen, twenty years old. He sits just off a jungle trail amongst foliage that will never see an autumn. He has used the jungle growth to tie his poncho into a makeshift lean-to. He is proud of his temporary home. He sits in front of the lean-to on his steel pot. It triples as a helmet and a sink. He's thumbing through a *Playboy* magazine, glancing at the advertisements, glaring at the full-color glossies. He runs his hand over close-cropped hair and along a stubbled chin. It has taken a week to grow.

He's thrown his pack, a captured rucksack taken from a dead NVA regular, under the shelter. The pack is gray, heavy duty cotton with three large pockets, one to each side—better suited for the carryall factors jungle living demands. It holds more and sits better than the

Army issue. He still wears an Army-issue pack harness and ammo belt. Every hook, clip and eyelet on the belt is a parking spot for a first aid pack, an ammo pouch, shrapnel grenade, another ammo pouch, a canteen, a smoke grenade, a flashlight, another ammo pouch, a canteen, white phosphorus grenade, ammo pouch, ammo pouch, ammo pouch.

His boots, stateside paratrooper style, are still wet from walking through rice paddies. While he turns the pages of the magazine, his toes work the sodden socks around to expel water through cracks in the boots. The fatigue pants are stateside cotton issue, lower legs still damp from the mucky walk. There's a split open at the crotch to keep that area properly ventilated—helps prevent jungle rot. Without too close an inspection, it's quite apparent, our man who reads *Playboy* doesn't wear undershorts.

The fatigue shirt hangs outside the pants. Only the bottom button is fastened. The ammo belt and pack harness wrap around the shirt and secure it in place. The sleeves are rolled up, exposing scratches on the hands, wrists and forearms, the result of hand-to-hand combat with some wait-a-minute bushes when walking point yesterday and the day before. Of course, he doesn't wear an undershirt, this sort of man dresses correctly! All underwear or no underwear.

His jewelry is dog tags. No watch, no rings. The M-16 rifle lies across his lap, balanced on crossed legs. The *Playboy* is spread across the rifle, centerfold turned out. A Winston curls smoke between nicotine-stained fingers. He turns back a page, covering half the foldout.

Thunk!

The sound of a mortar round being dropped into a mortar tube. It's not that far away if you can hear it. We don't have a mortar with us. Must be . . .

Our man who reads *Playboy*, who has just started to lie up alongside the centerfold, leaps to his feet. The magazine goes flying, ripping the Playmate of the Month in two.

"Incoming!" our man screams. He dives into the jungle. Will he live long enough to vote for Playmate of the Year?

• • •

I quit watching the news. A painful routine, it opens with a war scene; then an administration spokesman at the Paris peace talks; anti-war demonstration; then back to a war scene. In each skirmish portrayed, I can identify just about what happened by the looks of the jungle, villages, roads, people, our men.

The news finishes with a Who's Winning, Who's Losing scenario. I can identify who is winning and who is losing. Everybody. I quit watching the news.

• • •

Got to get some sleep, tick tock tick tock, don't want to look at the bedside clock. Pull down the shade. Is it night? When's my next class? Got to make up to catch up to work up to pay up to grow up to throw up to lights out by crushing eyes shut, rolling left then rolling right. Sit up, lie down, fight, fight, fight the pillow curled around a replay of "what if . . . ?" to "how come . . . ?" Pace the room in a chain of smoke as Crazy Horse happens again at 1:00 A.M., the Happy Valley scene at 2:15, Ia Drang Valley on the run at 3:51, tick tock screams for Doc at five o'clock. It's only me at 5:23. Tick at 6:00, tock at 6:11.

Brrrrinngg!

• • •

I'm confused. Enraged. I can't prevent her from leaving me but she hasn't left yet. I know she's going, but I can't stop her.

I race to the line of pay phones. Enter the first booth, yank the receiver off its hook. I struggle to pull a coin from my pocket.

What's that number? What's the fucking number?

I tear out a coin. Jam it in the coin slot. It wedges, too

big. I try to pull it out. My fingers slip from the coin. Great, I used a penny. It's stuck. Dammit! I throw the receiver at the phone. It ricochets back, hitting me at the right shoulder joint.

"Ouch! Motherfucker!"

I dart to the next booth.

OUT OF ORDER.

I pull out my pen, print under the sign: Fuck you.

I'm so mad I can hear the anger's roar rushing in my ears. I'm so mad . . . The third booth cooperates. The phone takes a dime. A line clicks open. I dial.

Got to fucking tell her off. No. Ask first if she's leaving you. Then tell her off! It would help if you dialed the number. Fuck you too, 555-2237. The phone company goes into action. I spit blood on the floor of the booth. Must have bit my tongue. Come on, you sneaky bitch, answer the fucking phone.

"Good Morning, County General Hospital. May I help you?"

"Oh, County . . . Bonnie? I mean, extension 617, please."

"Extension 617, thank you, sir."

Click, click, click.

Now, what was I going to say?

"Medical records."

"Yes. Hi. Is that you, Bonnie?"

"Yes, Rod. What do you want this time?"

My mind is racing, it's a scramble. I'm confused.

"I, ah, thought I was calling you at home. Got mixed up or something. Uh. So are you going, uh, leaving, er, soon? Are we getting together again? Tonight? You and me? What's wrong?"

"What's wrong?" she repeats impatiently. "What's wrong is you keep calling me at work to ask what's wrong. We had agreed to meet tonight after I get off work. What may be wrong is I dread going through another discussion about us. We spend all our time together talking about breaking up. I would love for us to get together and have it not be so negative."

"Yeah. Well. It's real important to me . . ."

"Me too, Rod, but let's lighten up. Let things just happen."

I try to accept that. I try to figure out why I feel so insecure. I can't. I'm blank.

"I'm all for letting things happen, Bonnie. I really am."

"Good. So am I. We'll get together after work and have a few beers, a few laughs. Now, I have to get back to work, okay?"

"Okay."

"Bye."

"Bye."

Click.

I put the receiver back near its cradle. It drops to the metal tray under the phone. I reach for a cigarette, step out of the booth. I feel like I've just been put in my place. I don't know where my place is. I was angry. She handled me. Now I'm empty. Lonely. No closer to being sure of what's going to happen down the trail than when I called her.

• • •

Two ways of thinking have developed in this country. One line of thought follows the anthem of Country Joe and the Fish's "Fixin' to Die Rag."

Everyone sings along at Woodstock.

" . . . be the first ones on your block to have your boy brought home in a box."

Comforting thought, having been there and with a brother there now.

The other philosophy can be found on the bumpers of pickup trucks.

America. Love it or leave it.

I'm going to have a cookout. Invite "Fixin' to Die Rag." Invite "Love it or leave it." It will be called the last supper. I won't be alone in my sleepless nights with upset stomachs.

• • •

VETERAN'S DAY

for the u.s. of a.

war is the folly
of a peacetime rally.
with honor to defend
it is the dead who comprehend.

we are numb
in the heart
by war's revival.
admit it
America,
you overlooked the arrival.

bleeding brains,
minds bent to vast proportions.
dying fear,
last thought,
we are the country's abortion.

while, in the kitchen,
cabinets manipulate
stainless steel misconceptions.
and the operations,

performed by us,
are more than just deceptions.

make it clear to the living veteran,
"get an education."
if we dress right, dress
and cover up mutations.

a guilty son tries to rid himself
of this social disease.
can he live above
the code of survival?

no one will believe it,
st. thomas had to see it.

we are the unknown soldiers of america.

English teacher gave me a B+ on that one, even though it was "grammatically inconsistent and technically inept."

I'm running out of steam on this college education bullshit. The G.I. Bill is always a day late and a dollar short. The campus is utilized for throwing Frisbees or taking over buildings to voice disapproval of the war. No shit.

My bosses at work are still hassling me about the length of my hair. Bonnie and I are closer to breaking up. I sat down to watch the World Series this year, pushed myself off the floor ten days later. The picture is rolling on the TV. A sportscaster is shouting something about the "miracle Mets." There are five half-gallon wine jugs rolling around the living room floor. Did I have a good time? Who won? Is the war over yet? Did my brother Gene make it back?

• • •

"Rod, please take your boots off. I'm tired of asking you every time we meet. You are in continual rebellion, aren't you?" She whirls about and walks into the den before I can answer. I clench my teeth, working the jaw so hard I feel my ears wiggle. There is such a thrill to being so pissed. I sit right down in the hall and yank off the boots, letting each one fly with force.

Crash. Crash.

This is your introduction to my course called Psych III E, "Introduction to Group Therapy." We meet in an encounter-type group setting. We started out with twelve participants. That was three-quarters of a semester ago. There are seven of us now. This is an intellectual confessional for people who have never done anything, but have thought about doing everything.

So, what the hell am I doing here?

I could say that my major is psychology and this is a required course, but I'm an honest type of guy. I show up because I won't back down from Debbie. She's the facilitator of our encounter group. We meet at her home. By the way, I didn't take my boots off outside because the damn water sprinkler had soaked the front steps. I'm going to sit in the water? What am I, expendable? The challenge between Deb and me has evolved because I am able to get off the group hot seat as quickly as I'm put on it. She doesn't like that.

Seriously, I think this group encounter thing may be of some help to me. I could use some way to release, get to the bottom of, find out why I feel so . . . something . . . I don't cry. I can't cry. I believe I'll burst. I hope this group will open me up. I'm in pain. It would help if I released some . . . something. Never mind. I am strong. I can handle it. I'm just joking. Really.

"Then, when he had to go back for the second tour," she sobs, piling more shag rug pickings in front of her, "I didn't really believe he had to go. I believe he's just stringing me along to get the extra separation pay. Then when he comes back, when the war is over, he'll divorce me."

She bows her head. Tears drip on the shag rug pile. I recross my legs because one foot has fallen asleep. It looks like more than half the group is sleeping. Debbie must be daydreaming because she hasn't challenged me in five minutes. I question Saundra.

"Saundra, he hasn't shown or acted out that he's stringing you along, has he?"

She looks up from her pity, shakes her head.

"Well, don't think the worst of him yet." I look at the others to see if anyone is paying attention. No, but it did wake a couple.

"Is he an officer or an enlisted man?" I ask.

"Officer."

"Well, then, one reason he is over there is because it's an asset to his career."

She nods her head as she blows her nose. "That's what he said."

"Saundra, has he cheated on you? Has he been cruel?"

She shakes her head.

"Has he kept in touch?"

"He writes every week. Calls at least once a month."

"I don't see how you can think the worst of him. Whether you know it or not, Saundra, you are in the Air Force now." I smile, trying to lighten the moment. She returns the smile. I like these sessions. I can console, be Doc again.

"What's his job over there?"

"He's a flight operations officer in Cam Ranh Bay."

"Oh." That information cuts into my sympathy. She continues.

"He's always under the threat of attack from the Viet Congs. He sees their campfires every night. In his last letter, the helicopters went off to bomb the campfires as he was writing."

Huh? He's surrounded by campfires? Where's he stationed, Frontierland? From what I understand about Cam Ranh Bay, about base camp there, you can get pizza to go. It's been reported to be safer there than Chicago or Boston. It's the L.A. of Viet Nam. If he's a flight operations officer he could sign himself onto any air transport flying back to the States. He could fly right into McClellan Air Base, right down the road from this house. He could catch a cab home, make love to Saundra, hustle back to the air base and catch the next flight back to Cam Ranh Bay. He'd be in time for mail call and the letter she sent yesterday. Christ! She's so fucking lucky. He's lucky. All these fuckers sitting here are lucky.

"Rod. You just changed completely right before my very eyes," Debbie interrupts. I jerk around to her, defensive.

"You were working so well with Saundra," she continues. "Consoling. Reassuring. Then it was like a dark cloud passed over you. Your expression changed. Your manner." She stops talking. Stares at me. I'm caught in the open. I stare back. The whole group is awake. A few fidget.

"Why don't you talk about Viet Nam, Rod?" Debbie starts to chip away.

"I do talk about Viet Nam." I straighten. The shooting pains begin in my lower back.

"No, you don't. Not as much as you think," she challenges. "Does he, everyone?"

A few in the group shake their heads at her beckoning. Others fidget. Everyone is attentive.

"You see, Rod. You don't talk about it for yourself. Viet Nam, I mean. You talk about it for others. Why don't you answer some of the same questions you ask?"

This is the hot seat. I can't get off it.

"Were you an officer or an enlisted man?" Debbie asks.

"Enlisted."

"Air Force?"

"Army Airborne."

"What does that mean?" Saundra says through sniffles.

"It means I jumped out of planes, Saundra."

"Were you on the front lines?" She wipes her eyes.

"There were no front lines." I begin to pull shag rug into a pile.

"Did you do any killing?" asks another member of the group.

Christ! I hate these questions. They bring back the visuals. The dead. The booby traps. The wounds. Ambushes.

"I was a medic. I killed to defend my wounded, my dead."

"But you saw your friends wounded. Killed."

I hear those words. I recall that rice paddy. In the rain, at least I thought it was rain. I crush my eyelids to shut out the group. My ears block up as the tension within me builds. I won't hear anything. There is a faint muted calling of my name. I burrow my head down deeper into my chest. I mustn't crack. They don't realize that letting go means exploding. I'm not going to allow myself to do that. I won't be vulnerable around these people. I don't know them, I don't trust them, I want to be with my boys. I want everyone to be safe. I don't want to be around selfish, pampered, civilized, ignorant people who live high on the hog off our experience, our horror and terror. The sacrifice does not fit into this circle.

•   •   •

"Hello."

"Roddie?"

"Hi, Mom, how's it going?"

"Roddie, your father's home. He's back from Viet."

"Great."

"He's eating my pepper sandwiches. Do you want to talk to him?"

"Let him eat."

She doesn't hear that. She shouts away from the phone. "Eddie, Eddie, Roddie's on the phone. I have him on the phone this minute."

"Mom, Mom. Don't bother him. Let him eat. Mom."

"Rod!"

"Dad!"

"How are you, son?"

"I didn't want Mom to bother your eating. I'm good, Dad. How are you?"

"Feel fine, son. Still sober. Tired but okay. Boy, that's quite a hellhole over there, Rod. I don't know how you made it. I was amazed and scared. Some of those G.I.s we were around, who we saw come in from those jungles. Animals. I mean, Rod, they were animals."

Am I supposed to agree or disagree? He continues.

"We'd see guys come in off the helicopters. Filthy, I mean, dirty, sweaty, filthy. They hadn't bathed in weeks."

I recall the T-shirt tearing up my back as I tried to pull it over my head. It had been a month without a bath.

"One of those guys had an ear hanging on a necklace around his neck."

I don't know what to say. I recall instead the comedy of Kelly and me, both determined to get clean. It was a creek in the Ia Drang. We dressed in helmets, boots, M-16s and soap. Couldn't stand it any longer. The sniper opened up. Pow! We didn't even flinch, just kept washing. Pow! That did it. We took off after the fucker. Running through the water was our rinse.

"It was cruel, Rod. An ear, a human ear."

I envision R. O. with his necklace of ears. He stashed them when we were coming back to base. I can't believe any infantry people coming back to base would be so stupid as to flaunt it. I would have told the asshole to take the ear off. Put it away.

"Rod. Those paratroopers were animals. Animals. I don't know why we let them do such things . . ."

"Dad. Dad. I was a paratrooper over there. I was in the infantry. You don't have to tell me about it."

"For God's sake, we were in a jeep, driving by an air transport. These guys were loading off. Rod, I swear, I saw heads."

Christ, how do you fight a war nicely? Cong gets ahold of any of us, our dead, he peels off any tattooed skin. No tattoos, then he cuts off our cocks, our balls, stuffs them in our mouths. God, I'm so glad I didn't see that. Maybe it's not true, maybe Mac was lying about that ambush up by Kontum City, I don't know. Doesn't anyone realize that in Nam, in war, anyone can do anything at any given time? He was in World War II. What's so shocking?

"Rod? Son?"

"Yes, Dad."

"Did you hang up?"

"No. No, I'm here."

"I guess I'm not used to using the phone. I saw your brother Gene while I was there. He's fine. He's safe. Working in a pharmacy in a field hospital."

"I know. I read a letter he sent Mom."

"After about two months over there, Rod, I got really

fed up. I have to confess, I'm not in favor of that war. Son, things are a bit different with us in the civil service. We can get fed up with the waste. The waste of everything, including lives. It's so crazy, Rod. I don't mean to offend what you went through over there, son, but it's sick. I told them before I came back. It's sick. So many animals.''

"Dad, maybe you ought to settle down. I'll talk to you later. Mom's invited me to a spaghetti dinner for you tonight.''

"She just fixed me two of her patented pepper sandwiches.''

"Good. Good.''

"I'm going to vote for Eugene McCarthy now that Bobby Kennedy's dead. God, it's crazy . . .''

"Whatever, Dad. I'm glad you made it back.''

"So am I, son, I missed you.''

"I'll see you this evening.''

"Right. Bye.''

What is war about? It is about killing families off. Bleeding them dry. Number 2 is back from Nam. That's my brother, Gene. He's in one piece except for his mind, he left some of that over there.

No, he wasn't wounded. He didn't see any actual combat. He says he would "help unload dead and wounded when the occasion did arise but . . .'' then he just wanders off. He's hurt but it's not something that can be seen or touched. We are all concerned. There is so much confusion. Bad drugs. Rock stars dying. Riots. Black Panther shoot-out. Anti-war demonstrations. Then Number 3 brother, Greg, comes to me with this:

"Hey, Rod.''

It is a faint but familiar salutation.

"Hey, Greg, how's it going?'' I shout, bent under the hood of the truck.

"Guess what?''

"What?''

"No, guess."

"You're pregnant."

"Naw. I just got my draft notice in the mail. I gotta report."

I drop the crescent wrench down below the fan. It gets caught between the radiator and the engine block. I try to reach for it. It's just out of fingertip range. I stretch, balancing on a tiptoe, grazing the cool metal alloy. Shit. Try the other foot. Don't get pissed. Try to think in some sort of nonviolent manner. Be reasonable. It's been three or four years since coming back from Nam. It's 1969 and the war keeps on. Time is running out. This brother could be the one that doesn't come back. Why the fuck does he have to go? Why does this fucking war drag on and on and on and on . . . ?

"What should I do, Rod?"

I step from underneath the hood of the truck. Straighten, oooh, my goddam back. Shit! I want to kick stone, break wood, throw earth, spit blood. I wipe my hands on a greasy rag.

"What do you think I should do, Rod?"

I turn to face him. I can't look him in the eye. I look at the greasy rag. I am so tired. Exhausted. I didn't sleep well again last night. Wet creek ambush, it comes around so often.

"What do you think, Rod? What should I do?"

I start to look him in the eye but pass by his gaze for the meadow beyond. I watch the golden grasses sway lightly in the hot breeze. He's too young and decent and jovial to have to live the war life. Maybe I could build some bunkers in that meadow. Put the family there. Hide them. Show Greg how to dig his own spider hole. Camouflage it properly. He could hide there.

"Rod?"

"Go to Canada, Greg. Or jail."

I'm so disgusted. I throw the greasy rag through the open window of the truck. I turn and look at him. He looks at me in surprise. Then the surprise turns to dismay. What did I just say? He bows his head. I bow mine. He turns one way. I turn the other. I've let him down. I should have stayed over there "till the mother-fucker is over." Could have hung out with Henderson. Could have saved lives. Could have kept my brothers out of it.

I hear the engine start. I turn to see him backing Mom's car out of the driveway. I want to call out. It catches in my throat. I know the unspoken fact. I went. I proved myself. He has to go. What else can he do. What are the choices? Hide? Run? Serve? Die? Time is running out on this family.

He will go. He won't make it back. He'll get it from behind, in the neck, from the tree line. Maybe he'll hear it. Maybe he won't. I step back under the hood of the truck, stretch for the wrench.

• • •

Alvarez and the boys came up on a Memorial Day weekend to see me. Al had turned me on to Harleys last summer when I went to visit him. I haven't said much about him because he and I haven't been in touch. He doesn't live but one hundred or so miles to the south but he lives in Chicano land. I live in Disney World. What I'm trying to say, folks, is that those of us who were so close to each other in survivalization have split apart since coming back to civilization. Society failed us. Anyways, it ain't that uncontrollable, I guess. Al and I do get to see each other on occasion. Which is more than some can say.

So we are heading our Harleys down Interstate 80, going down to the state capital for a demonstration. I take that back. I'm gonna demonstrate. Al and his boys are going to watch.

"Belbo, Raymond, Sergeant, U.S. Army. Viet Nam '66–'67, fire team leader. I would like President Nixon and President Johnson really, because he sent me over there, I'd like them to have these medals back. Viet

Nam campaign ribbon, Viet Nam service ribbon, National Defense ribbon, Good Conduct medal, Air medal, Purple Heart. I do this after much thought and pain. I'm sorry it happened. Thank you."

The fella throws the card into a handmade casket, bows his head and steps away from the microphone. The next veteran steps up to the mike.

"Airman First Class Michael Seward. I was stationed on Guam. I loaded bombs on B-52s. I get sick when I think of how many people I killed. I'm turning in these medals."

He drops two medals into the casket. He steps slowly away. The next man takes his place behind the mike. I move up a step, trying to practice my speech, fingering my 3 x 5 card of decorations. I'm sick, thinking of the wasted lives, the wasted wounds, the wasted time. Never have so few done so much for nothing.

"Step up, man, step up."

I turn around to the command behind me. "Don't fucking tell me what to do."

A black vet dressed in black, including beret, points over my shoulder. "The 'phone, dude, your turn at the 'phone."

I look to the microphone. The guy in front of me is disappearing down the steps on the other side.

"I'm sorry, man. I'm a little uptight."

"It's cool. It's cool. Go tell them."

I step up to the mike. I start to say something, but gulp. The casket in front of me is full of so many painful stories.

"Ah, Doc, er, Kane with the Army Airborne. Central highlands, '65–'66."

I toss the medals in the casket . . . watch them blend in with the others. I reach in my back pocket for my Combat Medical badge and jump wings. Fuck it. Throw it all back.

No!

"You want to share the mike with me, brother?"

I turn to face the black beret again. "Oh. Sorry."

"No, you can stay, brother. Listen to this." He holds my arm. I stop. He faces into the microphone, adjusting his sunglasses. "Yeah, O'Conner, 'Scooter,' 173rd Airborne, II Corps, 1966. Ain't got any of his medals but he died in my arms. Before he did he asked me if I made it back could I say something about it. Say it's no good. Say it's gotta stop. So I am, you dig?"

He steps away from the microphone, walks by me, saying, "Right on, Nam vets."

I watch him step into the crowd. It opens for him. I look over the TV cameras as they watch us perform this rite of passage. The crowd is peppered with VFW and American Legion caps. They are not being very friendly about the event. I look past them, trying to find Alvarez and the others. Al sees me and waves. I head toward him but on impulse detour so I can walk through a pack of VFW and Legion veterans. They are hooting and hollering at the vets as they toss their medals.

"Where the fuck were you motherfuckers when I came home?"

We're spinning down Sunrise Boulevard coming back in from the foothills. Rumble, rumble, putt putt. Alvarez and his friends came to my rescue in that crowd. I tried to tear this one fat asshole's throat out. We got out of the city without too much trouble. I really had to get rid of my edge. Once we got into the foothills I did up a tab of mescaline, smoked a bunch of joints of Thai tea, shared a couple of sixes of beers with the boys. Now we're sucking randomly on a quart of José Cuervo tequila. I got dibs on the worm.

Hey, did I tell you about this Harley I'm riding? I really missed the rush of those air assaults we did in Nam, clipping the hedge rows, rice paddies and stream beds at 110 knots.

Whooop!

'Bout ten feet off the ground, machine guns blasting.

Whooop!

I just slowed down from turning 107 on this thing. Could have done better if I had laid flat but I got the bottle of tequila between my legs. Don't want to break the bottle, man. Did I tell you 'bout the great motorcycle wreck I got in after breaking up with Bonnie. She's the one who wouldn't put out. We broke up. Wow! What a rush. Leaving her, I took a turn too wide too late to lean back upright. Downfall.

Crash! . . .

•   •   •

Alvarez tells me we are coming back out of the foothills, rumble, rumble, putt putt. I'm leading the pack. Six of us, low riding down the boulevard, rumble, rumble, putt putt. We are all pretty loaded. All sizes, shapes and colors, rumble, rumble, putt putt. That's bikes and bikers.

I had just slowed from trying to push the Harley over one hundred.

Crash!

That's where I left you. Crash! Auditioning for the job that guy on "Laugh-In" has. Dresses in a rain slicker, pedals a tricycle, fast as hell. Runs into the curb. Blam! I'm going to take his job away from him. I pull up to a stop sign on the Harley. Stop. Forgot to put my feet down.

Crash!

Al says they parked their bikes right at the stop sign. Picked up me and my bike. Put me back on. I struggled off, grabbed up the half empty bottle of tequila and got back on. I stuck the tequila between my legs. Drove off, leaving Al and the guys standing there. He laughed so hard telling me the story. Rumble, rumble, putt putt. Stop sign. Stop. Balance. Crash! I don't remember any of it. I don't want to know. It's a bad moon rising. I gotta do something or I'm going to die on that motorcycle.

•   •   •

What happens when a brick is thrown at a gun? If the brick doesn't score a hit, the gun picks up the brick and throws it back. Right? Wrong! What you have is the Kent State Syndrome. First, send American combat troops from Viet Nam into Cambodia. It's not like they've never been in Cambodia before, we walked back and forth across those jungles all the time. There are no border lines. Nixon sends a concerted effort into another country. The campuses in the U.S. have been in an upheaval for two years. They don't need much for an excuse. It's student demonstration time across the land. Every state with trouble calls out its National Guard.

Oooops! Don't throw that brick at that gun!

Pow! Four dead in O-high-O.

Fuck it, folks. I'm getting out of here. Before I kill myself and someone else. I'm leaving. I'm selling my Harley and taking up a summer school tour in Ireland and the European mainland. I have to find some hope somewhere or I'm checking out. If Greg gets killed in Nam, I'll miss the funeral. So what, funerals are for the living. I gotta get out of here before I'm one of the dead.

•   •   •

I step up behind two young women standing by the hotel registration desk. The taller one whirls toward me. "We were here first."

I stare at her while sliding the backpack from my shoulders. Whatever confrontation we might have started ends with the entrance of an elderly woman from the room behind the desk. Preoccupied with pinning a lace hankie to a sweater draped over her shoulders, she finally looks up. "Oh, I'm sorry. I didn't hear any of you come in. What have we? Room and board for three?"

"Oh, we're not together. Not with him," blurts the tall one.

"But we would like separate rooms," the other one adds, looking at me, then the clerk.

"I need a bed and a place to clean up."

"Just fill these out," the matron assures us, placing

registration cards before us. "We have room for all three of you."

We each scribble out the necessary information and return the cards. The clerk flips through them quickly.

"You're all Americans!" she exclaims with delight.

We look at each other, the other two nod. I shrug.

"Are you all here for the parade?"

"Yes," they say in unison. All three look at me.

"Yeah, if I can get some sleep and clean up," I growl. I spent the previous night sleeping in mountain mist outside the city. Now I don't know if I'm uncomfortable because of my damp, musty clothing or because I'm Irish Catholic. I come back from that thought to meet the gaze of the shorter, prettier woman.

"Sir, that will be three pounds six shillings from you," the clerk says, distracting me. "With sufficient facilities for proper rest and cleaning," she adds, proudly, offering a room key in trade. I fish through my pockets for pounds and shillings, feeling pensive.

"Where are you from in the States?" the pretty one asks.

I pull my hands from my pockets and pences spew, rolling all over the floor.

"Oops."

I stoop to retrieve the strange coins. She joins me.

"Where are you from in the States?" she repeats, kneeling at eye level.

"Uh, California."

"Really!" She smiles, handing me what she has collected.

"Oh, boy. A California hippie," smugs her girlfriend from above.

I stand, hand a satisfactory payment to the clerk, then shoot a glare at the last comment. The clerk counts out my payment, smiles, and rips off a receipt.

"Will you be staying on after tomorrow's festivities?" she inquires.

"I'm not sure."

"Well, checkout is 1:00 P.M. Let us know before then."

"I surely will."

She turns her attention to the big mouth. I turn my attention to the pursed lips.

"Where are you from?" I ask, feeling more comfortable with the room key in hand.

"Minnesota," she claims matter-of-factly.

"Darlene. Darlene. Do you have any English money?"

Darling!

Darlene turns, groping in her pocketbook. "Yes, here, Sarah. How much?"

"How much?" Sarah asks.

"Six pounds even," smiles the old woman.

"Six even, Darlene. I'll pay you later."

Darlene counts out, precisely, the pound notes. She hands them to Sarah. I stare at her. She stands five feet seven, at least 120 pounds, long, long, brown hair that has curled some in the dampness. Big green eyes make up most of the milk-white face. The rest is taken up by a pug nose and full red lips. No make-up.

Her task completed, she turns to me. "So, are you just passing through, or are you interested in this parade?"

What eyes!

"Um, I'm in a summer school program at a college in southern Ireland, in Kilkenny."

"Kilkenny! We're going to go there, aren't we, Darlene? If we have time." Sarah pecks between us like a hen. Oh, God, I hope these two are separable.

"Yes, Sarah, that's where all the craft shops are." She turns to me. "This is my friend, Sarah. My name is Darlene."

Will Sarah let me ignore her?

"My name is Rod. I've just come from one of the hills overlooking the city. I slept there last night." I pick up my backpack. Head toward the elevator. God, I'm tired. "Are you two heading up?"

"We're waiting for our luggage to come from the ferry," Sarah says.

"Maybe we could get together for dinner later," Darlene adds.

I turn in the elevator, smile at her. "Sounds good."

Sarah interrupts, "Darlene, he's a hippie."

Darlene scowls at Sarah. "So?" She turns to me as the elevator door closes. "We'll get together later. What floor are you on? What's your room number?"

"607."

The elevator doors open at six. I drag myself and belongings down the hall in the direction of 607. I'm glad to get away from that one. I couldn't stand much more of Sarah's insinuations. I find the room, lean my pack and my shoulder against the wall. Where did I put the room key? God, I'm exhausted.

It seems like forever since last night. I sat up in the shroud of light fog, chain smoking cigarettes, watching the bonfires burn in the city. I ditched the last Camel and slid between the folds of the sleeping bag.

I didn't sleep. Dreamt instead of Nana Kane cautioning me to be wary of nasty old Orangemen. "They slaughtered Catholics at the River Boyne in 1690, Roddie, then stayed on with Cromwell to search for Catholics in our own Ulster County. They impaled the defenseless souls on stakes."

My slumber shuddered under senses strained by centuries of tension surrounding this city. Damp with sea salt dew, I got up at the first gray light of day. I gathered my damp belongings along with my ethnic troubles and stumbled down the hill to a tram waiting at the end of its line. I climbed aboard in a disarray of gear, feeling very out of place sitting alongside suburban residents traveling to the inner city. We edged down the hill, passing the smoldering bonfires that had burned so brightly the night before.

I shiver, finding the key. It opens the door. Backpack and I fall through the entrance. I kick the door shut. Relaxation and privacy; what the hell am I doing here? I review my intention, climbing out of wet clothes. I came here to evaluate who is sticking it to whom. I want to witness, as an Irish-American Roman Catholic, what is the sense in a centuries-old conflict.

I twist on the hot water in the sink and begin to scrub down.

It isn't too hard to figure which side to be on. Right now I'm on the exhausted side.

I empty the sink of gritty water, pull out my toothbrush. The bonfires are damned intimidating, if you ask me. The British flags, too. Union Jacks and Irish Republic flags hanging outside houses, proclaiming whole blocks of homes in allegiance to Britain or Ireland. Barricades of sheet metal and barbed wire split streets right down the middle. You are either assimilated with or isolated from your neighbor.

I brush out wet hair.

Across the street from each other, right next door!

I inspect myself in front of a full-length mirror.

Playing for keeps.

Yawn.

I tear the blankets back to the sheets. Oh, God, am I tired. Slip in between the sheets to nestle, to sleep. Welcome to Belfast, Northern Ireland, Doc . . . good day . . . good night.

Rap. Rap. Rap.

A machine gun drums out a staccato of whining, ricocheting tracers. Sparks fly. I'm trying to adapt my jungle warfare experience to the street fighting in downtown Belfast.

Rap. Rap. Rap.

"Rod?"

"Huh?" I bolt upright. It's Doc, not Rod. Doc!

"Rod?"

Where am I?

"Yeah." I shout.

"I'm sorry. Did I surprise you?"

A distant voice.

"Oh, no." I swing out of the nightmare, stand unsteady.

"Hi, how are you?" I blurt to the walls, trying to sound relaxed, unaffected.

"Are you okay?" comes from the other side of the door.

"Huh? Yeah, I'm okay, just nappin'," I shout at the door.

"Oh, I'm sorry. . . . It's me, Darlene."

"That's okay, glad to be out of it." I cough to clear the fear from my throat. I step to the door. Talk through it. "Thanks for waking me, really. So what's up?"

"Sarah and I are going for a walk, then maybe have some dinner. Would you want to come along?" She has such a sweet voice.

"Hey, that sounds great. What time is it?"

"Three-thirty."

I slept dead.

"Sounds great. How soon? Give me fifteen minutes."

"No hurry."

I bounce down six flights of stairs in a euphoria, and burst into the lobby. My escorts whirl in surprise at my entrance.

"Hi." I grin, foolishly.

"Hi," returns Darlene, breaking into a smile.

"Hello," deadpans Sarah.

We all appear rested, refreshed.

"Shall we go?" I ask.

"I have a map," claims Sarah, looking for a little control.

"Okay, lead on," I say, smiling at Darlene.

We step out into the seaport's haze and stand in front of our hotel, the Christian Hostel. I hadn't bothered to look closely at the name this morning.

The city square that the hostel faces is blanketed with barbed wire rolls.

"This is supposed to be Victoria Square. Ugh! Look at all the barbed wire. How ugly," Sarah judges.

"Let's go this way." She turns to lead.

"Keep your voice down, Sarah," Darlene admonishes.

"What?" Sarah says, turning to look at me.

"You ain't seen nothing yet." I glare.

"Oh." She turns away to stay ahead of us.

"What did you mean by that?" Darlene asks quietly.

"Oh, nothing really," I reply. "Just that this is an armed camp trying not to be an armed camp."

"You know something about armed camps?"

"Sort of." I watch our scout suspiciously.

"Viet Nam?" she questions cautiously.

"Sort of."

"When?"

" '65–'66."

"Did you get involved in killing?"

"Let's talk about something else. Let's talk about how much we love parades." I look at her, exchanging sarcasm for marvel. "You have beautiful hair."

"Thank you."

I slow down to get some distance from Sarah.

". . . in Minnesota all your life?"

"Yes. Where do you live in California?" Darlene asks.

"Sacramento. Are you in school?"

"No. I just graduated from the University of Minnesota with an M.A. in music. Do you go to school in the States?"

"Yes, outside Sacramento, a commuter school. I'm in liberal arts till I figure out what I'm going to do. Do you play any instruments?"

"No, I sing opera." She beams. We walk in silence, digesting the information, formulating more questions.

"Do you like it out there, in California?"

"Some of it."

"What are you doing here?"

"I'm in a summer study program at a school in Kilkenny. Didn't I tell you that?"

"Not specifically."

"Are you traveling about, you and Sarah?"

"She and I flew from St. Paul to New York to Edinburgh to visit St. Andrews. We wanted to see the parade, so here we are. We go to London next, if we don't go south. Then she goes back to the States and I go to Germany."

"Wow! Hey, you guys, look at this. Oh, my God." Sarah gets our attention. We hurry our step. There is a hint of charcoal in the air. I reach the corner. The smell of burnt wood hits me full force. The avenue crossing us, passing west to east, its dwellings are burnt, charred beyond repair. Broken walls and shattered glass were homes, a community, once.

"Oh dear," laments Darlene.

"What happened there?" Sarah bristles.

"Well, where are we?" I wonder, looking about for a street sign. One is above me.

Falls Road.

I trace the sign back along the thoroughfare. The road winds its way through the middle of destruction.

"Falls area?" I wonder aloud. "This is the Falls area. The Catholic ghetto that was burned to the ground in riots earlier this summer."

"How awful," Sarah says.

I stare at the mess. I hear myself say, "Somewhere, in there, that fucking mess, are my father's relatives. Was where my father's relatives lived."

The stare becomes a glare.

"Are you Irish Catholic?" spurts Sarah.

"Some, most of the family is, I was just raised that way."

I somehow feel myself returning to the "faith," in a militant sense. A soldier for Christ's sake. What the hell are we doing in Viet Nam with this shit going on?

"Come on," says Darlene, turning back.

"Wow, I didn't know this had happened," Sarah proclaims.

"You must not be an Irish Catholic," I challenge.

Darlene reaches back and pulls me away from the chip on my shoulder.

"Come on, Sarah, let's go find something to eat," she says, pushing me down the street. I allow it.

We slowly separate on the walk back toward the city's center. Belfast becomes more personal for me. In the street, the traffic flows in a cadence of taxis, a jeep mounted with machine gun, privately owned vehicles, a bus, an armored personnel carrier, trams, water gun tank, military truck with a load of troops. I look up. Paratroopers, singularly and in pairs, are sandbag protected at rooftop corners. They peer through binoculars, staring down into the streets.

"Everything seems to be shut down," Darlene says, hands on hips, looking over Victoria Square.

"Looks like it," I say. I stop beside her, reach for her hand and squeeze.

"Thanks for keeping me from Sarah's throat."

"No problem," she says, staring straight ahead. "I don't know you very well, but I know that Sarah can be quite glib."

I release her hand.

"Nowhere, nowhere is there anything open," Sarah says, arriving between us.

"Well, what do you want to do?" I inquire.

"I'm hungry," Sarah says.

There is silence, confusion amongst us. We can't stand around. We have to decide.

"Say, the Christian Hostile we're staying at serves dinner till 5:30. Shall we eat there?" I volunteer.

"Yes, I was thinking the same thing," says Darlene.

"Great, how do we get there from here?" Sarah challenges.

"Right behind you."

We enjoy a quiet meal. They don't go hungry, these Christians. I still wonder why they didn't have religion on the hostel registration card. Everybody looks alike, especially if they're naked, so how the hell does one tell if you're Catholic or Protestant?

"I'm full," says Sarah, pushing herself away from the table, sliding into a slouch.

"Good food." I burp, pulling out an after-dinner cigarette.

"I have to go to the bathroom." Sarah straightens in alarm.

"If there isn't something close by, get on the elevator, squat out, but keep your thumb on the pass button."

Ouch!

I get a kick from Darlene underneath the table. Sarah jumps up, leaves to search for a bathroom.

"Sorry, I couldn't resist," I say apologetically.

Darlene looks at me sternly, then breaks into an uncontrollable giggle.

"So it was good, a good comment."

She nods approval.

"Say, what do you have planned for this evening?"

"I don't know," she says, gathering her composure, "I have to ask Sarah."

"Are you two separable?"

"It's possible, but she is so spastic on her own, I wouldn't let her out in this city by herself."

"I can respect that."

"What did you have planned?"

"I don't know. Do you smoke?"

"No, I really don't even like the smell," she says sheepishly.

"Oh, sorry." I relent, smashing out my cigarette. "But, that's not the kind of smoke I meant. You know what I mean, don't you?"

"Oh, smoke! Well, no, not often. It affects my voice. Do you have any?"

"Yeah, if you wanted to . . . ?"

She peers over my shoulder, looks suspiciously around the room. "What do you think?" she whispers.

"Well, before we do anything tonight, would you want to?"

"Uh, I guess I could get separated."

"Good, come to my room."

Sarah approaches, hitching at her slacks. "I don't know what your plans are for tonight but I'd like to go up to my room and freshen up, change my clothes."

Thank you, Sarah.

"Okay," I say, standing. "How 'bout we meet in the lobby in half an hour?"

"That's enough time," Sarah says. "Darlene, how about you?"

"Half an hour is fine with me."

"Okay. See you then." I take my leave.

I tune in Radio Luxembourg on the house radio. Nothin' like a little Top 40 in a combat zone. I sit down to roll some reefer.

Rap. Rap. Rap.

There goes that machine gun again. I shout at the door. "Yes!"

"It's me."

"Do you have identification?"

"Shut up and open the door."

"Yes, ma'am!"

I go to the door, swing it open. Darlene strides in. I stand, like a mimic.

"Close the door, Rod," she says curtly.

I obey. "Is something wrong?"

"No. It's just Sarah. She is so strange, but I understand it." She sits resignedly on the bed.

"Well, let me offer." I go to the desk and light up a rolled one, turn and hand it to her.

"Yes, I think it will help. Do you think it will smell out in the hallway?" she cautions.

"Not with the window open. I've already checked."

"Good," she says, taking it and pulling in a healthy Midwestern draw.

"We have to go soon," she worries, while holding in the smoke.

"We don't have to smoke much. Will you be okay out in the street?"

"Yes, just as long as you're close by," she says, exhaling. "We both decided it would be safest to stick close to you. Do whatever you want to do."

"If we can't find a good pub or movie, I'd like to explore, see the city."

"Whatever . . ." she says, taking another draw on the smoke, then offering it back to me. I take my turn.

She watches, then says, "Tell me somethin', Rod."

"Huh."

"Do you look for trouble?"

"Huh?"

"I mean, it sounds like you have seen enough trouble already. Why are you here in Belfast?"

I'm confused at such a pointed inquiry. Hmmmmm?

"I guess I'm sort of asking for it," I say. "You see, after almost losing my ass in Viet Nam, I did want to get the feeling for a struggle, conflict, revolution, police action that was more related to my past."

She sits, quiet, drawing in smoke, turning my rationale over in her head. "Okay," she confirms, gazing at me openly. "Just don't get us into any trouble."

"Trust me. I've been here before. I mean, I came back from something like this. I know what I'm doing."

"I'll trust you."

"Thank you."

"You're welcome. Good grass."

"Thank you again."

"We should get going soon."

"Whatever you say, hon."

I'm won.

We stumble from the stairway into the lobby, looking entirely suspect. Sarah spies us, comes right at me. "Where are we going to go?"

"A movie, a pub, or exploring."

"You know, you are in charge of our safekeeping."

"Said and done."

"You know that the movie houses and pubs are all closed."

"Says who?"

"Because the police and the army are afraid of I.R.A. bombings, retaliation for some Catholics who were shot here in Bally Murphy the day before yesterday." She holds a newspaper under my nose.

"So we explore." I shrug, ignoring the newspaper.

"I don't want to go into any bad areas."

"Sarah, I don't want to go into any 'bad' areas either."

"How will you know? How can you tell?"

"By sight, by smell, by a shiver up and down my spine."

"Darlene, are you ready?"

"Yes, Sarah."

"Okay," she says. "Let's go. I brought my camera. I want to get some pictures before it gets dark."

It's early evening and quiet in the streets as we step out of the hostel. There is a congregation of people milling around in front of the church off to our right.

"Let's check that out," I point.

We keep pace and move toward the crowd. The people are dressed in their Sunday best and carry themselves that way. We move around the outer fringes of the group.

"Who are they?" Sarah asks, loudly, and those within earshot turn.

"Sarah, this is no time to be playing Lois Lane," Darlene admonishes.

"Well, I want to know," she rebuts, blustering into the crowd.

"She needs some dope."

"She is a dope."

"Let's just hang back here, don't want to get caught in any crowds. First lesson."

"You're the leader."

Sarah darts back out from the group. She turns and begins to take pictures of the crowd. That raises eyebrows.

"Let's get her out of here!"

We remove Sarah, each of us at an elbow, from the crowd's consciousness.

"Who's the Reverend Ian Paisley?" she queries, as we move away.

"Oh, God." My heart sinks.

"That's his church," she says, pointing back over her shoulder.

"Great. We're getting as far away from there as possible." I quicken my pace.

"Why?"

"He's a Unionist, a great target for the I.R.A."

"How do you know? Are you in the I.R.A.?"

"Fuck off, Sarah, I'm leading this group. We do as I say."

We retreat in silence. I settle our pace back to a tourist walk. We venture into another area of the city.

"It's too bad everything is closed," Darlene laments. "These pubs and shops look very interesting from the outside."

My mind is still on the congregation of the Reverend Ian Paisley. I'm not really paying attention to where we are. Where we're going. I turn a corner.

"Ooops!" I come face to face with a soldier in camouflage fatigues. The uniform is definitely out of place amid the city rubble. The shotgun he carries is not. The rest of the combat patrol is evenly paced behind him.

"Excuse me," I request meekly.

"Ya don't belong here, mate." He stares into my eyes.

"Right." I whirl. Bump into Darlene, who is rear-ended by Sarah.

"Let's go, kids," I command.

"Why?" asks Sarah.

"I have a shiver up and down my spine."

"Oh." She turns. "Wait, let me get a picture." She turns back. The trooper stands his ground, shotgun at hip trained over our heads.

"Move the fuck out, Sarah." I grab her arm and twist her back the way we came. Darlene needs no explanation. We scurry back to busier streets.

"What was that?" asks Sarah.

"A combat patrol. A real, live ammunition, combat patrol."

"Oh, I wish I could have gotten a picture."

"Right, Sarah. Well, I suggest, as it's getting dark, that we head back to the Christian Hostile."

"Why do you say Hostile?"

"Speech impediment."

We walk.

"There will still be a parade tomorrow," Sarah says, not being able to stay silent for very long.

"I'm sure it will be a very interesting spectacle, amid all this," I remark, apprehensive as to how that event will affect me. "But for now, let's head for cover."

"I guess we should just look forward to an uneventful night," sighs Darlene. Thunder rumbles in the distance. "Anyway, it's going to rain."

Back in the safety of the lobby, we stand uncomfortably amid the easy chairs. The tensions from outside ebb from my bones, but not from my mind.

"Well, shall we bid adieu until morning, maybe meet for breakfast?" suggests Sarah.

"I reckon," I say. Darlene is mute, staring into the empty cafeteria.

"How about eight o'clock?" Sarah continues.

"Fine," I say, anxiously.

"Darlene, would you mind if I borrowed your iron?" Sarah asks.

"No," Darlene says, vacantly.

"Are you all right, Darlene?"

She turns to me, out of her daze.

"Yes, I'm okay. It's been a long day."

"Well, I'm bushed, too. Darlene, are you coming, so I can get the iron?" Sarah heads toward the elevator.

"Huh? Yes." Darlene murmurs, and heads in the same direction.

Damn! Good night, darling.

"Good night, girls, see you soon."

"Oh, aren't you coming?" Darlene turns to me.

"Yeah, I'll catch the next elevator up. I'll be in my room." I feel a bit bent in the heart.

I am following Bilbo Baggins along the path Gandalf has staked out for him. Maybe I'll learn something that I can use from this fantasy.

Ring . . .

A doorbell?

Ring . . .

A phone.

Ring . . .

I move in the direction of the sound.

Ring . . .

Where the hell is it?

Ring . . .

"Yeah?"

"Rod?"

"Yes."

"Uh, this is Darlene. Are you busy?"

"Not really. I just realized I had a phone. No, I'm not busy, just reading."

"Oh, what are you reading?"

"Lord of the Rings."

"That's a wonderful book."

"It's fun, I guess."

"Well, I'm calling because I didn't know what you were doing and, uh, well, I wondered if you had any more of the ah . . . ?"

"Sure do!"

"Could I . . . ?"

"You sure can."

"Ah . . ."

"Come on over."

"Are you sure?"

"Positive."

"Okay."

"Bye."

"Bye."

Whoop de do! I bounce from wall to wall in delight. Better put on some clothes.

Rap. Rap. Rap.

Wow, that was quick. I struggle into clean Levis. Can't keep Darlene waiting. I whip open the door. She stands there, looking so-o-o-o fine.

"Hello."

"Hi." She stares into my eyes.

"Come in," I offer, turning to escape the gaze, leaving the door open. I search for a shirt. The door shuts behind me as I pull on the covering. I turn. "Well, has it been an experience?"

She stands, pressed against the door. "Yes, it has."

"Did you get an education?"

"One I hadn't really expected."

"Well, have a seat," I offer, sitting at the desk to do the usual. Darlene walks to the bed, sits on the corner of it, close to me.

"Are you sure this is all right?"

"Is it all right with you?"

"I didn't want to interrupt anything."

"Darlene, this is a pleasure." I hand her the rolled reefer.

She puts it to her lips. I light it. She draws. Here we go.

"How long has it been? How long since you've been back from Viet Nam?" she asks, languishing on the bed.

"Four years."

"You went early."

"Everyone goes early."

"Did you see any action?"

140

"I believe I already told you that."

"No, you didn't."

"More than my share."

"Oh." She reflects on that. I look away self-consciously.

"Do you have anything to drink?" she asks politely.

"Tap water?"

"Oh, no. No thanks."

I fall into a quiet disappointment.

"I have a bottle of Glenlivet scotch in my room. I bought it in St. Andrews. Sarah doesn't know."

"Never heard of it."

"Do you want to try some?"

"Sure. What about Sarah? Will we see her?"

"She's already in curlers, locked in her room. She won't bother us."

She pushes herself off the bed, stands in front of me. I look up. She bends over and kisses me softly on the lips, so lightly as to tingle. The moment hangs. Straightening, she growls, "Grab your glass and move your ass over to my place."

Wow!

She turns and walks out the door, leaving it open. I sit, mouth agape. The total effect of her tenderness crashes down around me. I jump to follow, as a puppy would, glass in one hand, cigarettes in the other, so foolish, and so what?

I scrutinize her room from the doorway. The interior is the same as mine, though she has a window overlooking the street, the city. A bag of ice sits in the sink, a bottle of scotch sits on the bureau.

She stands at the door. "Come in."

I step into the middle of the room, wondering what to say.

"Nice place you got here."

"Thank you." She shuts the door. Locks and chains it. "Have a drink?"

"Sure," I offer my glass.

"I had some already," she confesses, preparing the drink. "To get up the nerve to call you."

"Oh?"

She hands me three fingersful, with ice. "Go ahead, it's good." She turns back to serve herself.

Should I be drinking in a combat zone? That's right, idiot, walk around town stoned out of your mind, then confront yourself with drinkin' whiskey in the woman's room. What's the matter, boy, afraid to lose control?

"Yes, I didn't know whether I could trust you," she comments. "Then I realized that you had the experience in Viet Nam. You got us through the day."

She looks at me and shrugs, pouring a short straight one. "Cheers," she says, swallowing the whole thing.

"Is that a left-handed compliment?"

"I have nothing but compliments for you," she says, putting ice in her glass and pouring another.

I am being overwhelmed.

"Sit down," she casually commands. I obey, sitting on the bed.

"Well," I pause and sip the bittersweet, "it's nice to know that you trust me."

She does not comment, rather goes to the radio on the bureau and turns it on. Immediately, symphony music floats about the room. It might be good to be out of control.

She sits back down, staring at me. "Don't let it go to your head."

Go to my head, hell! There is a war going on outside. I'm sitting in here, half buzzed, with a round-eyed white woman on my hands. What would those fools out there in the streets do to trade places with me? What would I have done four or five years ago, to be in this situation? So involved am I with the struggle over whether to be a lover or a fighter, my ear only catches the end of her comment.

". . . and I know you hide your feelings, fears, experience, behind a cool exterior."

Uh oh.

"You've been through a lot. A lot you don't share. A lot most of us don't understand. That we're sheltered from."

Would someone get this woman off me?

"So?" I rebut.

"So," she growls, leaning toward me, "let the outside go. Be with me, here, tonight."

I am being disarmed.

She leans forward, approaching slowly. My defenses melt, face to face, eyelids begin to shutter. Lips touch, tingle, stirring up the desire. What if it's a tease? Lips touch softly then part, yet the taste, the smell lingers.

"Let the outside go? What do you mean?" I croak.

"You know what I mean," she says, leaning back casually.

"Uh," I flounder, "could I open the window?"

"Go ahead."

I leap for the window, tug it open to a damp, pleasant draft. It's raining softly.

"It's raining out."

"Yes, the breeze feels good."

I return, sit on the bed.

"We need it."

"We know what we need."

"Huh?"

I'm showing my colors.

"Don't worry, relax."

"Okay," I say obediently, slipping down to the floor, leaning against the bed. Can't go any further.

"What are you doing?"

"Relaxing."

"Yes, but what are you doing on the floor?"

"I've heard that question before."

She chuckles and sips. I don't chuckle. I swallow my drink.

"Could I have another one?" I ask, holding my glass aloft.

"Sure." She bounces up, grabs the glass, goes to fill it. The symphony on the radio and the drizzle outside blend melody with rhythm.

She returns to me with three fingers of scotch in ice. I know someone is losing his inhibitions. I hear other familiar sounds over the symphony, the drizzle. A moving army lumbers through the streets. I hear tank treads, whining jeeps, the crackle of a two-way radio. There's a struggle for control going on. It seems to be everywhere.

"Would you want to smoke another one? I brought it with me."

She looks into me. "Sure. Bring it here."

I struggle up from the floor, sit on the edge of the bed, pulling out another.

"How old are you, Darlene?" I ask. Back on the bed, I slide back to the wall, back to basics.

"Twenty-three." She stares at me.

I light the reefer.

"Oh." I inhale the smoke and hold it. "You don't look it."

"People say I look to be about nineteen."

"You do."

"I know." She stares. I try to maintain eye-to-eye contact, look at the smoldering cinder instead.

"How old am I?" I dare, foolishly, passing her the smoke. She takes it, pauses in thought. She draws the smoke in, holding it inhumanly long, then releases it in a relaxed exhale.

"I'd say you are . . . seventy-two."

"What?"

"Somewhere up in there."

"Huh?"

She offers the smoke. I come forward, reaching for it. She slides to the edge of her chair. Again, we are so close. I take the smoke, lean back.

"Come on, old man, act your age," she goads.

"Mama, you're gettin' awful close."

"I started this morning, first time I looked into your

eyes," she whispers. "I saw the pain, from too many lifetimes. You are so young."

Silence.

She straightens, changing the mood. "I'd say you're my age, a little older."

I shrug. Puff on the reefer.

Bearing down again, she continues. "Age doesn't make much difference in your case."

I puff more.

"I've never met anyone like you before," she continues, leaning forward.

Puff. Puff. Puff.

"Give me that stuff," she commands, taking candy from a baby. "You're too shy," she adds, taking a couple of quick hits off the cinder. I reach for it. She pulls back. "Wait your turn," she scolds, taking a long draw. I reach for my scotch. Gulp!

"Okay," she says, handing it back.

I take the smoke, what's left of it. Look at it, then up. She leans right into my face. I close my eyes. Warm, wet, soft lips touch mine. She stays, nibbling at, around, my mouth, following the nips with her tongue. Soothing. The warmth of her breath, as she exhales, is a soft breeze on my cheek. She slowly leaves. Lips linger. Once we're apart, she sits down.

"I'm a little high," she apologizes.

"So am I. That doesn't mean you have to stop."

"I agree."

Her tongue leads the way back to the corners of my mouth. I open up. My latency provoked, returning tongue for tongue. A corner of my intellect interrupts: "How is the war doing?" I pull back, quickly.

"I'm a heavy breather."

"Prove it." She pulls me back by the nape of the neck.

Yeah, prove it.

Our lips touch again. Tongues dart. My hands caress her shoulders. I stand and lift her, a feather. We move together, knees rub, thighs push, hips, nipples, chest, close, closer. We sway, necks twist as noses nip, in passing. Lips leave for cheeks, then to ears, breathing like in a wind tunnel, heavenly sounds. Caress, such stirring. Rock, sway, each other in bearable hugs. Move as one. Darlene, oh, darling!

"Let's lie on the bed," she whispers hoarsely. I drip.

What are they doing outside?

I pull off my T-shirt, draw out of my pants. She turns to face me, so supple. "My God, you have beautiful breasts."

"My God, you have hair everywhere," she soothes.

I'm hard. It's easier.

Are they on patrol, stalking that fear of an ambush?

We reach for each other, still standing in the thrill of the caress, hugging, rubbing against each other. Chest hair rubs the rise of two round mounds. My hands reach to touch the dimples above the buttocks' rise. Erect, I rub between her legs. We begin the motions, breathless, moaning, knees weakening. She steps back, away, and draws the covers from the bed. I feel, at once, naked and alone.

. . . they must be cruising, bait for urban guerilla booby traps.

"Come lie down. I want you close to me." She gently pulls me down. Supine, we fondle each other. Oh, why do I resist? Resist no more! "Are you all right?" she whispers. I melt over her.

The snipers, sharpshooters and lookouts, are they watching?

Her tongue darts, teases my nipple, goosebumps rise as her lips pull gently at my chest hair. Gone stiff, I'm lost in a revelry.

"Come inside me," she moans, beckoning by stretching open as the sheets crackle static.

I drop my guard.

We transported each other back and forth in ecstasy far into the night. We sampled, tasted, whetted thirsts in selfless splendor. Then sometime after yet another successful sojourn, she fell into a fitful sleep. I have the moment alone, while we are together. I leave her side, go to sit on the window sill. I tingle at the lick of the seacoast breeze. So alive! I gaze down into the street. They are still there. Where I had left them.

A combat patrol files along the concrete streets. A troop transport, covered in wire mesh to deflect the direct hits of homemade bombs, trucks slowly down the avenue. Sandbags that provide cover for machine guns and sharpshooters slowly wash away under the cleansing drizzle. The weather never gets in the way of war.

My ears still chime from our last cumming. I start to get dizzy from my intense focus on the street activity. I bow my head to rest on bended knee. Tears well up, roll, fall, flow off my cheeks and down the inside of my thighs, mixing with sexual smells I never would have thought to wash off.

I snap to, suddenly. Wet, vulnerable in a window overlooking a combat zone, I look back to her. She rests wonderfully on her side. I stir again.

Torn between two worlds. Hope and hopelessness. Love and hate. Here at war's door, I plant a seed. The risk is great. The danger is fearsome. The exposure obvious. How many of us opt to be fighters because we think we're protecting our lovers? Yet, we have never lived.

We are suckers to our own violence, I guess. I can't think that it was not worth it. We lost too much to scorn it. So many men never will be able to feel, share, believe in being gentle, in being in love.

She groans as she rolls to where I should be lying. Her eyelids flutter as she reaches blindly for me. I leave the window, the war. Duty calls.

WIGGLE YOUR TOES

by Doc Kane

I'd rather lay
in cum stains than in blood stains.
I don't care if you recoil at the fact.
I'd rather lay
in cum stains than in blood stains.
I now know which is the natural act.

Oh, and by the way, lovers,
when you are cumming on to being,
wiggle your toes, wiggle your toes!

• • •

Tone,

I hope this letter finds you well. I'm doing okay,
I guess. I'm writing this sort of as a farewell. I
don't know if you got the postcard I sent from
Germany last summer, but I was over there for a
while. I'd advise avoiding Belfast, Northern Ireland
(boy, did I get laid there!), but Europe is the place
to be. I traveled from Ireland to Istanbul, partly
with this American girl and mostly on my own.
Then I came home. Now I'm going back.

I've been waiting out here in California to see if
my brother, Greg, would make it back from Nam.
(Four of us Kanes have been there.) He got back
last week. Not very sociable, but he's alive. So
now that that's over with, I'm getting the hell out of
the U.S.A. Peace freaks say we did too much to
those Vietnamese. Then some war freak says we
didn't do enough. I still haven't been able to get a
decent job.

Anyways, I'm sure you don't have much good to
say about all this. Were you anywhere near that

shoot-out with Fred Hampton? Damn! Man, the whole thing is all fucked up! Want to come with me? They treat black people better in Europe.

Yeah, right. Well, send all correspondence to my mom's address. I'll be in touch with you through your grams. Be careful, Tone, it's a fucking jungle everywhere.

My thoughts, buddy,
Doc

• • •

"We got some pretty mellow dudes living here," he boasts, stretching back on the couch. I sit in an over-stuffed chair, facing him. We're both in an altered state. The only things I can move are my ears. The only thing he can move is his mouth.

"Let's see. I'm the only one in the house with a straight job. There's Pietranowicz. He works as the move-ment printer. There's Mike. Mike rented 4130. He was active for our big demonstration in April, now he's back in school, at Georgetown. Let's see. Boy, this is really good smoke. Oh, yeah. There's Tim. He's a movement heavy. He's an active organizer. Where did you say you got this hash from, man? Appalled?"

"Nepal."

"Nepal?"

"It's called Nepalese temple ball. The monks make it over there."

"Out of sight. Sure does make me mellow. Let's see. Jack. That's right. Jack lives here too. He's away right now, traveling around the country. You can stay in his room. He's a mellow dude. He was a captain in Special Forces."

"What about you?"

"Oh, I'm a mellow dude," he admits. Then he stares out the window, silent. The pulse of the house skips a beat. I look closely at him. If his mouth stops moving for any length of time I may have to call an ambulance.

"Bruce. Bruce, what did you do in Nam? Where were you stationed?"

"Oh, I'm a social worker here in the District. That's why I'm a little edgy. After work, need to get mellow."

"What did you do in Viet Nam?"

"Oh. I was a clerk in Hue, First Marines. Hey, man, if you want to listen to some mellow notes, come up to my room. I have a great stereo and great albums. Yeah, use my headphones too. Hey, did you ever fuck on a waterbed? Man, I got a waterbed. You ever get a chick you want to ball, man, you can use my waterbed. Unless I'm using it, of course. Hey, you want to see it? You want to hear some mellow notes, man?" He rises like Lazarus from the dead. A minute ago I was anticipating saving his life. He heads out of the room. I labor out of the chair.

"C'mon, man. Dope this good has got to have some mellow tunes. I got the new Rod Stewart album. Wanna hear it? You can listen on my headphones."

He stops at the stairs. "Yep, you're going to like this house, Rod. Nothing but mellow dudes. Each floor, there lives a mellow dude. You too, a mellow dude with mellow dope."

"Hey, that was some pretty strong dope."

I turn. "Oh?"

A big, bearded, blond fellow, dressed in a jungle fatigue jacket and blue jeans offers me a hand.

"My name is Tom Pietranowicz. I wasn't here last night to meet you. I'm the movement printer and house chauffeur."

That rings a bell. We shake.

"Oh, yeah. Bruce talked about you. You want some smoke?"

"No. No thanks. I don't do dope. I drink beer. I get high on Jesus." He laughs. "Have you met everybody?"

"I have no idea. I met Mike. Tim. Bruce. Let's see,

I've heard about Jack. Now you. How many live here, anyway?''

"We have five. Could handle more. Where are you coming from?''

"I'm from California. I'm on my way back to Europe. I've stopped here in Washington to apply for visas and work permits. I slept in a church basement in Georgetown my first night here. The priest there told me about Viet Nam Veterans Against the War, gave me your phone number. I talked to Bruce. He said to come over. That's how you found out about the dope. Anyways, I was in Nam, then my brother, my Dad, my other brother. It didn't do any of us much good and it still goes on. I'm fed up with it.''

"When were you there?''

" '65–'66. I was a medic. A 'Doc.' ''

"I was a medic too.''

"Oh yeah? So you took the training in Texas, at Fort Sam Houston?''

"1967.''

"Quite a while after me. Where were you in Nam?''

"I wasn't in Nam.''

"Oh?''

"I was lucky. They sent me to Germany. I worked my tour in a dispensary in Nuremburg.''

"Oh.''

"Did you see a lot of action?''

"You could say that, though I ain't complaining. I'm alive, with all five appendages.''

"Where'd you get your dope from? Bring it back with you? Have it sent?''

"I brought it with me from California. Some of the stuff is from there. Some is from Thailand. The hash is from Nepal.''

"Are you going to stay with us a while?''

"If you guys will take dope as barter, I'll crash here while my visas and work permits clear. Then I'm heading back to Europe.''

"Yeah. Well, maybe you'll like it here, stay a while. It's all right with me if it's all right with the other guys, except Bruce. His vote doesn't count in my book. But the other guys will probably let you stay as long as you share your dope. Are you going to sell any? How much you got?"

"Maybe I'll sell some. I have some cash, so selling it isn't important."

"Well, in the meantime, what are you doing? What are your plans? I'm asking because I could use some help down at the office. We've got a demonstration coming up day after tomorrow. I got leaflets to print and distribute. You doing anything today?"

"Well, I was going to pick up some visa applications at a couple of embassies, but I'd like to see D.C."

"Embassies are too busy on Mondays. Help me run off some leaflets down at the office, I'll buy you lunch. Help me distribute the leaflets, I'll give you a tour of the city."

"Sounds to me like you need help. What about the other guys?"

"Oh, for most of them the revolution doesn't start until ten, sometimes noon."

"Really?"

"Yeah. If you hang around long enough, see the way things are run, you may come up with the same question I have."

"Oh yeah? What's that?"

"When the revolution is over, who's gonna deliver the milk?"

Pi and I cranked out over 5,000 leaflets on a dilapidated mimeograph machine. It announced a demonstration in Washington to bring the war to its knees. We bundled up the leaflets, dumped them in the car, had lunch, then Pi gave me the tour.

This town is covered with leaflets and posters announcing anti-war demonstrations as far back as when I got out of the Army in 1967. I know because I saw the damned things everywhere we went. I jumped in and out of that car at Pi's direction, delivering bundles of leaflets. As we cruised, Pi pointed out the famous landmarks of our nation's capital. I littered leaflets. He pointed out the infamous landmarks. Leaflets here leaflets there. Pi filled me in on the anti-war movement. More leaflets here. More leaflets there. Here a leaflet. There a leaflet. Everywhere there are anti-war leaflets. And anti-war posters. Everywhere.

"Hey, Jack, now that you're back we'll move Rod down to the couch. You don't mind, do you, Rod?" Pi says as he flips the burgers.

"Sure, the couch is okay. I'm not going to be here that long." I stretch up, handing the pipe to Jack.

"As long as your dope holds out, you're welcome," Jack says, and puffs.

"That ain't a nice thing to say to a brother," Bruce snaps, grabbing the pipe and sucking in his share.

"He knows what I mean," Jack says, swigging off a beer. Bruce attempts to pass the pipe to Pi, who just shakes his head. Tim takes the pipe, goes back to the terrace edge overlooking the street. He puffs, lost in thought, then suddenly turns to me.

"Hey, you may be able to help us out in other ways, Rod. You know, for room and board?"

"How so, Tim?"

"Well, we are in kind of a bind with this demonstration coming up day after tomorrow," he says.

"Oh, oh," Pi cautions, "Tim is delegating responsibility again."

"Fuck you, Pi." He turns to me. "You said you were a combat vet, right?"

"Right."

"Yeah, well, I'm supposed to speak at this demonstration, as a representative of Viet Nam Veterans Against the War." He takes a long pull on the pipe. Holding his breath in, he says, "I ain't got anything ready. How would you like to give a speech?"

I'm speechless.

"Didn't you say you could write?" Pi reminds me.

"Well, ah, yeah. I've done some writing . . ."

"So, if you can write, you can speak!" he concludes.

"Not necessarily . . ."

"It's settled," Tim cuts me off, raising his beer. "Rod Kane will speak for us at the demonstration."

They all raise their beers. I look at the pipe. It's out.

"What the fuck am I supposed to say?"

"Talk about what you did over there. Did you commit any atrocities?" Tim asks.

"I was a medic," I bristle.

"So?" says Jack.

"I don't know if I could talk about any shit like that. But me and my brothers, we filled in quite a few years over there."

"Far out!" Tim exclaims. "Talk about how the war fucked over your family."

I'm standing in a roped-off area behind a speakers' platform in a circle called the Ellipse, between the White House and the Washington Monument. The area is packed full of demonstrators.

I hate crowds. I'm sick to my stomach. I'm supposed to speak next. What am I doing here? Goddam this fucking war! Look at all the people. Damn. What would the guys say if they knew I was going to do this? Henderson would be pissed!

"Ron King."

That sounds familiar enough.

"Yes." I answer, turning left and right.

A black man steps down off the back of the speakers' platform with the help of crutches. He hobbles toward me, stops, offers a hand.

"Peace now. My name is Julius Hobson. How do you do?"

"Hi, Julius." I return the strong grip.

"Ron, I'm going to be the next speaker. The program says that you follow me."

"I guess."

"You do. So, I'm going to do my speech, then lead the crowd in the chant, 'Out Now.' I'm not sure how long the chant will last but it looks like we have a lively bunch here today, so it might take a couple of minutes. When I feel the time is right, I'll introduce you as a combat veteran with Viet Vets Against the War who would like to say a few words."

"Whatever you say, Julius. Oh, by the way. It's Rod Kane."

OUT NOW! OUT NOW! OUT NOW!

"Next on the program, people . . ."

OUT NOW! OUT NOW! OUT NOW!

". . . a combat veteran, a member of the Viet Vets Against the War, who fought over there . . ."

OUT NOW! OUT NOW! YAY VETS. BOO VETS. OUT NOW! BABY KILLER.

". . . Ron King."

OUT NOW! YAY VETS. DOWN WITH THE KING. OUT NOW! OUT NOW! BOO BABY KILLERS. OUT NOW!

I step up to the podium without looking at the crowd. It's easier to jump out of a plane without a parachute. I start to say something, but I choke. I look up from the podium at the sea of faces, lean into the microphone.

"I was there. I made it back. My father was there. He made it back. My brothers were drafted and sent over. They made it back. We are one burned-out family. And it still goes on. The same old shit. So I'm here to say: NO MORE WAR! NO MORE WAR! NO MORE WAR!"

The crowd takes up the chant. I step off the podium, become dizzy, confused . . . slow down . . . can't stay here . . . got to get away . . .

• • •

I cross the room, touch her shoulder. The blouse
slides off, baring twin rose tattoos at the shoulder blades.
As I would come in after the fight to get fucked, so I can
find relief after the peace march to . . . She turns to me,
breasts sitting firm and upturned. The nipples, light brown,
turn bright red at the touch. I step back from the taste.
She slides her pants off, then sits down and takes off her
leg. She leans it against the bedstead. We roll over each
other to the middle of the waterbed. Anchored, rocking
in the undulating waves, we sweep over each other like
two sailboats slicing across each other's wake. Pulling in
the ebb tide, we ride together down the water slide.
Lulled to sleep in the midnight motions, we cum up on a
crystal dawn.

She rolls to the edge of the bed. Picks her leg up off
the floor, puts it on then slides into her pants. Buttoning
her blouse, she casts a glance over her shoulder.

"Thanks, Steve."

She walks out the door. It wasn't until much later that
I realized I had just been fucked.

Tim said it was because they were all burned out. Pi
said he was doing just fine, so don't speak for him. Mike
did look burned out. Bruce is never around unless it's
for dope call. Jack just reads and belches.

So, I have been duly appointed representative of the
District of Columbia chapter of the Viet Nam Veterans
Against the War. My credentials? I'm a Nam combat
vet. I also have good dope. I am being sent to the
National Steering Committee meeting in St. Louis.

"Hey, leave some of your hash behind for emergencies."

•   •   •

"Hey, brother."
"How do, brother."
"Hey, brother."
"Welcome, brother."
"Hey, bro."
"What's your name, brother?"

"Doc. Er, Rod Kane. D.C. chapter."

"Hey, brother."

"How do, brother?"

"Brother."

"You brothers know where you're crashing?"

"Yeah. I just talked to your housing coordinator."

"You brothers know there's no dope smoking in the workshops? They're all being held in churches or schools."

"Aw, shucks, brother. How am I going to get home if I can't sell some of this homegrown?"

"Hey, brothers, it ain't funny. The St. Louis police are watching our every move. Keep that stuff out of sight."

"I wasn't joking, man." He turns his wheelchair toward me. "Hey, brother. Where did you get the coffee?"

"Over there." I point. "The mama with the jugs."

He peers across the room. "You mean the mama with the set of claymore mines?"

"Really."

"Where you from, brother? I'm from the Deep South."

"D.C."

"Stay put. I wanna sell you some honest to goodness homegrown."

"How 'bout after the workshop?"

The pot is better than the workshop, a power struggle among the chapters to unseat John Kerry as head spokesman of the organization. It has been implied that he is using the organization to further his political career. I think that being the leader of an organization of disgruntled veterans is political suicide to begin with. Goodbye, John! He steps down.

The meeting was adjourned for the day. I spent last night in the hospitality of the boys from Texas.

Whee doggie!

Still burping up a breakfast of Lone Star beer and donuts, I walk down the basement stairs of the elementary school. This is the future agenda workshop. Everyone is settling around a square of tables and chairs built for nine-year-olds.

"Awright, brothers. Lissen up. Lissen up."

The mumbling and rumbling continue.

"Okay, brothers. Cool it now! At ease!" It still isn't working.

"Ten HUT!"

Everybody shuts up.

"Uh, thanks, brother, whoever you are. Awright, brothers, I want to call the meeting to order. The different chapters are all present and accounted for. First we got to clear up a problem before we get started on the agenda. The chair recognizes the brother from New York."

"Thanks, brother." A vet gets up from the table across from me. "Yeah, we got a problem with the representative from D.C. We don't know who he is."

Everyone turns to look at me.

"We want verification from D.C. 'bout this guy 'cause he could be a pig or a narc for all we know."

The room starts buzzing.

My jaw drops. My heart leaps out of my mouth, runs around the adjoining tables, and tinkles on the brother from New York.

Everyone starts to hubba hubba.

The convention host stands. "Wait a minute. Tim called me from D.C. to say this guy is okay."

"Sit down, brother, the chair hasn't recognized you."

"Fuck, no. I won't sit down. I organized these workshops, this convention. I know about this guy."

"You better sit, brother, till the chair recognizes you."

"We sat up smoking homegrown with the brother all night. He's cool. The homegrown's on sale out in the parking lot. The van with Confederate flag plates."

The chair bangs on the table.

"Quiet! Quiet! Quiet! The meeting is out of order!"

More hubba hubba, chair shifting and creaking, the

meeting goes out of control. Many of the guys look to me. I don't know what the fuck to do. I shrug.

"Call Pietranowicz."

Well, Pi straightened everything out over the phone, but I didn't shake one more damn brother's hand at that convention. I returned to D.C. with the task of preparing Washington for a Christmas anti-war "media event" by the East Coast chapters. None of us at 4130 are happy with V.V.A.W.'s attitude toward us in D.C. Pi starts to talk about splitting with the organization and forming a District of Columbia Veteran's Coalition (D.C.V.C.). I still suffer the insult of the "pig" accusation. I don't think even getting drunk will numb the sting of political infighting.

Waking up with a crushing headache, I'm flat on my back. I'm in a pine box, my hands folded across my chest. I've died and gone to hangover heaven.

Fat chance.

I prop myself up on shaky arms, look around enough to recognize the foyer at 4130. What the hell happened after I finished that third bottle of Boone's Farm blackberry wine? A bunch of us had fasted yesterday— Thanksgiving Day. We sacrificed the ultimate meal to end the war. I drank instead.

I turn my head left and right, spy something above me. I focus. It's a pink helium balloon with the black letters OUT NOW! printed on it—leftover symbol of the October demonstration. How could it be floating in midair?

I realize a string is holding it in place. I follow the string to its anchor, peer closer. Oh, oh. My unit stretches upright out of the folds of my half-opened pants. I'm strung up like an outlaw being hung by the neck until dead as my privates take part in an obscene anti-war statement: "I need help getting it up for the Nam."

"Pi," I say in a loud whisper. "Pi?"

"Yeah?" He shouts.

"C'mon. You wanted me to wake you for this permit meeting I have with the Park Service this morning."

"Oh, yeah. Sure. Hold on, be right down."

I step back down off the landing, taking another swig off the Rolling Rock beer. A door opens on the second floor. I walk to the foyer. Pull out a reefer. Light it. Puff. I hear footsteps descend the stairs. I turn in anticipation. Yep. It's our resident girl-illa, Louise. She came to one of our parties a while back. She never left. She's slept with everyone in the house except Pi and Jack. One never knows which room she'll come out of next.

The demands of the Age of Aquarius have taken their toll. Louise's free love philosophy has disrupted communication between my housemates. She never takes the same vet to bed two nights in a row. Yet every night, like clockwork, she's balling someone's ears off in the middle of the eleven o'clock news. I know, because I'm sitting down here with the rest of the forsaken fuckers, watching them munch on shredded hearts and gulp back Rolling Rock tears.

"Roddie?"

She stands before me, her face screwed up underneath a mop of red hair. She pulls her robe closed.

"Roddie, can you remember where I put my clothes?"

"How 'bout downstairs in Mikey's room?"

"Oh." She stumbles toward the basement. Stops. Turns to me pushing her red hair back from her forehead. "Is he alone?"

"I don't think so."

"Damn."

She turns and heads downstairs. Pi comes bounding down from the third floor.

"Okay, let's go," he says, running a comb through wet hair. As usual, his sweatshirt is on backward.

"Lace up your shoes, Pi."

"Oh." He stops, puts a foot on the arm of a chair, and laces each shoe precisely. Pi's fashionable taste dates back to the fifth grade at Our Lady of Constant

Sorrow parochial school. I take a long draw on the reefer. He wrinkles his nose, stamps his feet, and pushes his aviator glasses up on his nose. "Okay, let's go."

He steps out the door.

"You look real dapper, Pi."

"It ain't gonna be a fashion show."

I follow him out to the car, thumbing out the reefer and replacing it with a cigarette. We get in.

"Crack the window." He cranks, then starts the car.

"I am, I am," I puff as I roll the window down. A chill November wind stirs dead leaves and dead leaflets. I close the window with a shiver, putting the cigarette out. We head down to National Park Service headquarters. I've filed permits to march Viet Nam Veterans Against the War from the U.S. Capitol, past the White House, to the Lincoln Memorial. We're gonna end the war.

"Okay, we're going to meet with Mr. Page, he's the permit representative for the Park Service," Pi finally says as we pull into the headquarters parking lot. "He's a permit-challenging pro. His credentials date back to Martin Luther King and the civil rights movement. He will challenge every aspect of the permit. If he confuses you, I'll step in."

"Hi, Mr. Page."

"Pietranowicz," a voice booms, "not you again! Are you in on this one too? I thought I got rid of you on the Capitol steps last April."

"I'm consulting on this one, Mr. Page."

I step into view as Pietranowicz turns to me.

"This is our new man, Mr. Page, Rod Kane. He's a real Viet Nam veteran." My neck hairs bristle at the implication. I look Mr. Page over. He's in his mid-fifties, a disheveled-looking civil servant.

"Kane, good morning. Call me Page." He stretches a hand out over his desk and looks right through me. "I hope you listen to what Pietranowicz has to say. Take his advice and we won't have any problems."

I just nod, returning the shake. All I ever do is shake hands. I never know which way to do it. The old way, like I'd do with Dad. The new way, like I would do with Nam vets.

"Now," he commands, "I have a surprise for you boys. I don't want to see your parade plan revisions. As far as I'm concerned, the demonstration stays on the sidewalk. You march from the Capitol up Pennsylvania Avenue, right on Fifteenth Street, back across Pennsylvania Avenue to the north side of the street. You stop in Lafayette Park across from the White House. There, you disband the group peacefully. You collect all signs and banners, especially those with wooden handles. I don't want any weapons."

He comes around the front of the desk, stopping six inches from my face. "If you guys are going to march on to the Lincoln Memorial, you'll have to do it as individuals, not as a group."

I start to challenge this. Page steps out the door. He disappears down the hallway. Pietranowicz follows. "C'mon."

I stand in the middle of my defense.

"Dammit!"

I go after them, catching Pietranowicz at a turn. Without slowing down, he says, "I dealt with him for every permit we needed for Dewey Canyon III. He knows what he's doing."

"Where are we going?"

"I don't know."

We spy Page at the end of the hall, hands on hips. When we reach him, he steps through a door marked CONFERENCE. We follow.

Holy God!

The conference room is packed full of police, in uniform and plainclothes. Everyone wears a badge but me, Page and Pietranowicz. Christ! I'm glad I brought my hash along, a pipe too. We can have a symbolic little peace pipe passing, then I can be escorted to jail.

We stand at the head of the conference table. Page says, "Pietranowicz, Kane, these gentlemen, these peace officers, represent the police forces of the Metropolitan area. Each man has an interest in the demonstration you've planned. You may know some of these men, at least recognize some faces. They know who both of you are. Now, if you will excuse me, gentlemen." He steps backward out the door, closing it.

It looks like the fucking war room at the Pentagon. At least fifteen bodies in police polyester blue with gold badges. Pi and I sit in the only chairs available. Under his breath, he says, "This has never happened before."

As we settle, a voice from the right side of the table starts up. "Rod . . . Rod. Remember me? Mike Rosario."

A plainclothesman leans forward. I recognize his face. "I'm with MPD–SOD. We met at the peace vigil in front of the White House, Thanksgiving Day."

"Oh, yeah. Hi." I don't remember too much about that day.

"I'm not going to bother introducing everyone here at the table. I'll have everyone sign this paper stating who is who and what police organization they represent." He slides the paper and pen toward me.

"You start."

I sign my name and V.V.A.W. Pi signs his name and pokes me to note that he put D.C.V.C. next to his name. The paper passes down the line.

"Kane."

I turn to an overweight police officer in a high-class uniform.

"My name is Gerry Wilson, Chief of the Metropolitan Police Department. What's this shit we hear that you people are going to defoliate the National Christmas Tree?"

I start at that accusation. One of our members was boasting of doing that at the house last night.

"And what's this I hear about your people throwing napalm canisters on the Christmas presents under said tree?" he finishes.

Pi leans into me, whispers, "Allegations, unfounded allegations."

"Ah, these, those are unfounded allegations, sir," I say.

"Ed Stone, Kane. Executive Protective Service."

I turn my attention to the other side of the table.

"We hear from our sources in Pittsburgh, Pennsylvania, that you have people coming into town who are going to take over the South Vietnamese embassy on Sheridan Circle. What can you tell me?"

"Nothing that I've heard about. That's a new one on me."

"Mr. Kane, Bill Williams, White House Police. We hear you have people who plan to throw blood bags on the White House lawn."

I turn to that accusation.

Gerry Wilson cuts in. "Yeah, we heard these guys are going to slit their wrists and drip the blood on the sidewalk."

"If they want to use their own blood, that's their business," I contend.

"Kane," Wilson answers, "we want to know if you're going to be able to control your people. We don't think you can. We don't want a bunch of crazy, doped-up veterans running amok in the nation's capital."

Pi leans into me. "Tell him it's all hearsay."

"I understand your concern, Chief Wilson," I interrupt at Pi's prompting, "but all your allegations are hearsay. We have no plans to do any such things. We have no plans for violence. Everywhere we go and everything we do that day is spelled out in the permit application."

"Alan Rhinehart, Kane. Capitol Police. Where is everyone going to go to the bathroom?"

I turn, taking a fold of paper from my jacket pocket. "I have a contract for ten Sani-Johns to be placed at Bacon Drive and Constitution Avenue."

"You can't march as a group to the Lincoln Memorial," Wilson butts in.

"Why not?" I turn to him.

"You need Sani-Johns at the beginning of the march as well as at the end," comes from somewhere.

"But you can't put them on Capitol grounds," Rhinehart insists.

"What about toilet paper?" comes from anywhere. I am being turned about. Pi starts chuckling. Wilson cuts back in.

"You can't start at the Peace Monument at the Capitol, go by the White House and on to the Lincoln Memorial."

"Why not?"

"Kane. Ernest Fry, Federal Protective Service. What's this we hear that guys are going to be carrying body bags with them? They are going to step out in the street, get in the bags, block traffic."

Pi whispers to me, "Street traffic isn't the concern of the Federal Protective Service."

I don't even listen to Pi, rather, I retort, "They won't be able to get any body bags. They're all being used in Viet Nam."

"Mr. Kane. Tom Kelly. National Park Service Police. What is this we hear that you guys are going to take over the Statue of Liberty?"

Okay. We got the toilet paper. I mean, after the Capitol Police giving me all that shit, the Sani-John people supplied the t.p. Big hassle, you know, like "who's going to deliver the milk?"

I'm parked in Pi's car at the Fifteenth Street elbow of Pennsylvania Avenue. I have an unobstructed view down to the Capitol. So do the plainclothes cops who are double-parked behind me. Isn't this exciting?

I watch as a couple of homemade V.V.A.W. banners come billowing up Pennsylvania Avenue. The vets carrying the banners could finish the march with hernias the way this wind is blowing. Pi is leading the parade marshals as they buffer our people from traffic and pedestrians. I hear the faint beat of drums as the group gets closer. I can't remember who is supposed to be on the drums, two or three guys. Four fellas are supposed to carry the casket.

The marchers pass the Department of Commerce and make the right turn in front of me. Christ! How many came for this? Pi told me to put down countless dozens on the parade permit. It's at least countless dozens.

One of the drummers is limping as the march goes up the incline of Fifteenth Street. He turns out of the line and steps gingerly over to the park bench next to the car. I try to remember his name as I roll down the window. A little squirmy guy, he's been over to 4130 a few times. Dennis Apple? What's the name they called him?

"Hey, drummer."

"Hey, Doc. I didn't see you sitting there." He gets up and limps over to me. "What do you think of the action? Not bad. Lots of brothers from Boston and New York. Couple from Florida. Hey, mind if I sit in the car? I don't think I'm going to make the blood spattering at the White House."

"Shhh!"

I glance into the rearview mirror. My police tail is busy taking pictures or talking on the two-way radios. I motion the kid around to the passenger side as I stretch to unlock the door.

"Thanks, man," he says, cramming himself and the drum into the front seat. There's only room for the drum, but he seems to fit himself in.

"Yeah. Settle down. What happened to your foot?"

"Blister. Used to happen in Nam all the time. But I wouldn't come in from the field. Nope. Had to stay out there with my brothers. How come you ain't marching with the others?"

"Don't really care for crowds."

"I know what you mean. You the one, the medic who saw all the action in the central highlands?"

"Yes."

"Yeah, it was a bitch. Hey, you want to smoke some? I got some great smoke." He lifts his ass, pushing the drum on me, pulling out a bag of reefer. I look into the rearview mirror. The cops behind me are using binoculars. They've turned their attention to the Ellipse. I look over there. A couple of Park Police on horseback are watching a group of yippies perform for the "Newswatch Action News." The news is always around to get the full story for whoever watches "Newswatch Action News" at 6 and 11 . . .

"Put the dope down," I command.

The car double-parked behind me pulls past us as the last of the marchers disappear. It makes a left turn to bring up the rear of the demonstration. In my rearview mirror I note two occupants in the car that stays behind. I recognize one cop from the permit meeting. He gets out, waltzes up on my side.

"Keep the fucking dope out of sight!" I roll the window down. "Hi, Mike."

He bends over to face me. "Well, not a hitch yet, Rod. Not bad, not bad. You got quite an organization."

"Right, Mike. Looks like a little trouble over there on the Ellipse. They aren't my people."

"We know, Rod. We know. It's been a pleasure following you. You take care now. See you at the next permit meeting."

"Right, Mike." I roll the window up.

He walks around the front of the car, joins his buddy. They head over toward the Ellipse.

"Fucking pig," my passenger growls, pulling his bag of grass out from under the drum. I sigh with relief. The whole thing is out of my hands now.

"Fucking pigs, man. Really fucking pisses me off, man. You know? Fucking pigs, man," the kid says. He spreads the dope out on the skin of the drum.

"What's your name again?"

"Dennis Apple, but they call me Turk. They called

me Turk in the Nam. I was a tunnel rat," he states proudly, while rolling one.

I check all sides for silent observers. No one around. I look over at the Ellipse. The Park Police horsemen are following the "Newswatch Action" team camera, which is following the yippies. We're safe.

"Didn't anybody tell you about me?" he asks, lighting the reefer.

"We don't keep a file on everyone, Turk. We don't check IDs. You're Turk, the tunnel rat, if you say you were."

"Did you do any tunnel work in the highlands?" he asks.

I ignore the question and take the reefer he offers. I draw long and hold it. It impresses me, immediately.

"Did you? Do any tunnels?"

"No, Turk. We let white phosphorus grenades do the tunnel work for us." I take another hit and the march doesn't seem that important. The Ellipse disappears. . . . Okay, Turk, it's good smoke, keep talking.

"It wasn't that easy where we were."

"It wasn't that easy anywhere, man."

"Right. You are right. You don't mind if I talk about it, do you, man?" He peers at me defensively.

"Shut up and talk, Turk." I hold on to the smoldering herb. The car's interior becomes one big cloud.

"I was with the Big Red One in the area north of Saigon. There was a picture in the paper this morning. Did you see it?"

"I was real busy this morning."

"Right. The picture showed this big tunnel they found north of Saigon. Tunnel led to a huge underground city. It had living quarters, mess halls, hospitals, a school." I pass him the nub. He pauses. A couple of Park Police motor scooters pass by, heading toward the Ellipse. I look ahead. See the band of yippies carousing by the intersection of Pennsylvania Avenue and Fifteenth Street. They head south on Fifteenth. The news follows them, then the police.

"That city was something, wasn't it?"

"I guess so," I say, distracted. I don't know if I want to hear it.

He rolls another, then piles the rest into the baggie. He puts it away. Wipes the drum skin clean, then peers off to where he assumes I'm looking.

"Man, I remember this one time . . ." He strikes a match, puffs. Hands me the smoke . . . "I don't know how I did it. It was in the Iron Triangle. Know where that is?"

I inhale more smoke. "North of Saigon."

"Right. We'd been out three weeks, crisscrossing some plateau. It was early afternoon, real hot. Everyone was kicked back in the shade because the captain had called a halt. There I am, cooling it, when this call comes up the line, 'Where's the Rat?' 'Send up the Rat,' 'Rat up front!' They called me the Rat," he states proudly. Does he realize how obvious he looks? "But I like Turk better."

"Turk better."

"So I lace up my boots, grab up my gear, and head up front. The captain and others are standing around this large clump of bamboo. 'Sir, here's our tunnel rat,' the lieutenant says. The captain turns to me, 'You know what you're doing, son?' 'Yes, sir,' I say, snapping to. 'Find out what's in that hole.' He points to a hole back in the bamboo bush. 'Yes, sir,' I say, saluting him, I take off my gear, hang two grenades around my neck on commo wire, check the .45 on my hip, flick the flashlight on and off in my left hand, grab the bayonet in my right."

Why did he salute?

"I step into the bamboo, smell around the hole, feel the dirt for moisture. Not damp. Old hole. I decide to go in headfirst." He pauses, pulls on the smoke, exhales his explanation.

"So, I get in the hole, out of the direct sunlight. I sit till my eyes get used to the dark.

"As I was able to see better 'n better, I slid deeper into the hole. The tunnel widened, I could almost stand up. It must have been a supply hole. Anyway, it was pitch black and quiet, real peaceful. I couldn't feel any strong drafts, so I knew this was something big. The air always settles in large holes. I decided to use my flashlight, a quick flash off the ceiling to see what was ahead."

He stops. Drops his eyes to the drum, as if to see the scene on its skin. I look over at the Ellipse. Park police, news, yippies, are all in view. Can't tell who's watching who.

"From the shadows off the flashlight I note the C-ration cans hanging from the ceiling. Probably had rocks in them, I don't know. I crouched down and stepped under them. I was lucky to be moving cautiously 'cause a rush of cool air stopped me at the edge of a drop-off. Ain't it funny how tunnels breathe?"

"It's a real scream."

"No, I didn't scream, but I sure was scared. I felt below me with the bayonet. Felt for ladder rungs dug into the sides of the drop-off. I stopped to listen real hard, you know what I mean?"

"I hear ya." I finish off the second reefer, pop the nub in my mouth. Lunch.

"Yeah, so I don't hear anything. I kind of turn around on my stomach, go over the side feetfirst. I catch a rung of the ladder. Step down slowly, feeling for the bottom. Is the dope gone?"

I belch. "Just finished it."

"Want me to roll another one?"

"No."

"Oh." He looks down at the drum skin again.

"So . . . ?"

"So, I touch bottom, carefully. Sometimes they have punji stakes setting there."

"Makes sense."

"I use my flash again, against the ceiling. It had been about a fifteen-foot drop, so I know I'm onto something big. It's like an intersection with tunnels going left, right, and straight ahead. Which way does I go . . . ?"

He starts to act real vacant-minded.

". . . you know, I bet I could pass for a gook if I got my eyes slitted, or however their eyes are. And shave my head."

I look at him through the pall of smoke. Where did that idea come from?

"I decide to go to the left. With a quick flick of the flashlight I can tell it looks like the easiest way to go. Kind of bends . . ."

His voice trails off. I check the Ellipse. Yippies, Park Police, "Action News" is nowhere to be seen. I come back to the rat. He's in a daze.

"You know, I don't have to hear this, man, if it's too heavy for you."

He jerks his head around. Glares at me as if I just insulted him. I glare right back. "You could give us both a break."

"I think I got to say something, man."

"Then speak."

"So, I go around to the left. Standing up. Real cool it was down there. That's what's nice about tunnel work. It's cool. Comfortable." He grins. I don't. It fades.

"As I follow the tunnel around," he continues, "I begin to see light. I put my flash away, take the .45 out of the holster with my left hand. Bayonet in my right. I move real slow, keeping my ears open, adjusting my eyes. The air is getting warmer again. I feel a tug at my foot. Freeze!" His eyes widen. "I look down. Foot caught on a wire. It's stretched across the floor, then follows up the wall and runs into the ceiling. I back my foot off, release the pressure. Nothing happens. I still don't know what it was, but nothing happened. I stepped over it, soaking wet."

"Someone let you live, man," I shrug. "We've all been there."

"Really. I got careful. Kinda inched along the wall.

That's where I made my mistake. I shoulda turned right around there and gone back to tell the captain.''

He pauses, takes a deep breath. "As I edge around the bend, I get down on my hands and knees. I see that the tunnel ends in the ceiling of a large room. The place where the light is coming from. I can hear voices . . . at least a voice. . . . I put my bayonet away, put my .45 in the holster. Take the grenades from around my neck. Lay flat to listen and feel. I inch forward, not making any noise. As close as I get, I still can't tell what's going on down there. It's got to be a big room though, 'cause I can hear the voice echo."

He puts his hand to his ears, leans his elbows on the drum and speaks into it. "I get closer to the edge. I want to look, see what's up. Loose dirt lays at the edge. Could push it over the side if I'm not careful. The voice keeps yapping. I lay there, wondering. . . . The war room? Officers' quarters? Weapons room? Man, I'm gonna get me a medal!"

He brings his head up slowly, turns and looks at me. "I shimmy back from the edge to where I can kneel. I pull the grenade pins out with my teeth, wait a second, then let them fly, one after another. I turn, get up, and start running like hell. I'm back in the dark by the time they go off. Could hardly hear them. It didn't sound bad. But it was."

He leans over, drops his head on his arms. The drum thuds. I wait for the punch line, looking over at the Ellipse. The "News Action" team is putting its cameras in the trunk of a car. The undercover cops are coming back our way. Everything is breaking up. Turk is sobbing. I start the car. He lifts his head, inquiringly.

"Sorry, man. I want to get out of here before the plainclothes get close and whiff the reefer."

He sighs. "Okay."

"So, did you get your medal?"

He straightens, shakes his head.

"I blew up a teacher and a classroom full of kids."

I pull out onto Fifteenth Street. After a moment, I realize out loud, "Kindergarten Cong."

The door pops open. I glance at the travel clock on the mantle: 3:30 A.M.

"Shhh."

The shadow uses some caution closing the door.

"Who is it?"

"It's me, Mike."

"Watch your step, Mikey."

He steps gingerly across the various bodies stretched out on the living room floor—veterans and their supporters from out of town who didn't get arrested. Mike sits down with a thud next to me.

"What are you doing awake?"

"Radio watch."

"Oh."

"I'm also waiting for the guys who were in the Statue of Liberty. They're supposed to drive down from New York tonight."

"I thought they were still in jail up there."

"Someone hiked bail for them. They supposedly got out about midnight. Ray Grodecki called me. Said they were coming down to hold a press conference outside Superior Court with us tomorrow, when I go down to bail out the D.C. Ninety-four."

"Is everything ready?"

"Readier than we were for the Pageant of Peace demonstration."

"Are you still miffed about that?"

"You and Pi really didn't do what you said you were going to do."

"Hey, we had the stage set up by 7:30."

"It was supposed to start before . . . fuck it, never mind. Where you been? Out getting laid?"

"This great, voluptuous undergrad, Roddie. You should see her. From Michigan. Daddy is with General Motors."

"Is that like us being with General Westmoreland?"

"Better. She doesn't have to get weekly haircuts."

"Hey, that was a good one, Mikey. You must be stoned. You got any more on ya?"

"Here." He reaches into a pocket, draws out a hand-made smoke. "Compliments of General Motors. I got lab tomorrow, I got to get some sleep."

He stands and stretches.

"Mike, it's Christmas holidays. School is out!"

"But the labs stay open and I have a lot to catch up on. 'Night, Roddie."

"Be careful, Mikey. I'm not sure who's sleeping in your bed."

"Just as long as there's more than one."

"That's the spirit."

He bounds to the back of the house and down the stairs. I light the reefer, try to relax.

The commentator's remarks on the eleven o'clock news went something like this: "The well-coordinated effort of Viet Nam Veterans Against the War expressed itself again today. The third and final day of that group's occupation of the Statue of Liberty in New York was supported by a sit-down occupation of ninety-four veterans and their supporters at the Lincoln Memorial here in Washington . . ."

Well-coordinated, Christ. We weren't ready to go to jail. I haven't got bail money for ninety-four people. And in the middle of it all, Pi's screaming at me to post his bail immediately. Tim's spouting off into any microphone. Jack's profiling for the TV cameras. Christ, you'd think they disorganized the demonstration instead of me.

Anyway, the blood bags that were thrown in front of the White House didn't break.

The guys decided to block traffic by lying out in the street in body bags. Well, we know you can't get body bags because they are all being used in Nam. So these bozos hide lawn 'n' leaf bags under their coats, leap out at the intersection of Pennsylvania and Madison, climbing into the bags. Problem is, the bags aren't big enough. These guys are lying out in the middle of traffic looking like they just fell over in a potato sack race. Other guys wear lawn 'n' leaf bags over their heads, like half-finished Gumbies. No one convinced anyone that someone was dead. A new addition to the lyrics of "Fixin' to Die Rag" . . . "be the first one on your block to have your boy brought home in a lawn 'n' leaf bag." We are our own worst enemy.

As for the well-coordinated efforts of V.V.A.W. nationally, check the history of our takeover of the Statue of Liberty.

It was no surprise. The New York City chapter put out a press release announcing the event three days before it happened. Our guys land on the island by ferry. They enter the statue, tell everyone there of our intentions and why. All the folks leave on the next ferry. Our representatives proceed to pile the furniture from the Park Service offices in the statue up against the entrances, anticipating a military assault on our occupation. With the evacuation complete and the doors barricaded, a tourist appears at the steps leading down from the statue. It doesn't take him long to surmise what is going on. He sidesteps the furniture blockade, pushes the door open and walks out.

Oh, oh! The doors open out! Any idiot in the world can just open the doors and ask our bunch, "Hey, what are you guys doing sitting on a pile of furniture in the middle of the doorway?"

Feel foolish? I figured out how to solve that problem. Wake the whole country up. March them to the Statue of Liberty. Bring the furniture outside. March the country into the Statue. Pile the furniture against the outside of the doors. Don't let anyone out until the war ends!

Brrring?
Should have shut the damn thing off.
Brrring?

At least taken it off the hook.

Brrring?

Let's get it over with.

"Yeah!"

"Mr. Doc Kane, please."

"Speaking."

"Mr. Kane, Sergeant Benjamin O'Herlihey, National Park Police down at the West Potomac Park station."

"Oh. Oh."

"Mr. Kane, a gentleman by the name of Dennis Apple, also known as 'the Turk,' has referred us to you. Are you acquainted with this person?"

"Yes."

"He claims to be a brother of yours."

"What?" I sit up abruptly in bed. "A brother? No, sir, he can't go that far. What's he done? Banging on his drum and disturbing the peace?"

"A passing motorist reported an individual allegedly jumping from Memorial Bridge at approximately 12:30 A.M. Our choppers pulled Mr. Apple out of the water in the vicinity of the bridge approximately ten minutes later."

"No shit."

"Upon preliminary questioning, Mr. Apple gave us your name as an immediate family member living in this area. He said you were a brother and gave us this phone number."

"A brother? Wait a minute, what time is it?" I whirl around looking for a clock.

"It's 2:12 A.M., sir. I'm sorry for the inconvenience but we try . . ."

"That's okay. That's okay. Just didn't want to think I was dreaming. No, officer, no, he's not a member of my immediate family. He's a member of the same organization I am in, Viet Nam Veterans Against the War. He may infer being a brother in that sense but he's not a brother in blood."

"Well, sir, that may shed an interesting light onto Mr.

Apple's situation. Since our preliminary questioning of
the gentleman we have found a previous file on him. It
seems he's had a habit of jumping off that bridge since
he was fourteen. He has been frequently hospitalized at
St. Elizabeth's since that time for chronic suicidal
tendencies."

"Really."

"Which would mean that he could not have served in
any of the armed forces, or in Viet Nam. There is no
record of his having served any term of military service."

"No shit."

"That's affirmative."

"Why that lying, jiving, two-faced little twerp."

"That's why I was calling, to verify."

"Well, I ain't his brother and he ain't even a member
of the organization either."

"Sorry to have awakened you, Mr. Kane."

"That's cool. Anything else."

"No, sir, that's all, good night."

"Good night."

Click.

Is it in the darkness, trying to fit this latest information
in with the sympathy I had for "the Turk." I recall the
"tour" I took with him through that tunnel. There is a
stirring in the bed, she rolls my way.

"Trouble?"

I turn to her, thankfully. If I were alone I'd probably
start spitting blood and shitting on furniture.

"No. No, not really, just a case of mistaken identity."

"Oh. So what else is new. You know I still don't
know your real name. Do you have a real name, a last
name?"

"I told you, call me Doc, and besides, what's your
name? Wait, let me think . . . I seem to recall . . .
Tracy? No, Stacey."

She giggles. "Stop it, that's not fair."

"I bet you even believed me when I said I was in Viet
Nam, didn't you, Tracy?"

177

"Of course I did. You're with V.V.A.W. You look like you were in a war."

"Oh yeah, what did I do over there?"

"I don't know. You said your name was Doc. Were you a doctor over there?"

"No, my little wayward waif." I turn to her, slowly. She edges back on the pillow.

"What were you doing over there?"

"I was a tunnel rat."

"A what?" She squeaks, stuck.

"Yep." I hover above her. "I found tunnels, then climbed down into them."

I run a hand under the sheets.

"Oh. Oh. Is this a come-on?" She opens up. I bend to kiss her as a hand slides, searches, finds. I leave her lips and whisper.

"Oh? What have I found? A tunnel? I've found a . . ."

"Oh baby, a little higher and to the left."

Jack hands the pipe to me, exhaling into the pages of his book. I take it. Inhale. Hold it, step down to Tim.

"Thim," I say, in that unique voice that comes from holding in smoke. He turns absently, takes the responsibility from my hands.

"Thanks."

He smokes. Then steps up to Jack, hands it back. The circle is unbroken. We aren't going to have many more smoke-ins on the front porch of 4130. Bruce and Pi aren't with us anymore. Bruce took his headphones and skipped off to Ventura, California, in the middle of January. Pi went back to his sister's in Virginia. He said he was burned out. Finally! That was in February. We are now in early spring. Jack is going out to California to school. Tim is going back to Ohio. He says he really is burned out. Finally!

That leaves Mike and me. I have a job cleaning the outsides of government buildings, scaffold work. It's quick money. I have to get those visa applications in to the embassies. I hope to be in Frankfurt, West Germany, before Memorial Day.

"Hey, when is Memorial Day?" I think out loud. Neither of them pays any attention. "Jack? Tim?"

Jack looks up from his book, draws on the pipe. "What?"

"When is Memorial Day?"

"How the fuck should I know? It's out." He hands the pipe back to me.

"Tim. Hey, Tim."

"What?"

"When's Memorial Day?"

"In late May."

"Yeah, I know that, but when exactly? What day?"

"It varies, I think, from year to year. It's not like it used to be. The government floated the date so everyone could have three-day weekends every year, or some shit."

"That's real white of them."

"Really," he says and returns to his private musings. I look down at the ash in the pipe. There is enough for one more load then we have zilch dope.

"Hey, you guys."

I look up. Mike comes bounding down the street. "Guess what, you guys." He's grinning from ear to ear. He bounds up the front steps. "Guess who I just saw."

"Who, Mikey?" I give up easy these days.

"Pietranowicz."

"Where?" Jack says, looking up from his book.

"When?" Tim turns.

"Just now, Mikey?"

"He was over at the dry cleaners, picking up his uniform."

"Oh no, did he re-enlist? Did he go back in the Army?"

"Did he join the National Guard?"

"Fucking Pietranowicz. Couldn't make it out here in the real world. He had to go back in."

"No. No. That's not it." Mike pauses. The grin on his

face is so big he can't say anything. Jack snaps his book shut.

"Well, what is it?"

"He was picking up his policeman's uniform. He's a cop. Pietranowicz is a cop."

Silence.

We're dumbstruck. We look at each other. I try to reason. He taught me everything, introduced me, worked the hardest, ran the show.

"Of course!"

Jack stands.

Tim's chin hits his chest.

"He said he wasn't sure how to get the word to you guys. He said he hoped you all wouldn't be too pissed. He really enjoyed himself while here at the 4130."

"Really, Mike, where'd you see him?"

"I was walking across the Calvert Street Bridge, saw his car double-parked in front of the cleaners. As I checked closer, he came out with a uniform over his shoulder. His hat and nightstick were on the back seat. He showed me his badge."

"His gun?"

"Checked in at the station. By the way, Roddie, he says you could be in some trouble."

I look at the others. Jack starts to grin. Tim puts his hand over his mouth. Mike chuckles. They all begin to laugh. I don't think it's so funny, but I have to admit I couldn't have done it without him. We all begin to chuckle. He was the best worker we had. I look at the pipe. What an occasion for the last of the hash. I take it out, load the pipe, stoke it and offer.

"A toast, to Pietranowicz, whose immortal words I quote, 'Who's going to deliver the milk?' "

"Hear! Hear!" in unison. I pass the pipe. It puffs its way around the circle and arrives back at me, extinct. We stand in a silent circle.

"Roddie?"

"What, Mikey?"

"What are you going to do? Pi says you're in trouble."
"He's going to call a lawyer."
"He's going to call a priest."
"I'm going to call time-out!"

* * *

Doc,

Peace, white boy, that's where I'm at. I hope that isn't a surprise to you. It's a relief for me.

I'm not going to go into any great detail of how Islam has changed my life. I will say that I am at peace. Brother Malcolm has shown us the light. I work amongst our people as a paralegal, interpreting white laws for the sake of black defense. I hope you understand that the anger, the rage you hear from my people, is only an attempt to throw off the yoke of our own suppression.

I want you to know that I am doing well. I'm taking care of myself and those who I am responsible for. I wish the same for you.

My respects to you, Doc. Live a clean life and you will realize peace.

Sincerely,
Akim Ali Clark

* * *

Start the clock again.

First of all, my lawyer says I can't talk about being busted. All I can say is that I'm not going back to Europe, at least not in the near future.

I have removed myself from the professional veterans' ranks. I can't make a profession out of something that disturbs me. The war climbs in and out of my mind every night. Why go into an office and deal with it every day? As it is, the anti-war movement screams "vets to the front" every time there's a confrontation with police. It seems like we are pushed to the front no matter which way we turn. I'm tired of fighting. I want a change, the stereotype is so fatal.

Of course, I quit drinking and drugging. I hope for probation. I don't feel betrayed by Pietranowicz but I do wonder who he really is, printer or policeman? The war continues. I have a job. I'm back in school. My college advisor says, "Write about what you know. Write about what interests you." I want to make love.

I do not understand the sexual revolution. I'm not that far removed from revolution, having fought in one and witnessed another. Sometimes it feels like the only thing I'm qualified for is to wander around the world, from revolution to revolution, exercising my talent for saving lives, testing life's luck, living on the edge.

In armed revolution, like in Viet Nam or in Northern Ireland, it's a simple task. We try to kill them. They try to kill us. We try to ambush them. They try to ambush us. We booby-trap them. They booby-trap us. Cut and dried, live or die.

In the sexual revolution, like since the back seat of the car or since the invention of the birth control pill, things aren't so simple. We try to live with them. They want to be independent. We try to love them. They say they are getting fucked. We try to figure it out. They withhold information. Escape and evasion, laugh or cry.

I am going to report to you as a war correspondent in the trenches of love. Before taking up my position, let me make one admission. I know how to make war. I don't know how to make love.

●   ●   ●

I'm sitting in the bathroom, looking for something to read. I spy a U-shaped folded pamphlet on the edge of the sink. I pick it up, unfold it.

Aha!

It's the instruction sheet that comes in a Tampax box. I skim the instructions, flip it over. Great, a map. Christ, I can't make heads or tails out of the diagram. I turn the sheet one way, then the other. Where? What? How? Wait, damn, the printing is upside down. Ooops, there.

Hmmm, the maps we have to rely on in the sexual revolution are as bad as the maps we had in Viet Nam.

* * *

"No, not there. Don't you know anything?"

I tense, pulling my hand back from the fold.

"Don't you know where the clitoris is?"

Keep your voice down. I clear my throat. "Of course, I do."

What the hell is a clitoris?

She pushes herself away from me. I freeze, prone on the bed.

"Where are you going?"

"We have to do it differently. I just can't lie here and have you climb on me and pump up and down."

"I haven't had any complaints in the past."

"There just isn't any pleasure in it for me." She sits up, turns her back.

Pop! goes the ego. I scramble in my thoughts. Don't get out of bed. I put a hand on her shoulder, trying to turn her around. She stiffens.

"Honey?"

"What?"

"How about you show me. Let me go down there. I'll look. You point things out to me."

She relaxes, turning around. Damn, that was close. I thought I knew everything. I mean, you figure going through a war and looking at all those centerfolds every month gives a fella a pretty good lead in the bedroom.

"Now, you have to be real careful. . . ." She opens herself. I turn away, self-consciously. "Don't be embarrassed, I'm only going to show you the little man in the boat."

* * *

"Hey, Mona, which one was it? Which one threw the briefcase in the Potomac? You know, the 'deep six' trick. Who did they accuse? Erlichman? Was it Gray?"

"How do I know. You watched the Watergate hearings, not me. Where'd that come from, anyway?"

She hangs the necklace on the edge of the mirror, pulls the sweater over her head. The brown globes quiver, beautiful. I pause. "The F.B.I. stopped me again today. While I was working on the GSA building."

"God, the war is over. Why are they fucking with you? You didn't talk to them, did you?"

She kicks off her sandals, slides out of her pants and panties.

"He caught me by surprise. He asked about Tim. I said I didn't know anything about Tim. He asked about the American Serviceman's Union. I said I quit demos after the Bureau of Indian Affairs takeover in '72."

She stands, hands on hips, like an advertisement. She steps to me, putting me face to face with my main objective. I feign a nip. She draws back at the hips, pushing me down on the bed.

"It's like they don't have enough trouble with Watergate." I reach for those breasts. She leans forward. I thumb the nipples slowly. She undoes my belt, then goes below it. The zipper opens. It sounds like the slice of a knife.

"When I get you out of these, baby, I'm going to make sure you don't get back in them."

She starts to get up. I reach for her hair, pull her gently toward me. We use our tongues to trace slick paths from ear to ear. She sits back suddenly. Stands, stoops to pull off my pants.

"You still have your boots on. How come you men wear damn boots? They are so hard to get off!"

The boots go flying.

"Hey, I wasn't finished talking about the F.B.I."

"Fuck the F.B.I." She grabs the cuffs of the pants and yanks. They disappear. The coins from my pockets fly everywhere.

"Keep the change."

"It's probably pennies."

She comes back down on top of me. We lock into a sexual struggle. Twist and turn. Push and pull. Squat and squirm. She climbs on. I hang on. She tilts. I whirl. She pushes. I pull. We moan and groan. Riding. Ride. Ride.

"Oh. Oh. Oh."

"Christ."

We cum with a gush as skins turn red blush. She falls to the sheets. We slump side by side. Belly to belly, we rock. We cradle. Exhausted. Can't move. Unable.

"I lived with a cop, you know."

"Oh? Does that mean you're gay?"

"What? Gay? Has my dick been saying I'm gay for the last three or four months?"

"You could be bisexual."

"I could also be late for dinner. For Christ's sake, Mona, what has gotten into you? You know what I meant when I said I lived with a cop. I'm making innocent conversation about the disadvantages of being a Viet Nam veteran. No jobs. Being portrayed as crazy, fucked up."

"You've done a good job with that."

"Fuck you, I've cleaned my act up real good since I've been on probation."

"I'm just tired of hearing about it. The war is over. You should forget about it. It's your own damn fault you ended up in Viet Nam anyway. Don't come crying to me about it. It was your own fault."

The cigarette smolders close to my fingertips, the ash an inch long. I don't see it fall. I don't feel the burn.

"Where's more reefer? Let's get higher." She moves about the room, intently. I don't answer, even though there is reefer in my shirt hanging on the door.

"Here's some, in your shirt pocket." She turns to show me. "Put that cigarette out before you burn yourself. Look at the ashes all over."

I slide off the mattress, onto the floor, flattening the

cigarette ashes under me. I stretch to stub the cigarette out in the ashtray.

She kneels next to me. "Got a match?"

I bring the matches back from alongside the ashtray. She snaps them from my fingers, lights the reefer, blows the smoke in my face, then sits back out of reach.

"Want to do it some more?"

Mona puts me down. Teases, she would say, then expects me to hump her all the way to ecstasy. Why do I screw around with someone who fucks me flat then puts me down?

"C'mon macho man." She comes back alongside me, having realized I need encouragement. The sweet reefer aroma passes by. I look her in the eye.

"No thanks, Eve. Who put you up to this anyway? Was it the snake? Huh? It was the snake, wasn't it?"

"Oh, stop that bullshit. Take some of this, you're gonna need it."

I bristle but take the smoke. I have to try to relax. I'm supposed to look forward to getting laid. Her put-downs are like cold showers. I've been so raw since I quit drinking. Why put out if I'm constantly being put down? If it can happen to women, it can happen to men. I mean, it's great pussy, but it ain't that great.

"Give me that before you hurt yourself." She takes the reefer from me. I could use a drink. This is trouble.

"Come back to earth, Peter Pan. I want to take you for a ride." She leans into my face, planting a wet kiss. I draw my lips tight, turn. She licks a cheek, blows in my ear, searches below with her hand. She weighs on me. I fall back, hitting the mattress like a ton of bricks. She settles at my side, using hands, head and heart to stimulate. I'm trapped. I don't want to fuck, but I can't express it. I follow her lead. Men are supposed to always want to fuck.

She uses her experience, twisting, stroking. I respond halfheartedly. She disappears from view. I am a captive audience. She stays out of sight. Should I say something? She tries harder. It grows. I don't try. It shrinks. She works harder. It does. I don't work. It doesn't. She does. It does. I don't. Do. Don't. Will. Won't. Can. Can't. Was. Won't. Dammit. Do it. Don't.

"Oh. Oh. Oh."

"No. No. No."

I squirt something on the inside of her leg.

"Don't. No. Dammit. Not there," she mutters, looking down at a smitten little semen note.

"Ooops."

Wow! I am fucking up, caught in a relationship I don't want to be in. I'm afraid to leave. I need to be with someone. But if I stay, there are these various duties I'm supposed to perform. I'm afraid of something. I feel trapped. We try. I get to a point, when we're rocking and rolling, then I dam up . . . something puts a knot in my dick string.

The harder we try, the worse it gets. We foreplay. I go along. It's that or leave. I need to stay. We continue to play. She gets hot. I lose it. She froths in frustration. My sexuality seeps away. A part of me says, "Don't go. It feels good." The other part of me says, "Freeze. It's an ambush." She's ready. I'm not. She's open. I take a shot. It lands on the sheets. She moans. I gloat. This is war, bitch! If you can't respect my situation then I'm not going to respect yours.

I have to get away from here. This relationship is eroding my self-confidence. It's gnawing away at my self-esteem. I'm afraid of making it with anyone. What if this nonaction is permanent? No, it can't be. Maybe it is. Again and again and again and again.

•　•　•

"Honey, why don't you go lie down on the seat behind us."

"Mommy, I want to be next to you. Ask the man to move back there."

I can shut my eyes but I can't shut my ears.

"I can't ask the man to do that. Now you go back there."

"Excuse me, mister." I open my eyes as the little girl plows past me. She has a blanket tucked along one side of her head. She steps into the aisle. Putting her thumb back in her mouth, she gives the two of us a wary glance. She climbs up on the empty seats behind us.

"I'm sorry. She's been such a little snot since we left her dad's. They get along famously. At least now we won't be bothered. Where'd you say you live?"

With all the empty seats in the back of this bus, she has to sit next to me.

"I don't believe I said anything about where I lived. I told you where I was coming from."

"Where?"

I can't even doze.

"Where'd you say you were coming from?"

"The jungle. The woods, I mean, northern Minnesota."

"Oh, are you from there?"

"No, I'm from Washington, D.C."

"Why'd you . . . ?"

"I needed to get out of the city. A bad relationship was getting worse. I needed to get away, go back into the woods." I sit straight back on the seat, close my eyes.

"I know what you mean. I'm on my third husband, back in Cleveland. That's where we're going, back home. I dread it. I'm sorry, you probably want to sleep, don't you? I just want to touch you so."

I open one eye. Roll my head to the left. She looks at me in a pixie kind of way. She is serious.

"If you're not reading that magazine, I sure would appreciate it if you'd turn off the light."

"Of course." She reaches up to turn off the reading light. The darkness helps.

"Is that better?"

"Much. Good night."

"Good night."

The silence is golden on this pitch black cruise down a Wisconsin highway. There is a creak as the armrest is folded back. I feel a blanket being draped across my lap. Oh no! Why don't I just move to another empty seat? She slides close. Her warmth is very fresh. She snuggles up against me, resting a hand on my leg. Oh no!

She whispers, "I'm sorry. I just have to. Before I go back, please, be close."

"What about the kid?"

"She'll sleep."

It's quiet and warm. It becomes warm and sensual. I relax as she holds me close. No demands, no performances, no judgments, just a bus passing through the night.

• • •

The door creaks on its hinges. It always wakes me. It creaks again. She's in here. I feel the weight on the bed, a whisper.

"Baby."

It usually alarms me, but not this time. I must have gotten something good out of being away.

"Honey?"

I stir, turn slowly. She kisses my shoulder, looks into my eyes.

"Hi."

"Hey, Mona."

"You've slept quite a while."

"Yeah, I'm probably suffering from bus lag."

"I'll bet," she says sarcastically.

"Honey?" She can change, become so sweet.

"Yes?"

"I did miss you. I mean, the separation was good for us, but . . ."

She leans, exposing those great breasts. I stir, then choke.

No. Keep your mind on it.

I lie back. She leans close. I head up to her lower lip. Nip.

Her eyes flash open. She takes a quick suck of air. I palm a breast.

Slow down. Slowly, boy. Keep your mind on it.

She pulls back the covers.

I freeze. Should have gone to a shrink.

She stretches alongside, adding full-length warmth to my doubt. I return to desire. We share each other's shoulders. I stir. She slides on top. We work our hips, rubbing breast to breast. I stir stronger.

Keep on it. I want to. Keep on it. So much. Do it. Take it. Give it. Slow down. No hurry. It's there.

I enter warily, surprised at how stiff, how smooth. She melts down over me.

We groan.

The edge of the head rubs at a roof so wet, so warm.

Turn. Turn. Turn. I want it, to be back.

Let go.

Unhurt.

Sealed inside, so big as to be all sensation as blood pumps us to massive heights, moving as one. Jesus, how high. There's so much noise from all sides.

Deep. Deep. Deeper into the wild chasm of circles that spiral and swirl. She squirms slowly down this side of succumbing as I pulsate up against ruby red walls in the flight of homeless swallow sperm, swirl, circle free, me.

Blam! Oh. Blam! Oh. Blam! Oh.

Now I can get the hell out of here.

• • •

"It's ten, baby, I'm already two hours late. The dispatcher is going to be pissed."

She moves her head from my shoulder. The shirt is soaked in tears. This has been going on since last night. No, longer than that, since last week. Every day. Every night.

My feelings remain the same.

She pushes me away as if she heard that. She steps down the hallway to the living room. "Oh, boy," I sigh, gather up pens, pick up the motorcycle helmet. She can't stay here. I can't trust what she'll do. She just won't accept it. She's too young. I should have known better. Never again.

"Karen." I step into the dark living room, flicking the wall switch. Darkness. Damn, that's right, the bulb popped last night when we were arguing. I try to adjust my eyes to the vague light. The floor creaks in the darkest corner. I step to the window. It won't be much light. I prime the shade, snap. It jumps from my fingers, whirling on its roller. She moves out of the daylight.

"Come on, Karen. I have to go to work. You can't stay here."

"Leave me be. I want to be alone, to say goodbye to this place. I'll make sure the door is locked when I leave."

"No funny business."

Silence.

"Karen, no funny business."

Reassured, I step to give her a kiss.

"No," she commands.

"Okay. No offense. I'll see you sometime."

"No you won't," she growls.

I should not have left her alone, so wounded. I'll probably go home tonight, the chain will be slid across the door. I'll look down, blood will be seeping out of the crack under the door.

Honk! Honk! Honk!

I jerk the motorcycle into the driveway, offering a middle finger to the noise behind me.

"Motherfucker," he screams, driving by.

"If your father bends over, I'll do him too," I scream back.

I park the motorcycle, muttering accusations at the whole system. I step down into the dispatcher's office, checking the time: 1:33 P.M.

"Kane."

I turn to the dispatcher. He holds a phone receiver out to me as he pens on his clipboard. I take it.

"Hello?"

There's no sound. I press the receiver firmly to my ear. "Hello?"

"Sniff."

"Ah shit, Karen."

"Sob."

The other phones in the office start to ring. I stick a finger in my other ear, bending away from the noise.

"Sniff. Sniff. Sob."

"Karen, are you all right?"

"Sniff. Yes. Sob."

"Where are you? Karen?"

"Never mind . . ."

"Are you all right?" I try to listen for background noise at the other end of the line. The noise here wins out. I shut my eyes, trying to get a picture. I can only conjure up something opaque.

"C'mon, Kane, I need the phone."

"Karen, I hope you're okay. I have to hang up. Please don't call me here. I'm out in the street most of the time. You'll just be harassing the dispatcher. That could lose me my job. Understand?"

"Yes, sniff, I only wanted to hear your voice."

"Well, now that we've taken care of that, I have to go. Call me at home tonight, okay?"

Silence.

"Karen?"

"Okay. Sniff. Sob."

It's sevenish by the dots on the Guardian Federal clock. I groan as I get off the motorcycle in front of the house. Ride all night. Ride all day. Every night. Every day. Tonight, rest. I step up to the apartment. Oh, oh. The door is ajar. Three quick steps and I push it open.

"Karen?"

Shut the door. The living room walls quiver in shadows of flickering light. I step in. Two candles, a bottle of wine, food on the table. She sits on the other side. Her eyes glisten in the soft reflection. Her tears drop. My heart sinks.

"Dinner's cold," she sobs softly. I sit hurriedly, fork pasta with a couple of twists. Right, it's cold. I stab at the salad. The lettuce is so lifeless I can't get it on my fork. "It's good though," I mouth, biting into the crust of spongy garlic bread. Her head drops to her chest. My stomach turns to indigestion.

"I was so late getting to work this morning, I had to work through rush hour. You aren't supposed to be here, anyway."

She slowly lifts her head, such a fine beauty she is.

"I wanted to see you, Rod."

"Karen, it is all very nice but . . ."

". . . but it's not enough?"

"Karen, today is turning into yesterday."

"Will you at least have a glass of wine with me?"

"Baby, you know I can't drink alcohol."

Her head drops again.

We move too slowly, walking down the street. She has locked my hand in a fingertight grip. This is a replay of so many nights. As we get closer to her apartment building, she stops. I am so impatient. Let her go at her own speed, but let her go. She turns to me.

"I'm so sorry I've been such a pain. I became so obsessed with the relationship. In so short a time. It's like . . . it's like . . ." She turns away to wipe a tear, then comes back around. "I just let myself go so far, so fast. I wanted to be in love so bad. You're so easy to . . ." She turns away again. I let go of her hand. Wait. She turns back around slowly. "I lost my identity."

It's 11:00 P.M. by the Guardian Federal clock as I cut through the park. I'm winded from the feelings, from fleeing down the street when she finally closed that door. It's done. My own fault. She was very much a woman for being so young. How did I let it get so heavy? Why did I sweep her off her feet? I should be penalized. No fucking fair, Kane. You know you can turn those feelings off and on. They don't know that you have such experience.

I jam my hands deeper into my jacket pockets—feel a sudden prickly sensation as the hairs stand on the back of my neck. I whirl around. Stop. Someone disappears behind a tree. I step backward slowly, scanning the park. It was someone, I'm sure. I turn back around without missing a step. If it's a mugger, he'll have to catch me. He can try to mug me. Yeah, if he catches me. Poor Karen, she'd bitch about that, not being able to go out at night. Being afraid of muggers, rapists. Never dawned on me, protect them from communism. They get raped instead.

Yeah. I stop. Look back. The shadow disappears behind another tree. Yeah. I head back. Yeah. C'mon, motherfucker, try me. Choose me. Take my money. I approach the area where he disappeared. He darts out from behind another tree, moving like a bat out of hell. I give chase. He hurdles some bushes, then a park bench. Streaking across the street, he disappears into the night. I pull up at the crosswalk.

"Aw, fuck it."

• • •

I pace along the down side of the trail, looking over a marsh. I step off the trail to let Henderson and Two-Tone by. My feet start to sink into the damp earth. I look down. Through the vines, a fresh-cut edge of bamboo sticks pierces the fabric at my crotch. The stake appears to cradle my right nut in its hollow center. I look to step back but the muck sucks at my ankles, swallowing me deeper. I sink forward as the point tears at the fatigue pants' seam. I suck in air. I suck in stomach and intestines. I suck in nuts and pecker. I may have to squat to pee for the rest of my life. I bend at the

waist, slowly sinking forward. To be impaled or not to
be impaled, that is the question. I try to shout, but
nothing comes out. My arms flail backward, like two
windmills in a stiff breeze . . .

Jesus!

I jerk straight up out of sleep, grabbing for my nuts
and stomach. I am disemboweled. I feel for blood, gasping for breath. Look around. Henderson? Tone?

She lies on her side, turned away from me. I exhale
fear. Whatever I was going to say, I swallow. I am
relieved and embarrassed.

Damn!

I shudder, lie back. The pillow is soaked with sweat.
The sheets damp. I roll on my side, to her. She's dry.
She's warm. I curl up behind her. She mumbles, moves
her legs. I freeze. She settles. I readjust to her sleeping
form. I would like to wake her up. Scream. Tell her I'm
terrified. She is so at peace. I'm jealous. What's her
name? Linda? Belinda?

    •   •   •

Woof! Woof! Woof!

I grin to myself. He's a good dog. He would have
done good in Nam. Bark first, ask questions later. We
could have survived together, come home together, Boo
and I.

Locking the door, I head upstairs, exhausted.

Whack! Whack! Whack!

His tail slaps the doorway, as he stands at the top of
the stairs to greet me.

"Hi, Boo." I stroke his head and push him aside.
"Where's your mom?"

"I'm in here, honey."

Mary's in the kitchen, that means good food.

"Come on, Boo. Mary's got foods for us." He bounds
ahead of me. We greet at the kitchen door, he stands
between us as we grope for each other lustfully. I finger
her jet-black hair, pull back, peer into her emerald-green
eyes.

"Hi."

"Hi. How'd it go?"

"Oh, okay. Exhausted. Did she call?"

"Not that I know of. I work too, you know."

"I know. I know. Damn, she said she'd call." I peek over her shoulder, "Umm, smells good."

"Thank you. Now, out of my kitchen. Out! There's not enough room in here for three."

She pushes. I balk.

"Uh, uh. No way. If Boo gets to stay, I get to stay."

"Come, Boo-Boo. Go with Roddie." We exit with our tails dragging.

I comment over my shoulder, "Oh, by the way, I quit work today."

"What!" She drops her spatula. "What? You quit? Why?" She follows me into the dining room. I pick up the newspaper. Talk to it.

"It's just too much with school and my writing, besides I've got that job if she calls. She said she'd call. She said they always give Viet Nam vets special consideration. If not, I'll go back to courier work part-time. This paperwork mess with my G.I. Bill is supposed to clear up this month. We'll have that money."

Mary sits resignedly. Whatever is simmering in the kitchen begins to boil. She mumbles something. I look up from the paper.

"What?"

"I said, why don't you give up the writing. You can't write. I don't think she's going to call. Being a Viet Nam veteran can work against you more than for you, especially when all you do is write about something as negative as war."

"I beg your pardon?"

"I mean it. You should just forget about writing. Concentrate on something else. Take a course in real estate. You know how to renovate houses. Learn how to sell them.''

''Write about something as negative as Viet Nam, huh?''

''Well, it is. You got nothing out of that war.''

''And you break your neck to get in front of that TV every night to watch 'M*A*S*H.' ''

'' 'M*A*S*H' is funny. Your war wasn't.''

''If it weren't for medics like me with the troops, 'M*A*S*H' wouldn't have any casualties to wisecrack over.''

''Oh, God! I don't want to hear it.'' She gets up, saunters resignedly back to the kitchen. What's boiling over is about to burst. I flush in frustration. My war is negative? I didn't get anything out of that war? I can't write?

BACK TO THE LAND

by Doc Kane

I couldn't get a job so I thought I'd take a chance. Buying three pairs of black PJs and a one-way airline ticket on Northwest Orient, I headed back to the highlands. They might give me a shot, no pun intended.

Sure enough, I was needed. There was a shortage of medical expertise. The people still suffered from the usual tropical diseases and hygienic naïveté. I settled right in, providing a service, contributing to the common good.

Mama-san shared her betel nut with me. Papa-san presented me with his niece. We started a little family. I thought I had found some peace.

But like an old gunfighter who has hung up his guns, it's hard to put the past to rest. Especially when the people hold you in such high regard. Especially when you have their trust.

One day, in a lightheaded splendor, the pangs of guilt won out. I confessed to all the villagers. "I swept through here with the others way back in '65. I still remember all the destruction. I'm surprised so many of you survived."

Needless to say, they were speechless, some resentful with rage and tears. The memories of violence cannot be erased, no matter how many years. The reaction that struck me was how many refused to face such a twist. There was a depth to the silence as so many stared with eyes amist. There is no comfort to being the subject of such a gaze.

I sent to Qui Nhon for my airline ticket, contacted Ho Chi Minh City for an exit visa. As I was bent over my Air Viet Nam bag, putting away the last of my black PJs, a hand came to rest on my shoulder. I turned quickly. Here were a number of villagers, a mass of Oriental eyes, formed behind old papa-san, who said, "You have a home with us. G.I."

Kane,

Although it's pitiful, it has potential. Rewrite and submit it again. You also owe me two feature articles. As of now you'll get an F or an incomplete.

Prof. Barnes

P.S. Who is Doc Kane?

Somewhere above the wet creek, in a tree I guess, I watch over Happy Valley. I gaze down on the rice paddies, at the island of shrubs and trees in the middle of the paddies. A thatched reed roof pokes up amongst the foliage. We didn't notice the hut when we were standing at that dike on the lower end of the island. From up here it seems so clear.

He lies crumpled at the base of the wall, never to

move again. A slight drizzle falls on the whole scene, like a shroud covering a still life.

Over and over and over again it plays. Nothing moves, for weeks, months, years, night in, night out. The rain just sends a steady cleansing shower on Happy Valley.

Sooner or later, I have to go get him. Not alone, no I'll have help. We'll roll him out. Hoist him up. Carry him through the muck. His eyes open, a gaping hole in his neck. Absolution. Our Father, who art in heaven . . . Christ! Over and over. Night after night.

I sit up. Mary lies there, reading light on, thumbing the pages. God, I can't keep reliving, replaying that scene. I got to say something, get some help.

"Honey?"

I turn toward her, "Honey? Mary?"

"Oh, shut up! Go to sleep, will you please?"

Blam!

I slam her across the head. She falls back on the pillow, in complete surprise. So am I. Where did that come from? I flush in anger. Roll the other way out of bed. Fuck it. Just goddam fuck it!

I lie upwind so that the dog won't catch my drift. I move closer, under the hedge. Settle back. I'll bide my time right here. The subtle smell of charcoal passes over. I lean up on an elbow, watch the balloons strung around the patio, tugging at their ties.

Mary comes out of the house, her sister, Gwen, following. They each handle a crock pot.

Boo-Boo steps out the door, raises his nose to the wind. I freeze, hoping he doesn't go through one of his sprinkle routines. If he spots me, he'll stand at the fence, whining and wagging his tail. Why the hell did I come back here anyway?

A horn beeps at the other side of the house, pulls up at the carport.

Woof!

Boo-Boo goes for the car, the two turn from their conversation. I recognize the car as Mike's.

Beep! Beep!

Woof! Woof!

Boo disappears down the driveway as another car arrives. Mary follows. My arm is asleep from propping my head up. I lie on my back, keep an ear open.

"Boo-Boo, down. Hi, Suzie. Boo-Boo, down. Michael, could you hold on to the dog until the excitement settles down?"

"Sure, Mary. C'mere dog."

"Hi, Jim. Hi, Nancy. Hello, Mark. Glad you all could make it."

"Rod isn't here yet, is he, Mary?"

"No, he said he had extra work repairing someone's walkway. Thank God. I didn't have any idea how I was going to get him out of here. Unknown cooperation."

"How's he taking the big 3-0?" Mike asks.

"Wouldn't know it by looking at him, but deep down I think he's groaning."

I grin at that comment. The big 3-0. Ten years ago I was still in Nam, just relieved at making it out of teenagehood. God, ten fucking years since Nam. It seems like only yesterday. I never thought I'd make it to thirty. Never thought I'd make it to twenty. I'm exhausted. Nothing has changed. Wonder how Alvarez is? Haven't heard from him in . . . years. God, years! Got to lay my head down. Exhausted. Just sleep for a second. Henderson will wake me in a minute. Good old Henderson. He knows how to wake me.

"Doc, you got to be careful how you sleep, man. You sleep like you're dead, Doc. You got the dead man's sleep."

Good old Henderson. Dead man's sleep. Wonder where he is? If he's alive? Tired. Dead tired. Doze. Henderson. Off.

Sniff. Sniff.

My eyes blink all too quickly. Not dead. Dark though.

Dusk. I prop up on my elbow, nose to nose with the dog. He's trying to stick his head through the fence.

"Hi, Boo."

Bark! Bark! Bark!

"Shhh, Boo-Boo, shhh. Sit, Boo. Be quiet. You'll give me away."

He quiets. Drops on all fours. I sit up, try to get up. Too soon. I look past him to the patio. It's empty. The balloons hang limp on their strings. The coals die in the barbecue. Carport empty. No lights on in the house. Where is everybody?

I struggle up, as does the dog. A little wobbly, I walk down the hedgerow to the end of the fence. Step around it, pushing the dog away.

"Down, Boo, down. What happened? Where is everyone, puppy? What happened to the party?" I walk to the front door, unlock it. Step into the living room.

Snap. The lights show the trappings of a surprise birthday party. Wonder where the presents are? I step into the kitchen. It's immaculate.

"Have you eaten, puppy?"

He rubs his head against my hip, looks at his bowl, licks his chops.

"Right. You haven't been fed by me, just everyone else at the party."

He licks his chops and tilts his head in question.

"Okay. Okay, but only because it's my birthday and you're my bestest old friend in the whole wide world." I throw his favorite gulp together, slide it across the floor.

Gulp!

I go back into the living room to sift through the party debris. Looks like quite a few people showed. Wonder where Mary is? Probably took her sister home. Look at all those presents. Wow, that was awful nice of them. That was awful nice of her to gather everyone together. I'll leave the presents, open them when she gets home. I head out the door, leaving the lights on.

I walk down the driveway, trying to remember where

I parked the car. I get to the street. Stop. Pull the pint of whiskey out of my back pocket, shake it to hear how much is left. I have to stop and get more. I unscrew the cap, lift, swallow.

Burp!

Happy Birthday, Doc. You made it to thirty, as surprising as making it to twenty. Really surprising. Made it to thirty without being surprised. I hate surprises. I don't care what the purpose. I won't be caught off guard. No more ambushes. No more booby traps. No flashbulbs flashing. No balloons popping. No way. No crowds. No parties. Nope. Don't like it. Don't want it. Won't happen.

Sorry, Mary.

I feel behind me for the lamp switch, fingers walking across the nightstand.

Snap. Darkness.

My hand returns to the soft supple mound. I take a fold of silk and flick it back and forth across the nipple. Mary moans. I shift my weight, lie half on, half off. She drapes a leg over me. We are halfway there.

Slowly pumping a leg, she rides the silk gown up her thigh. I move, sliding a strap from her shoulder, it falls. I feel the nipple tighten. I start to nibble at her shoulder, lip walking my way to where that breast lies. She goes for the nape of my neck, where that bullet has yet to strike. She ricochets kisses across my shoulders, then down the spine line. I stiffen.

We make sounds like a good back-up group.

I move so I won't mess up her gown.

"Don't go," she whispers.

"I'm not going, baby. Just changing my point of attack. Do you need to put in the diaphragm?"

"No."

I set up on my knees without losing the lip lock on her left breast.

"Oh!"

I release and move behind her, massaging her lower back. Then range randomly upward leaving cool, damp tongue tracks to her shoulder blades. With my chin, I rub day-old beard across the nape of her neck. She reaches back to react, releasing the pins in her hair. It falls free as I reach under silk and sweat.

There is no noise but our noise. There is no world but our world.

I take the high side of silk, push it higher, above the hipbone. I reach around and down, catch my fingers in the curls, among them, feeling for the furrow.

"Oh!"

I find it. Spreading fingers, I slide between what is damp and what is wet. She backs into me slowly, searching for my strength. Legs bow. I fit into the space, so hard I slide.

"Oooh."

All the way inside.

We twitch and turn. All sweat and breath. We groan and grind. It can be so erotic from behind. Higher on high, what a drug to try.

Rrrring!

Bells are ringing.

Rrrring!

"I'll get it."

Mary rolls, twisting, snapping me out.

"Yeow!"

She trots out of the room.

Rrrring!

"Christ, why don't you break it off and take it with you?"

The phone stops ringing. I roll to the other side of the bed. Sit up holding you know who. She always has to answer the fucking phone. Imagine, being in heaven and wanting to come back down to earth to answer the phone.

I hear the muffled sound of a one-sided conversation in the next room. One time it wasn't her sister. We ended up with a year's subscription to a magazine called *Desire* or *Me,* I don't know. I look down to see if it's broken or bleeding. It's wet and wilting. Well, fuck that. I sit on the side of the bed and smoke a cigarette. The phone conversation continues. It's her sister. They probably arranged the call.

The passion disappears. I get up, dribbling the event down my leg. I don't even bother to wipe it off. Cover myself with blue jeans and a shirt. I step out into the hallway, almost trip over the phone cord.

"Goddam booby traps."

The cord trails under the bathroom door. Mumbles come from the other side. I go into the den. Sit. Light a cigarette and stare out the window through the smoke.

It ain't no good. The passion confuses itself. We fuck like fanatics then lie in bed on a laconic ledge. Our feet no sooner touch the floor, and we fight, resent and hate. It's no fucking good. We are so unhappy, we've accepted it. Well, I'm not going to accept it anymore.

The toilet flushes. Water runs in the sink. She's off the phone. I resettle myself on the couch, steeling for some petty bullshit about women. I've gone on with it long enough. I did the therapy thing with her. We moved to a better neighborhood. I've been working pretty much. She didn't mind when I started drinking again.

The cupboard door creaks out in the kitchen. She's putting on tea, didn't even bother to go back into the bedroom. Damn, I could still be sitting back there, trying to keep it up. Wondering? Hoping. Ah, we've been through it all before. I even know the next move. Water the plants.

Mary appears in the doorway, watering can in hand.

"Oh, there you are."

"Right," I answer.

She steps to the Swedish ivy that hangs in the window. The way things have been going lately, that plant should be drowned. I follow her motions, eyeballing the figure under the silk gown. There still is a wet spot.

"That was Gwen," she says to the ivy.

"It seems that Gwen's calls have become more important than some things that used to be important," I mumble into my cigarette. Taking a strong draw, I flick the butt into the fireplace.

She turns and looks at me. "That was Gwen on the phone."

I grunt.

She turns back around to the plants on the shelf. "When are we going to Sam and Sandy's?"

I don't say anything. I am afraid to open my mouth. I close my hand into a fist. My head begins to pressure cook, the rage, the anger, the frustration, the fear. There is no respect. The only thing we can do is fuck. We don't make love. We don't really even fuck. It's no good.

"Rod, when do we have to be there? Should I get dressed?" She floats to the wandering Jew hanging in another window. I don't have to watch this. I won't be a part of this anymore.

"We're not going to Sam and Sandy's," I growl.

"Well, make up your mind. Are we going or aren't we?"

Make up my mind. Make up my mind! Okay. I'll make up my mind. I stand, gripping my fury. She freezes over the Norwegian pine.

"We aren't going to Sam and Sandy's, Mary, at least not together. You can go if you please. I may go. We can't go. We can't do anything together, not even make love. Or fuck. Yeah, it even hurts to fuck. I may go to Sam and Sandy's, but I'll be damned if I'm going to go with you."

I walk out of the den, become confused in the hallway. Where do I go? Where will I go? I walk back to the kitchen. The dog comes out of nowhere, stands in the kitchen door.

"How you doing, Boo-Boo? Want a snack?" I throw him a strip of turkey jerky, his favorite. He watches it hit the floor. Lets it lie there. He knows we're having trouble.

"What are you talking about?" She steps up behind him.

"It's no fucking good. We don't share in anything. We aren't going to put any energy into the relationship. We'd never make it to the altar. There will never be a wedding. I am continually insulted by your silence. Your scorn. You aren't happy. I'm not happy. I haven't laughed, I haven't seen you laugh, in months. It's a sham. There's no respect. We are through. Fuck it. I'm not putting up with any of it." I step by the dog and past her. She knows. I know. I leave the room. I leave the house. I leave . . .

• • •

We've been chasing country music from the bottom to the top. Starting at the Merchant's Hotel, we ran the bars until we ended up backstage at the Grand Ole Opry. I met some of the worst and listened to some of the best. It's been a country music paradise.

It started at a bar in D.C., then Erica returned to Nashville. Her ex-boyfriend had moved out of the house. She called me.

"Please. Please. Please," began Erica's invitation. Before she hung up, I was leaving pecker tracks down the runway.

I set out to capture her heart, wanting to replace what I had lost. It was a trap, like one of those jungle trails that aren't found on any maps. Once setting foot on it, there's no way to get off until someone is hit.

Now I'm lying in the middle of this firefight, hoping for one last fuck. My regrets caused me to linger. Now I'm drawing all the fire. My heart is full of holes. I've lost all the desire. I told her I have to go back to D.C. These scribblings were likened to a babbling brook, not a blithering idiot. "I'm leaving on a jet plane, don't know when I'll be . . ."

• • •

We are parked on the turnout overlooking Hope's Valley. It is the twilight of our misunderstanding. It has been raining. The windshield wipers have left streaks of bitterness where mourning dew had fallen.

Sniff.

"Do you have a cold again?"

"What do you mean, again? Besides, it's just a little one."

Honk! I use the Kleenex Mary hands me. It clears my sinuses.

Sniff.

Almost.

"God knows I tried to take care of you. All you kept doing was reliving that damn stupid war." She pauses to watch my reaction. I don't react to that anymore. I just pretend I'm not a Viet Nam veteran. Sniff.

She hands me another Kleenex. I just hold on to it.

"It was when I was having that affair with Skip. That was when I realized we were through. You didn't care. You didn't care if I was sleeping with anyone."

"I was relieved to see you happy again. Besides, I had my fun." Sniff.

"It's not fun," she says in a frustrated tone, then looks out the window. "All you were doing was tossing and turning in that war."

"I have to take care of that." Sniff.

"And the drinking."

"The drinking helps me sleep."

"I tried to take care of you. I wanted to face the responsibility."

"I didn't ask you to take care of me. I take care of me. That is what our breaking up has allowed me to do, take care of me. Not dump it on you."

"Yeah, listen to you, all clogged up . . ."

Sniff.

". . . wrinkled shirt. No shave."

"No furrow lines in my forehead. No frown. I'll keep

the wrinkled shirts and save on the razor blades. Fuck it.''

''And you still use that same 'fucking' language.''

''Mary, I'm sorry, honey. You are right. It is offensive, but I feel as though I'm operating under some kind of restraint. I release the pressure through my language. I'm sorry. I don't mean anything personal.'' Sniff.

''Well, it doesn't come out that way.''

''Nothing we planned or hoped for came out that way.''

She bows her head. The sun disappears beyond the tip of Hope's Valley. I turn the key in the ignition. The car thunks. Mary jumps. Battery's dead. I press in the clutch, look out on the road for oncoming traffic. None. I release the emergency brake, putting the situation in final gear. We roll from the turnout onto the highway. I try the key again. Thunk. Sniff. She straightens in her seat. I leave the key on. Put it in second. We roll down the hill, picking up speed. Pop the clutch. Car lurches. Engine roars. Sniff. Sniff. Sniff. She's crying. Sniff. Sniff. Sniff. I don't cry. I get colds instead.

•　•　•

''Hello?''

''Mom.''

''Roddie, for god's sake, what's going on?''

''What's going on where, Mom?''

''Oh, you know what I mean. I called Mary's house to talk to you. She tells me you've split up. She says you ran off to Tennessee with another woman.''

''Well, I figured it would be better than running off to Tennessee with another man.''

''Dammit, Roddie. What did you do to that woman?''

''Back off, Mom. It wasn't just me. It takes two to make love. It takes two to make war.''

''I don't want to hear any of your damn philosophizing. What happened? Did you hit her?''

''We had our fights. She got her licks in. One night,

though, I cold cocked her, yeah. That was when it ended. That's when I knew it was over. I apologized, Mom. That's all I could do. It was like a flash, honest. I didn't even think. I was angry. Then blam! I hit her. I didn't beat her. It wasn't like what Dad did, but it was enough."

"Speaking of your father, that's why I called. He's drinking again. He's dropped out of sight."

"Ah, shit."

Silence. We start to talk at the same time.

"Did . . . ?

"But . . ."

"Can't . . . ?

We stop. I feel her start to break down. Three thousand miles away, I can feel her pain, the sobs. The last time he disappeared I had to go out there to find him. No one hides from me, not Cong, not Dad, not you, not anyone. He still disappears though.

"Roddie."

"Yes, Mom."

"I'm really sorry things haven't worked out with you and Mary."

"So am I, Mom."

"Do you think things can be put back together?"

"Naw, not as far as I'm concerned. It's over. How are my brothers doing?"

"Oh, God. Eugene signed himself out of the hospital again. He's living in the foothills, east of Sacramento. He's not doing well. He's so confused. He says he's going to buy a horse and ride east to see you and the president."

"Ride east on horseback?"

"That's what he says."

"And he wants to see Jimmy Carter."

"You know he's not well, Roddie."

"Oh, all right, what about Greg?"

"Still the same, I guess. I haven't heard from him.

He's still in the woods in northern Minnesota. He doesn't have a phone. He doesn't write. It's like he's totally withdrawn. What's the matter with him, Roddie?''

"Well, he probably doesn't want to be bothered, Mom. He probably doesn't want to put up with all this stateside bullshit.''

"It's not bullshit, Roddie, it's our life.''

"Well, not necessarily, Mom, not after Viet Nam. It's something I understand from being there. It's like you don't have the patience with the way things are going back here. The way things are. I've been up where he lives. He's just chopping wood and milking cows.''

"Well, at least he could call his mother. Or write!''

"Yes, I know, but . . . well . . . that's his choice.''

"Well, I'm tired of all of you just ramming around, up and down, here and there. Aren't any of you taking any responsibility? Why does Viet Nam have to keep coming into it? Where's your father, Roddie? Dammit!''

Click.

•   •   •

"Boogie.''

That's what Sherrie calls out when she wants me. I look up.

"Boogie, heresie cumsie.''

I tiptoe to her. She lies supine, so fine, be mine.

"Boogie?''

"Yes.''

"Comsie lazie flopsy by me.''

"Absolutely.''

I start down on her. She straight-arms me. Points.

"Baresey buttsie, Boogie.''

I slide out of the Levis as she lifts her sleepshirt. I drop alongside. We glide. My favorite ride. Slow motions lead to rocking on high, so wide she cries.

"Boogie. Boogie. Boogie.''

•   •   •

In the midst of it all, I had to put Boo-Boo to rest. He was my best friend. He was very old. He wouldn't even chase squirrels anymore.

Dear Boo-Boo

Ah, my dark, yet gray-haired friend. The pain of this passing isn't your loss, it's mine.

Yes, you deer eyes, loping over acres of good earth as our protector. A wanderer. The wonder. We were all impressed.

Head hugging at my hip, with a tennis ball as chaw. Stretching out in throaty groans of repose, you'd wake with tail tapping tunes. The puppy bounds and, bouncing about kitty woos. Oh, who could forget those stinky farts, no more leftovers for you.

There is nothing more I can do, with so much love for you. I'll accept this task with grace if you'll return, begin in the same place.

Sincerely,
Doc

• • •

The blackness is colorful in its dimension. That is how I become aware, the depth of the blackness. Then there is the sound, like a terrorized fugitive moving through the jungle. Out of the corner of this scene comes the arm of the trap, a bamboo shaft. Sprung from its contorted tie by a careless foot, it becomes the center of my attention. A three-foot mahogany stake is notched and tied crosswise into the end of the pole. It is a sharp gleaming point of fact heading toward my face. Jungle vines that once grew in its way now lie lifeless over the arm. It is too late to blame anyone for triggering the trap as it whips toward my mind's eye. It is just a tried-and-true weapon, having been relied upon for centuries to block the paths of any intruders, be they elephants or earthlings. The pole is so close I can count its ribs of growth. The tip of the weapon is so close I can hear its fire-hardened tip cross my eyes, piercing the crest of my nose.

Christ!

I jerk my head straight back, smashing into her head as she sleeps, curled up around me. Welcome to the war, whoever you are.

• • •

I believe I have implied that when it comes to loving, they come to me. You may accuse me of rampant conceit but remember, I am taking valuable time out of my love life to relate all this glamour. I am booked up solid. There is no more room at the inn. There are no more ins to the room. I have three going, every day, every night. I call them morning, nooner and night. It's a tough job but somebody has to do it.

Even as I speak, I'm coming from the middle of night on the way back to morning. I didn't mean for it to be so late but nooner kept me until early evening. I worked a half shift on the food line at the café, then along comes the night and I haven't even eaten. She just finished taking care of that. What's a fella to do? I'm not about to call in reinforcements.

Now I have to figure out some sort of explanation for being out so late. I share morning's bed so I have to answer to her. Christ, I don't even know if I'm explaining this right. I can't think straight. Besides being liquored out of my mind, exhausted beyond all demands, I'm pretty tired.

I know! I'll tell her Kevin lost the keys to the café. We couldn't lock up. He went home to get spare keys. I hung around the bar to make sure no one stole nothing.

Burp!

Yeah, that's a good story.

"Beverly Court, buddy." The cab halts.

"Great. Here, keep the change."

"Thank you. Good night."

"She sure was."

I roll out of the car. Wobble up the front steps. My armpits are hanging off my hipbones. Hmmmm. There is someone on the entrance telephone by the front door. Good, I won't have to search for my key.

I get to the landing. He hangs up the phone and rests a hand on the door, waiting for the buzzer to unfreeze the lock. I wait alongside him. Nothing happens.

"They supposed to beam you up?"

"Supposed to," he shrugs.

"Shit." I go through my pockets. Find the key.

"Here." I key the lock, pull the door open. He grabs its edge, holds it for me. I look at him, ask, "Where are you going, man?"

"Fourth floor."

"Oh, to Mitchell's."

"Yeah."

"Okay." I step in. Mumble on the way to the elevator, rehearsing what I'm going to tell morning about why I have to leave for nooner because she wants me back later when I've just come from last night.

Crack!

The whole world falls on the back of my head.

Ouch!

I turn around. He stands there, handling a choke collar chain. It takes a lot more than one whack to put Doc Kane out.

Whack!

He whips the chain down across the front of my head. It's a good thing I'm so loaded, that one could have hurt. I step around the concussion and through the stars. I reach for his throat. It fits into my hand. I can kill him and plead self-defense. I grip his windpipe. He grabs my wrist and swings the chain. I ward off the blow, tighten my grip. He tries to step away. I wrap an arm around his neck, bend him over, introduce him to my knee.

Squish!

I headlock and hold, getting a better grip on that throat. Rip it out. What a sensation the kill is. Poor bastard didn't even have a chance. It's almost unfair.

Commotion behind me on the stairs. He manages a shout. Shit! I try to look over my shoulder. Two of them. Black. One real tall. Bastard in my grasp starts to backpedal, using his weight.

"Hllgh!"

Slam!

Hit the wall. Knocked off balance. Maintain grip. Someone grabs my arms at the elbows. Go from winning to losing. He wiggles out from under my arm. Whack! Damn! Ooof! Blam! Damn! Thud! Can't. Too many. Smash! Thump! Ooff! Crack? Ribs! Rrrip! Taking everything. Ooof! Don't fight. Whack! Stop! Slam! Smash. Damn, I'll die. Got to relax. Hope. Dead weight. Stay still. Numb. Tired. Smash! Thud! Hurt. Stop. Tired. Quiet. Shhh. Quiet. Shhhh . . .

Don't remember how long I was out. I only remember coming around feeling like I'd just been ambushed. Beat. First time I've been caught off guard since Happy Valley. Losing my touch. I try to lift my head. It's stuck to the floor in a pool of blood, sticky, salty, smelly.

I roll out of the mess, hike to my hands and knees. Stand, unsurely. Dizzy. Whoa! Can't see very well. Can't breathe very well. Can't hear very well. Pants falling. Shirt torn off. Got to get to elevator. Got to get to morning. Forget nooner. It's still night.

I've been trying to settle down since that ambush. Can't. Lost another job. Had to move again. Having nightmares about Belfast and Darlene. Keep waking up. Booze. Doze. Booze. Doze. Booze, until there's nothing left to drink. Have to doze. Please, some sleep. Please, slumber. Please, peace. Please. Doze . . .

Damn!

I just realized something.

VETERAN'S DAY

IT'S MY JOB

by Doc Kane

First, I take care of them,
day by day,
athlete's foot, pyorrhea.
Then I watch them on the trails,
check them constantly for the fever.
The shit hits the fan.
Everyone tries to kill each other.
I have to try to save them.

Back in base, I diagnose,
hour to hour,
new eyeglasses, diarrhea.
On perimeter guard, we relax,
read old love letters from Maria.
The shit hits the fan.
Everyone tries to kill each other.
I have to try to save them.

It becomes a routine,
minute by minute,
self-inflicted wounds, gonorrhea.
We lie back, enjoy some beers,
nickname the new guy, Beaver Cleaver.
The shit hits the fan.
Everyone tries to kill each other.
I have to try to save them.

I'm running out of time,
nothing's changed,
since World War II or Korea.
The captain said I could go home.
I say "I don't fucking believe ya."
The shit hits the fan.
Everyone tries to kill each other.
I have to try to save them.

• • •

Today

Tone,

I hope you are still alive. I am. It is to celebrate such an occasion that I'm writing. Dear Tone, I'm alive. Are you? Did you get my postcard? I'm still in D.C.

For some reason I have this feeling you are a lawyer by now. Or dead.

So, I'm joking around like this 'cause I'm hurting, buddy. I don't know how to say it or who to say it to. I thought of you. It sounds like you are strong. How did you keep it from catching up with you? It's killing me. I ain't got nothing or nobody.

I'm proud for you doing as good as you sound. Haven't heard from Alvarez or Henderson.

Anyway, thanks for listening. I hope to hear from you. Write! Call! Send money! Dope!

Sincerely,
Doc Kane

Doctor Kane,

Mister Kane. My name is Ophelia Clark. My grandson was named Eugene Clark. He died a courageous man. He had requested that you be notified of his death. I have raised many grandsons who were without any other family or parents. None of my boys have ever faced the trouble Eugene faced in his life. None have ever been able to stand up in the midst of their troubles and make the sun shine. Eugene could. Eugene did.

He spoke highly of you, Doctor, which he didn't do with any other white people. I hope you learned something from Viet Nam, like my grandson did.

God bless you,
Ophelia Clark

Well, that just about does it folks. I've put myself right into a hole. The only things I have with me down here are cigarettes, barbiturates, a loaf of three-day-old bread and a quart of Glenlivet scotch. I am going to sleep. I don't care how I do it. I am going to get some sleep.

•   •   •

"Have you been eating?"

"No, I mean, yes. I must be eating. I'm still alive."

"I see, not eating."

"I'm not sleeping, either. Just quit another job, before they fired me. It was close."

"I see, where do you live?"

"Anywhere I can."

"Do you think that might be a cause of your not sleeping?"

"Naw, I've been not sleeping since Viet Nam."

"You were in Viet Nam?"

"Yes."

"How long?"

"Eleven months."

"How long ago?"

"Ten years. Fifteen years. Twenty?"

"So, you didn't make a full tour?"

"What do you mean?"

"You said eleven months."

I sit up straight. Try to pay attention.

"Yes, I made it eleven months."

"Wasn't a full tour a year?"

"Yes, well there weren't many of us left. It got pretty rough. We slept on the ground. Just had C-rations to eat. Had some rough firefights. Disease. We weren't many in the end. They sent what was left back early."

"I see. Yes. Well, it was a terrible thing, that war was. Are you married? Single? Divorced?"

I try to think. Thinking hasn't worked in years.

"Single."

"Hmmm."

"Can I smoke?"

"Uh, no, you can't. Not in here, not around oxygen. No ashtrays. We try to keep the emergency area clean."

"Yes, I understand. I was a medic."

"So, you say you're at the end of your rope."

"So to speak."

"Yes, no job. No fixed address. No attachments. Those could be reasons you're not eating or sleeping."

"Yeah, well, whatever. I used to eat."

"Have you ever taken a sedative for sleep?"

"Yes."

"What?"

"Alcohol."

"You drink to sleep?"

"Used to. I stopped for a while. Started again. It hasn't worked lately, though. Drink, get drunk, start to slump off, pass out. Pop! Wide awake. Sleep ten, maybe fifteen minutes."

"I see. Do you think fatigue may be behind this calling it quits?"

I try to hear that differently. Do I give that impression, calling it quits?

"I just want a good night's sleep."

"You weren't really planning to commit suicide, were you?"

"If it would help me sleep, I would."

He drops his eyes to the chart. Starts writing. Stops.

"You don't plan on going anywhere, do you?"

"Don't have anywhere to go."

"Why don't you step out in the hallway. You can smoke there."

"Oh."

"By the way, when did you say you got in that fight?"

"Sir?"

"That was six weeks ago, wasn't it?"

"I guess."

"Healing quite well?"

"Yes."

"Good. I'm going to fill out this admission report. I want to admit you to the hospital for psychiatric observation and alcohol abuse."

I turn the other way in the seat, fish for a cigarette. Remember I can't smoke. Take out the cigarette anyway and finger it.

"What about your family?"

"What about them?"

"What about your family?"

"What about them?"

"Are they alive?"

"I guess, last I checked."

"Where?"

"California."

"Why are you back here?"

"I was born and raised here in the East." I lean forward, reach for matches. Toy with them, straighten up. No position is comfortable.

"You know you shouldn't be smoking."

"That's what I hear."

"So why do you stay so far from your family?"

"Because they are there."

"You know you are not being very helpful."

"Neither are you."

"Why do you say that?"

"All I get from you people about my situation is that I'm under observation. You want to watch me to figure out where I'm coming from. I've told you, I'm coming from Viet Nam. I showed you my writing. I'm coming from Viet Nam."

"We feel you are coming from the bottom of a bottle."

"Okay, so I go to AA. Why can't I go to the Viet Nam veterans' meeting?"

"Because we don't feel that is where you are coming from."

219

"I feel that is where I'm coming from."

"Okay. Once again. Are you married?"

"I'm single."

"Ever been married?"

"No!"

"Do you abuse alcohol or drugs?"

"Sometimes I'll drink too much."

"Then why fight me on going to AA?"

"Fuck AA."

"Why do you continue to say that?"

"Because my father was drunk all the time in bars or sober all the time in AA meetings."

"So, you've got some bones to pick with your father."

"For a while I did, for a while I didn't. During the war we were close. It's been bad lately."

"Where is he now?"

"I don't know. California."

"What about the rest of your family?"

"What about them?"

"Okay, Mr. Lee, all present and accounted for. You may start the meeting."

"Thank you, Mrs. Corn. Okay, gentlemen, community meeting of August 23, 1981, will now come to order."

Mr. Lee taps his Styrofoam cup on the table. "Secretary will read the minutes of our last meeting."

"Thank you, Mister President. August 16, 1981, meeting called to order by you. You said you were being discharged from the hospital so we would need a new president for the ward. The room was open to nominations. Nominated: Mr. Kane, Mr. Sprague, Mr. Phillips. Mr. Phillips tried to withdraw his name because he said the Thorazine fucked him . . . kept him from functioning. Mrs. Corn advised that he would have to learn to function with it. His nomination stood. Mr. Rowen spoke up about Mr. Sprague. He shouldn't be president because he was on ward restriction and a poor example for the rest of the patients. Sprague said it was a God-given right for him to be elected president. He said he hadn't been convicted of a felony so he would be a good example to the other patients on the ward. Mr. Kane had no comment.

"The election was held. The final tally: Mr. Phillips, 3; Mr. Sprague, 7; Mr. Kane, 17; 3 abstentions. Mr. Sprague interrupted to say the vote was fixed. He said Mr. Kane intimidated everyone into voting for him because he was from Viet Nam. President Lee called Mr. Sprague out of order. Mr. Sprague called President Lee out into the hallway. Mrs. Corn called the security guards . . ."

"That is enough, Mr. Spence. President Lee, carry on with the business at hand."

"Yes, Mrs. Corn. Thank you, Mr. Secretary. Could we have the treasurer's report, please?"

"Thank you, Mr. President. Treasurer's report, September 23, 1981. Balance $3.23. Collected 75¢ in smoking fines from Sergeant-at-Arms McGriff. Two PX books of $1.00 were turned in, found in latrine. Coffee fund, $1.65."

"Thank you, Mr. Treasurer. Is there any other old business?"

The group is collectively trying to add up the treasurer's report.

"Okay. If there is no old business, I would like to resign and turn the presidency over to Mr. Kane. It's been a real pleasure representing you fellas but I hope I never have to be in here again. President Kane, are you ready to take over your responsibilities?"

Even in the cuckoo's nest, I suffer the spasms of success.

"You should make peace with your father."
"You shouldn't feel guilty about your brothers."
"You must realize why you abuse yourself."

That's the only feedback I've gotten from my shrink, unless you want to consider the following encounter:

We have smaller, more personable satellite therapy sessions on this ward, two-to-one patient/staff ratio. Our ages and backgrounds span forty years, with illiterates rubbing elbows with trilinguals. We meet three times a week, one hour at a time. We sit in a silent circle clearing our throats and cleaning our fingernails.

Today we are listening to this ex-Army homosexual as he narrates his first "love" experience in the bomb shelter underneath Walter Reed Army Hospital. I cut in.

"For many years I've been real uncomfortable, like not sleeping well and stuff. It seems about seven or seven-thirty every evening, I'm ready to go sleep. By eleven or eleven-thirty, when I should be headed for bed, I'm wide awake. Even in here, same thing. Once I do doze off, for some reason, I think it's for radio watch, I wake up. Sometimes I'll lie awake the rest of the night, at least till dawn. I've used the drinking thing as a sedative. But now, even that doesn't work. I don't want sleep medication because that gives me a worse hangover than booze. I just sit up chain smoking all night. Then, when I'm supposed to get up for work, suddenly I'm ready to sleep. It fucks me up . . ."

"Mr. Kane."

"Huh?"

"Mr. Kane, Mr. Barry has a question for you."

"Oh, sorry."

"Yeah, Kane. What do you mean, you wake up to watch your radio in the middle of the night. We aren't supposed to have radios on the ward."

"No, Barry, I mean radio watch, like in the field in Viet Nam. We took turns at night, giving situation reports of our positions on PRC-25s."

"Huh?"

"Mr. Barry," the doctor slides forward in his seat. "Mr. Kane alleges to have been in Viet Nam. Mr. Kane, I thought we made it clear . . ."

"What do you mean, I allege to have been in Viet Nam?"

The doctor freezes. The group freezes.

"Are you trying to bait me, doctor? What do you mean, 'Mr. Kane alleges to have been in Viet Nam'?"

"I think we should let him sign out if he wants to go."

"We can't really hold him. He's shown no overt signs of suicide. He's not specifically antisocial. No real danger to himself or others."

"He won't take responsibility for his relationships with women. He has severe relationship problems with his father, with his family."

"His writing speaks strongly of traumatic experience in Viet Nam."

"It confuses too many issues. We have to concentrate on his alcohol abuse."

"He isn't on any medication, is he?"

"Nothing that we are responsible for."

"He's resigned the ward presidency, says his contract with you expires this Friday."

"I don't want him telling us what to do. He has no right to do that. He's a patient. If he signs himself out, let's make him sign out against medical advice."

The first thing I did when I got out of there was get drunk. That straightened me out. You won't catch me going near that hole again. That's what I get for going to a Veterans Administration Hospital to start with.

The doctor was right though. I should get in touch with my father, wherever he is. I should check with my brothers. Yeah, I'm going to square myself away. I'm going to get my shit together. If I can make it through Nam I can make it anywhere.

• • •

I found my dad. He's dead. He died drunk and destitute. I'm relieved. He's out of his misery and I know where to find him. I'm not relieved because in my intent to find him, I sent a letter ahead, warning him I was on his trail. In the letter, I called him every kind of drunken, wife-beating, child-abusing son of a bitch he is, was. It was the last he heard of me.

In recollecting our relationship, now that it's over, two things he said to me in sober moments stick in my craw.

He lamented being taken sick and being pulled off that troop ship before his combat unit, with all his buddies, assaulted the beach at Normandy, D day, 1944. From the way he talked, I can guess he felt guilty he didn't go down with them.

The other thing he admitted was that his brother, my Uncle Paul, did not die so mysteriously after serving in combat in Korea. He died by his own hand, after making it back. Hung himself. I never did get to know Uncle Paul but I always wanted to grow up to be like him.

Part Three

M R. KANE?"

I try to lift my head. It's stuck.

"Mr. Kane?"

I try to open my eyes. They seem sealed shut.

"Mr. Kane? Can you hear me?"

Don't panic, use the sense of smell. Sniff, sniff. Hospital? Try to lift the head again, stuck. Blood? Where am I? On a road? In a creek bed? What am I? Alive? Dead?

"Are you awake, Mr. Kane?"

I wake up on the inside before I wake up on the outside. I will appear to be asleep on the outside, but on the inside I'm wide awake. I'll be lying in bed all night, thinking about the Nam. Realizing how close I came to getting it. Wondering why he got it and I didn't. I doze. I dream, but I'm awake.

"Mr. Kane, wake up!"

I lie there. I wonder if I'm dead or alive. Hoping for the best, which is dead. I suddenly wake up. I'm disappointed.

"Mr. Kane." The voice rises. I need some sleep, goddammit! Let me die!

"Mr. Kane. This is Nurse Jenkins. I'm supposed to wake you to tell you that you are scheduled to meet with Dr. Smith in five minutes. Now I've done my job. It's up to you to get up."

I move my hand to check my crotch. I don't know why, except that the whole world is watching when you think you've pissed your pants.

I grope. Nope. Just sweat-soaked sheets balled up on a plastic-covered mattress. Well, the hand moved, let's try something else.

I lift my head. It peels itself from the plastic mattress, pounding like all hell. I push up to a sitting position, opening my eyes to the surroundings. A hospital bed in a hospital room with a hospital nightstand.

I slide the nightstand drawer open. There are cigarettes in there. Instead, I pull out a greeting card:

"Happy Valentine's Day!"

Christ, have I been carrying this card around? I grope through the drawer as I recall this is March, not February. I've been on a drinking binge since . . . since . . . Valentine's Day. I find the cigarette pack and lighter, take a cigarette out as I remember something else:

Ward Rule 1: Smoking is permitted in the Day Room and the Reading Room only.

I unstick myself from the bed and slip into loafers. I wrestle into a robe and step out of the room. Looking both ways, I move down the hallway, past the nurses' station.

READING ROOM. I step through the doorway, lighting the cigarette as the door closes behind me. I walk to the window, peer out at the hospital grounds. Almost a prison, but not quite.

The door swings open. I whirl to it.

"Good morning, Mr. Kane. Relax."

A white-haired white man with snow-white St. Nick's eyebrows and a handlebar moustache of the same color steps into the room. He's dressed in casual but expensive clothes covered by a white lab coat. He holds a steaming moustache mug in one hand and a large folder in the other.

"Good morning." He pauses.

"Mourning."

"You are Kane, aren't you?"

"I am."

I step to an end table strewn with veterans' service magazines and an ashtray. I flick the match toward it. He sets his cup and folder on another end table and sits in the chair next to it. I sit across from him and get a better look. Missed his wearing glasses. He adjusts them as he opens the flap of the folder. My name is on it.

"Kane, I'm Dr. Smith. You may continue to smoke." He thumbs through the chart and reaches for the mug, taking a long draught. Setting it back down, he traces something on the chart with his finger. He looks up at me.

"So, what happened?"

I bend to the ashtray, stub out the cigarette.

"What?"

"You tell me what."

I sit back, trying to think. What? When? Can't think, that's one reason I'm here.

"When?"

"I said, you tell me what happened when."

"I turned myself in. Went on a drinking binge last month. Wouldn't stop. It's happened before. Can't sleep. Drink heavy for days, weeks. This time I got busted for drunk driving. Stupid. Fucking up. It's happened before, but I never got busted. So I turned myself in. Took myself out of the game before I hurt someone."

I look at him for reaction. His clear blue eyes meet my cloudy gray eyes. He looks back at the chart. I reach for another cigarette, light it.

"Do you hear voices? Have hallucinations?"

"No." I pause, looking at him cautiously. "I've been known to talk to myself."

229

"Me too," he volunteers. "You were here once before?"

"About four months ago, next door, next ward."

"What happened then?"

I shrug. "I don't know. The guy thought I had one problem, I thought I had another."

"What's your problem?"

Boy, did I walk into that one! I shift in my seat, take a strong draw off the cigarette, crush it in the ashtray.

"My problem . . . problems? Right now, my problem is I'm out of hand with my drinking. I'm dangerous and I don't like it."

He nods. "Anything else?"

I shoot a piercing glance at him. "Isn't that enough?"

"Well, there are some reasons people turn to drink. To deaden pain. Have you had any recent traumatic episodes?"

"Got into a bad fight last year, couple of car wrecks . . . oh, yeah . . . my father just died."

"When?"

"Around Christmas, maybe earlier, Thanksgiving. Had to put my dog to sleep, too." I look at him. He sits, immobile, waiting.

"You know something, man. I mean, Doctor . . . you know, I think I'm still having problems with . . . the war."

I feel ashamed, saying that. Sort of like admitting I couldn't take it. After all these years, I'm finally caving in.

"The war?"

I look at the bookshelf. "Yeah. Nam. Years ago . . . fifteen? Sixteen years?"

"Were you in combat?"

I want to belch it out. Throw it up. The whole fucking horrible experience. The thoughts choke in my throat. If I answer, I'll spew terror all over this white, white, white man. Answer the question, Kane. "I was a paratrooper, infantry, a medic. Spent most of my time in the field, walking into ambushes, waiting to be ambushed or bailing out some poor fuckers who had been ambushed."

He leans to the side in his seat, places the chart on the table, flips pages. I sit back as far as I can, checking my anxiety level. I didn't realize it was that high. It almost came up. God! I'd been afraid of admitting to being a veteran.

"Do you know we have a meeting every Monday and Thursday here in the hospital for Viet Nam veterans, especially combat veterans?"

"I heard about that last time I was here. The doctor who had my case said he would refer me. I waited on that ward for three months. Nothing happened, so I checked out."

"Who was your doctor?"

"Weas . . . , er, Wenzell."

"He's moved on, but he was a good doctor. I wonder why he didn't send you to us?"

He looks at me as if I'll give him an answer. I shrug. "I showed him my writing."

"Well." He closes the chart in preoccupation, takes a draw off the mug, looks right at me. "Kane, as your in-house physician, I am going to make some recommendations. You may adhere to these while under my care. You may or may not adhere to them when you leave. It's all up to you. What you put into it, you'll get out of it. First of all, you have to participate in the regular ward program, just like all the other patients. You have the same things to deal with in our little society here on this ward as in that big society in that world out there. I feel you should also start on an alcohol abuse program as soon as possible, like AA meetings."

He pauses to check my reaction. I grind my back teeth.

"I also feel it may help if you attend our Viet Nam veterans' group that meets twice a week. I will see to it that your schedule works around that. Do you have anything to say?"

"Well, I sure would like to do that veterans' meeting."

He nods.

"And I know I have to get a handle on the alcohol thing."

"You have a family history of it."

"I know."

He stands. "Good." He offers a hand. I stand, take it, a firm, confident grasp. He lets go, bends to retrieve chart and mug. "Now, what's this about writing?"

"I've been writing stuff on and off since . . . the war has been with me." I pause, trying to think. "Anyway, Nam's bugged me for so long, I've been writing it down to get it out."

"I'd like to see it. Do you have any of it here?"

"I can get it."

"Good. Whenever you can, I'd be interested." He looks me in the eye again. "I think it was a good move on your part to turn yourself in."

"Thank you, sir. That's the first compliment I've heard in . . . years."

"You're welcome."

· · ·

I hesitate, then stand in the crowded, smoky room. "Uh, yeah, my name is Doc Kane, uh, I'm a fucking drunk. Am I supposed to say something?"

Someone says, "Only if you want to, Doc. You needn't give your whole name, either. Anonymous is just that."

"Well, thanks, I guess." I pause, trying to figure out what it is I have to say. "I know something about alcohol. My old man taught me. He was always either trying to be drunk or trying to be sober . . . drinkin' and fighting or abstaining and praying . . . no middle ground . . . war or peace."

I pause, think about how the old man was always either drunk or running off to AA meetings. Talk about feeling abandoned, why that bastard, and these people . . .

"Doc Kane?"

I look up. What am I doing? Where am I? Why am I here?

"Doc Kane, if you don't have anything to say, we can go on to the next person."

"No! No! I have something to say. It's just a shock to be here. There's a lot of conflict in me. I guess I'm really pissed off at myself, angry for having gotten myself into this situation. I could blame my father, resent you people, be pissed with the cop who busted me for DWI, be angry with the system for the war. But I can't . . . to be honest . . . 'cause, like, it wasn't the first time I ever drove drunk. That was eighteen, nineteen years ago. This was just the first time I got caught. I was bitter at first, but three or four days after it happened, then I realized something I'd never realized before. I was so drunk I couldn't remember if I had hit someone or not. I could remember being angry, belligerent, when I was stopped, but I couldn't remember where I'd been or what I'd done . . ."

I pause, try to adjust myself to admit, "I've done some things in my life I'm proud of . . . showed guts, courage, then I drive drunk. I can't think of a more spineless bastard than one who could kill someone, especially a child or a woman, or anyone innocent, and not remember it. And there I am, someone I despise. A coward. If I'm killing someone, I want to face it. If someone tries to kill me, I want them to remember it. A drunk driver is a coward. It's an atrocity. I've sunk so low. I'm glad I'm here to say that, no matter what happens."

* * *

"Mr. Kane, you have a visitor," the loudspeaker announces.

"I'm not here," I shout at it.

"Mr. Kane, you have a visitor!"

"I don't want a visitor!"

"Kane, quit shouting," one of the guys shouts over the TV program.

"Mr. Kane, someone came out here to see you."

"There's got to be something wrong with them. I'll see them in the isolation room after they've been put in restraints!"

"Kane, shut up!"

"Mr. Kane, go to the visitors' room."

"Yes, Ms. Nurse-in-the-Ceiling."

"Kane, we're trying to watch TV."

"Doesn't that loudspeaker in the ceiling bug you guys who hear voices?"

"Fuck you, Kane. Go molest your visitor."

"It can hear everything you say."

"No, it can't. Not when we turn the TV way up."

"Kane, get the hell out of here so we can watch 'M*A*S*H.' "

"Yeah, right. It's too bad you all have to get the war thirty years later. I wonder when Viet Nam will be funny."

I throw the magazine onto the dayroom table and head toward the visitors' room. I guess I'm being a bastard about everything, but I'm defensive. I know who the visitor is. I told her not to come by. It ain't gonna work. She was willing to put up with a drunken maniac, so there's something wrong with her, too. How could she do it?

You have to get out of this yourself. Don't blame her. If she's not good for you, she's not good for you. You have to find your own ground. Some place to put your own feet. Not step on hers, she'll step on yours. It will just be a distraction. Even blaming her is a distraction.

"Hi."

"Hey! How're you doing? You shouldn't have come out here."

"I know, but I just had to. I'm so worried."

"You don't have to worry with me being in here. No

booze. No drugs. No guns. Out there, you didn't worry. Why worry with me in here? They lock the doors at ten."

"I know. But you are going through so much, I didn't know what to do . . ."

"Carla, sometimes things happen because other things happened before us, before we were together. You got problems, too. We are both over our heads. I finally realized I'm dangerous. I'm out of control. I don't know how you put up with it. There's something wrong. Let me go. If I can get things settled . . . maybe . . . even the things I've said to you . . . I love you. I want you. Hey, I'm not sure if that's . . . if it's . . ."

Her head drops. She starts to turn away. Stops. Sets her jaw, shoots me a look that could wound, then reaches into her oversized purse. "Here, I brought you your toothbrush."

She hands it to me matter-of-factly.

"And your manuscript. You've worked so hard on it."

I take it from her. "Thanks. You helped so much."

"No, I didn't. If I had helped, you wouldn't be here."

"Stop it. Get off your case. That's part of your problem, you don't credit yourself."

"I learned some of that from you." She feigns a smile, steps to me, and brushes my cheek with her lips. They are dry. "Take care of yourself, wild man."

"Thanks for trying, Carla. Thanks for hanging in there."

Is it fifteen years? Sixteen! God! I don't know. If I had some place to go to I'd be there. Wonder what this meeting is going to be like. I won't sit around and listen to some supply clerk tell war stories about black-marketing jungle fatigues. If someone starts in on shit like that, I'll tear his throat out. Motherfuckers sitting on their asses in the rear, ripping each other off, and us too. If there are any guys like that in this meeting, I'll drop a frag in

235

the middle of the fucking room and clean out the fucking place. If I had a frag . . .

"Ready?"

"Jesus!" I jump seventy fucking feet in the air, exorcising a fart of fear as the manuscript goes flying across the hallway.

"Oh! Sorry," Dr. Smith says.

I flush, catching my breath as relief turns to embarrassment, then anger. My jaw grinds teeth into eardrums as a deep hollow roar rushes air, air everywhere from my lungs. He walks over, picks up the clipped copy of writings from the floor, returns it to me. "I'm sorry!"

"You got to watch out how you come up on me, man, I mean Doctor."

"I know, I know. I've been around enough of you men, I should have noticed."

"I'm a little edgy anyway, without any booze or dope, and this meeting, this group might be . . ."

"Yes, I understand. This group might be just the thing you need. It will be okay. Everyone is a little shaky at first. Come."

He hands me the manuscript, then heads off the ward. I follow. He stops at the elevator, pushes the button, turns to me.

"This is for you, Dr. Smith. My writing. You wanted to see it."

"Oh, thank you." He takes it back. "I still have the referral interview scheduled for you with the alcohol treatment ward. You did agree to a possible referral to the AT ward."

"Yeah, I know. Whatever . . ."

The elevator door opens and we get in and go up . . . get out a couple of floors above. I stuff a cigarette in my mouth, light it, then run to catch up to him.

"You'll have to put that out."

"I know, I know. I got this place pretty much figured out."

He stops at an unmarked door. I look for a place to

butt the cigarette. He slips into the room. Running back to the elevator, I douse the butt in the ashtray, then turn back. Which door did he go into?

I step into a room sized for about a dozen chairs and three bookcases with very few books. There is a map of South Viet Nam on the wall. Must be in the right place.

"Here he is. Kane."

I turn to the call, Dr. Smith sitting to my right. I take the seat next to him, looking around the room as he talks.

"Welcome to the group, Kane. The procedure here, we introduce ourselves, then you give us background information on your war experience, along with what brought you to this point in your hospital stay. Gentlemen, introduce yourselves to Kane."

"Point Man," comes the retort from my immediate left.

I turn to an average-size black man with a jagged scar on his right cheek. Have I seen him before?

"You can just call me Point. They did in Viet Nam. I was with Third Marines, I Corps, '67–'68."

"Sergeant Pepper, that's really my name," erupts a big, robust man across from me. "Twenty-fifth Division, '66, 196th Light Infantry, '68–'69."

"Berns, Major Berns, call me Bernie," comes from beside Sergeant Pepper.

"Or Major," Point Man adds.

"Don't listen to Point. Call me Bernie. I was with the First Cavalry, MACV, Ninth Infantry, Seventy-fifth Rangers. You name it, I was assigned to them."

"I'm Dr. Gates, Mr. Kane."

A petite woman peeks around Dr. Smith. She must have been hiding behind him. What the hell is a woman doing in here?

"My name is Paxton." Another fella leans forward, the other side of Smith. A stocky black man, he stretches across the doctor, offering a hand, interrupting my consternation. I distractedly return his grasp. "You can call me Pax. Third Marines, I Corps. Tet through '69."

"You know who I am, Kane," Dr. Smith says. "We are missing a couple members of the group, but that's usual as these meetings aren't mandatory and some of the fellas are outpatients with work schedules."

"Yeah, I wonder if Sully will make it today?"

"Is he at that memorial meeting?"

"We're building a memorial to ourselves, Kane, did you hear about it?"

"It isn't a memorial, it's a tombstone."

"It isn't even that, it's a ditch lined with names of all the guys who didn't make it back."

I twist my head to the various comments, still not sure who is who.

"Really?"

"Yeah, fifty-five thousand names of all the dead, etched in black marble stuck in the ground. You have to walk down one side and up the other."

"They'll probably charge admission to see it."

"No, they won't. All the money is being raised privately by Viet Nam veterans, Kane. A contest was held to pick the most unique architectural design."

"Yeah, it just happened to be done by a gook."

"She wasn't a gook, she's a Chinese chick, er, woman."

"She's still a gook."

I try to slow down the conversation. "Where's this at?"

"It's the Viet Nam veterans' memorial," Sergeant Pepper says. "Sullivan, one of our group members, is at a meeting of the memorial committee that is arguing over the design and where to put it."

"They'll probably put it out on the beltway so everyone can drive over it," Point Man says.

"Gentlemen! Gentlemen, please. All we are doing is confusing Mr. Kane," Dr. Gates interrupts. The group shuts up at her command. "Besides, we are ignoring protocol. Mr. Kane has not introduced himself or given us a short history of his experiences from Southeast Asia to the present. Mr. Kane, would you do us the honor, give us a little background information leading up to your arrival at the hospital?"

"Sure, I guess." I straighten in my seat. "I'm, er, Doc Kane. I was Army Airborne, assigned to 185th airborne infantry in Fort Benning, March '65. We trained in airborne/air assault using choppers. Didn't know at the time that the Pentagon and LBJ had a plan, but in July '65, we got orders to move the whole kit 'n' kaboodle to some boats in Savannah, Georgia, and in August '65, we sailed to Viet Nam under the colors of the 1st Brigade (Airborne), First Cavalry Division. We landed in Qui Nhon, September '65, and choppered into the central highlands, a place called An Khe. I still don't know what corps that is. . . ."

"Second Corps," someone in the group says. I look about as each member of the group looks at me, eye-to-eye. Christ. It is good to see eye-to-eye with so many others.

"Mr. Kane."

"Yes?" I turn to the woman.

"Don't stop, fill us in . . . more. What did you do?"

"I was a medic, Doc, paratrooper in the infantry. I thought I said that?" I look about at the guys. They nod. I look at her.

"But we don't know that, Mr. Kane, Dr. Smith and I, many people back here in the States, we need better clarifications. By the way, Mr. Kane, do you have trouble with your concentration?"

"Trouble with concentration?" I stare at her defensively. I forgot her name already. "Not necessarily, I concentrate on the war, or drinking. I'm afraid I've forgotten your name already, though."

"My name is Dr. Gates."

"Right. Dr. Gates. No, Dr. Gates, I think I'm a little confused with meeting all you people and hearing about this memorial thing, but I'm not here because of my concentration problems, or my memory. I will say that if I've had trouble with anything since Nam, it's been sleeping."

"For sure!" someone in the group reinforces.

"Nightmares?" Dr. Smith inquires.

"Yes. One reason I drink so much, so I could pass out and not have to worry about nightmares. Of course, after a while, all the booze in the world couldn't keep them down."

"Can you recall any for us now?" Dr. Gates asks.

"Do I have to?" I wonder . . . this is all happening so fast. "I mean, there are booby-trap nightmares that speak for themselves. Instant replay nightmares where, asleep or awake, I play the same scene over and over again. There are nightmares that combine Viet Nam action with stateside stuff. Christ! Do I have to get into all this right away?"

I look around at the group somewhat bewildered, this is going a bit too fast.

"Not if you don't want to, Mr. Kane," Dr. Gates allows.

"Thanks. Besides, my sleep problems don't come just from nightmares. It seems that, since Nam, I still wake up in the middle of the night for radio watch."

"That happens to me," Pax admits. "Not so much now, but the first six or eight years I was back, it did."

"What's radio watch?" Dr. Gates asks.

"The platoon leader, platoon sergeant, RTO and medic used to take turns sitting up at night to monitor any incursion by the Viet Cong around our perimeters," I say. "Or, if we sent out listening posts or night ambushes and there was action, someone had to be awake and ready to report on the radio to the company or battalion."

"They were called situation reports," Major Berns inserts.

"Sit reps," Sergeant Pepper adds.

"That's it," I recall, "Cong used to like to keep as many of us awake all night as he could. We had to report every hour on the hour our sit reps. My time for radio watch is . . . was . . . between one and three in the morning. I still do it. I still wake up somewhere in that time. Then I lie there, going over one instant replay or another, sometimes till dawn. Then I have to go to work."

I pause, recalling my poor sleep habits over the last fifteen years, compared to how I slept in Nam. "You know something? Now that I think about it, I slept better in Nam than I have back here. I mean, over there, if I wasn't doing my radio watch, I slept through the night—no problem. Sometimes, I'd even sleep through Cong's probe of our perimeters. One time, I slept through a mortar barrage."

"Dead man's sleep, Doc."

I turn to that comment. It came from Pax. "Yeah, that's what Henderson called it, dead man's sleep. 'Doc,' he said, 'I don't know how you are going to make it through a tour sleepin' so heavy.' Funny thing is, I never fell asleep during radio watch."

"I had a foxhole buddy who slept through everything," Point Man adds. "When I was in the rear getting my athletic feets fixed, they put a FNG with him. Cong snuck up on them that night and got both of them with a grenade."

"You don't fall asleep on guard and last long in the bush," Sergeant Pepper reinforces.

"Henderson had me med evac sleepers to the rear with FUO," I recall.

"Excuse me," Dr. Gates interrupts, "What's an FNG?"

"Fucking new guy," someone answers.

She scribbles that on her pad, then turns to me.

"And FUO is . . . ?"

"Fever of unknown origin."

"I thought so." She adds that to her notes, then

returns to me. "Mr. Kane, what's interesting is, you say you have trouble sleeping back here in the States, but in Viet Nam, you say you slept well, or 'dead,' as you put it. It seems to be a contradiction. Can you explain?"

My brow furrows.

"I think I can answer that," Major Berns volunteers. "There was a sense of security among the troops in the field. We could relax at night as each of us took the responsibility of vigilance from the other. That was why the camaraderie was so important."

"But why should Mr. Kane be so uneasy back here in the States?"

" 'Cause he ain't got anyone pulling guard for him while he sleeps?" Point Man pipes up.

"Hey!" I turn to his comment. "You might be right there. I sleep better when I sleep with someone. I still may wake for radio watch, but I feel much better when I wake and see her lying there." Pause again. "And then, I can be lying there and a feeling passes over me. Real uneasy-like. It can be when I'm awake, asleep, just dozing; all of a sudden, I know something is happening. I get up. Go to the window. There'll be a cat slinking across the yard."

"That's known as being hyperalert, Kane," Dr. Smith confirms.

"Whatever it's called, it cheats me out of a lot of sleep. On more than one night, I've lain awake reliving Happy Valley, or Ia Drang Valley. . . ."

"You were in Ia Drang Valley?" someone asks.

I turn around to Berns—I guess he asked it. "Just last night, for the thousandth time, man. . . ."

Blam! The door bursts open. I leap in my seat.

"Sorry I'm late, guys. Hope I'm not interrupting anything. Christ, I've just come from one of the most fucked-up meetings I've ever been to since Viet Nam!"

A middle-aged, overweight white man, dressed in a business suit, stops in the middle of the room. "Hey, did I interrupt anyone?"

242

"Hey, Sully, what happened?"

"Doc Kane just wants to sleep, Sully."

"We got a new member of the group, Sul. We got a Doc for our group."

"Oh." He looks around the room, spies me. "Sorry to interrupt you, er, Doc." He walks to me, offers a hand. "Pat Sullivan, Eighty-second Airborne, III Corps, '68–'69. I'm a National Service Officer for a veterans' organization. That's like a cross between a lawyer and a social worker. Lately, I've been monitoring the infighting over the particulars associated with building the Viet Nam veterans' memorial." He turns from me, goes to an empty chair, and slumps into it. "Whew! Well, there was a vote today to add a statue and a flagpole, which would satisfy the Webb-Perot faction, and it passed. So Interior Secretary Watt signed the papers releasing the land on the Mall so the Scruggs faction could dig the hole and put up the names of the fifty-five thousand who died over there."

"You mean they are going ahead with that eyesore?" Major Berns says.

" 'Fraid so, Bernsy, compromise decision. You'll have your statue in due time. The ground-breaking is being set up for next week."

Sully reaches into a briefcase and pulls out some paper. "I checked with the hospital administration and got the okay to reserve a bus for those of us veterans here at the hospital to go down to the ceremony as a group."

"Can we?"

He hands me pen and paper. "Sign it, Doc, and pass it around. I need to know how many are going. If you are an inpatient, you have to get the okay of your attending physician, and permission of your ward."

"What about you doctors?"

"If we are not your attending physicians, we can't give you permission to go," Dr. Gates says.

"Yeah, but you doctors could go with us."

"When?" Dr. Smith asks.

"This Monday."

"That's our next group meeting."

"So tell your chief Doc we're going to meet on the Mall."

"What about other vets, say . . . like guys who are combat vets but don't come to the group?"

"They're welcome to come. Just put their names down on the list. If they're inpatients, they must have doctors' permission and so on."

"But, if Dr. Gates and I go, that doesn't give everyone carte blanche," Dr. Smith says.

"What's carte blanche?"

"Some other time, Point Man, please."

The group starts to break up.

"I can't believe we're getting a memorial!"

"It ain't a memorial. It's a fucking hole in the ground."

"It's better than nothing."

· · ·

There are about twenty-five of us on the bus, all Viet Nam veterans from the therapy group, or from the various hospital wards at the VA. We all look like we've been through a war, bent, spent, and unspoken for. Our appearance would be enough to give the spit-shine veterans tight jaws.

The bus pulls up to the same spot on the Mall where I had Sani-Johns placed for an anti-war demonstration eleven years earlier. I have a passing thought of Pietranowicz. Wonder if he's still a cop?

"Okay, you guys," Sully calls for our attention from the top step of the exit. "We'll look for somewhere all of us can sit, to stay together. Head back here ASAP when it's all over."

"It ain't never over!"

We step off the bus into the brisk March air. As a group, we wander around the edge of the roped-off staging area. This will be a test for those of us who don't care to be in crowds.

The gathering is as diverse as the garb—military uniforms of the Pentagon, pin-striped suits of Capitol Hill. Field jackets and full beards. Sweaters with yellow armbands. Those folks must be marshals, filtering through the crowd giving directions, calling out instructions, strategically placing shovels on the ground. We limp and lope past a military band.

"Hey! Get your hands off that!" one of the marshals shouts. Point Man stops, caught with a shovel in his hand.

"I want to help dig," he says, lamely.

"We already have enough people helping." The marshal takes the shovel from Point and walks into the crowd.

"First time I've been turned down from digging a hole!"

"You even volunteered, man."

"If it was a war, they'd a made ya dig, Point."

"We'll sit over there," Sully shouts, pointing to seats on the far side of the crowd.

"Hey, front-row seats!" shouts Sergeant Pepper. We all move down a makeshift aisle.

"Where are you going? Who do you guys think you are? You can't sit there!" a woman shouts after us, then comes stomping over toward the group. Sully intercepts her. They huddle, as Sergeant Pepper announces to whosoever cares to listen: "We're Nam vets. We're combat vets. We're from the VA hospital. We came to see what kind of memorial you're dedicating to us and our dead comrades."

"Yeah, and our black and Spanish brothers."

The woman looks over Sully's shoulder, scowling. We fill in the rows of empty seats. She nods hesitatingly as the two doctors sit among us. I take a front-row seat and try to figure out what the hell this thing is going to look like. I had seen a drawing of it in the newspaper. How in hell are they going to put all those names on one monument? Kind of nervy thing to do, anyway. I crane my neck to the left and right, taking in the pattern of the shovels lying on the ground in kind of a wide V. How deep will they have to dig? I don't know if I'll want to walk down into it when it's finished.

Someone said they heard someone say someone else said he would blow it up if it were built. There are vets who don't care for a hole dug into the ground being called a memorial to our service in Nam. Others want the tone to be white marble rather than black. No flag to mark it. One flag to mark it. Fifty flags to signify it. Light the memorial. Don't light it. Names. No names. Dug into the ground. Reach for the sky. A statue. An obelisk. A wall. Viet Nam will be a conflict to the very end.

"Testing. Testing. Testing." The loudspeaker blares, passing the sound test.

The crowd begins to settle. Well-dressed dignitaries filter into the seats to our right. The difference between our two groups can best be described as the difference between those on the front lines versus those passing down the orders and policies from back here in Washington.

"Excuse us," a young, well-dressed woman says to me as if she'd like me to get up and leave. I look at her and nod, then look past her at the old man she has come with. She turns to help seat him. He is very old. Then she sits down next to me with much chagrin.

"Welcome everyone. Good afternoon and welcome," the loudspeaker erupts in a feminine voice. "This day we are gathered to dedicate . . ."

The ceremony begins on a salutation I don't care to follow. As the formalities drone on, I survey the area. Muddy ground, tree line not too distant, off to the right of the Lincoln Memorial. Christ! I remember the D.C. Ninety-four, Viet Nam Veterans Against the War, who perched atop that monument not more than ten years ago. They weren't going to leave until the war ended. Eventually, Park Police were escorting everyone off to jail. I ran around trying to raise bail money that put the chapter in debt. The war raged on another two years. That was eight years after I came back, and more than nine years after we were trapped in that creek bed in Happy Valley. Which was noted as the first . . .

"Everyone please take your places," the loudspeaker requests. "Those designated ground-breakers please step up behind the shovel with your corresponding number."

The old man near me starts to get up. The March wind whipping through the ceremony sets him back in his seat. His young guardian presses him back in the chair. "I'll find it for you. You sit and wait here." She turns and glares at me like I'd better not rob him while she's gone. I look at him, something about him is familiar.

"Howdy," I nod.

He tries to focus on me, but failing eyesight seems to be one of his burdens.

"Ambassador Bunker, come, I've found your spot," she says, returning.

Ho, ho! Ambassador Bunker. Our man in Saigon. The civilian counterpart to General Westmoreland. Well, this dedication surely has some big guns.

With the help of his escort, Bunker gets up slowly. Arm in arm, they step to the rank forming behind the shovels. The sun breaks through the overcast sky for a brief moment, then disappears. God took a picture. Bunker is led about four spaces down from our seats. Other participants become apparent besides the military and the pin-stripe crew. Women dressed in white and gold. Men in wheelchairs. Men leaning on crutches. High-ranking spit-and-polish officers next to long-haired and bearded men in dungarees and field jackets. Women in their Sunday best, children in . . . goddam! even kids. I'll bet those kids are orphans.

"Kane." A tap on the shoulder startles me.

"Oh! Sorry, Kane." It's Dr. Smith.

"Damn, man! Warn me, will you?"

"I'm sorry. Are you okay?"

"I'm okay. Why?"

"You looked to be tightening up. Starting to flush."

"This is pretty strong stuff, being around some strong reminders. Haven't seen this many military personnel since . . . Nam, or the Eighty-second in Fayetteville."

"Try to relax."

"I will. I will. Hey, Dr. Smith. Who are those women in white and gold?"

"Those are gold star mothers. Mothers who lost sons or daughters in Viet Nam."

"Oh. That makes sense. Thanks."

"Here, take this program. It explains who some of these people are."

He hands me an orange flyer and returns to his seat. I flip over the folded page as the speeches continue. I ignore the remarks by reading through the list of people designated as ground-breakers. There's Ellsworth Bunker's name. I look up. Where is he? There, between a pressed uniform and a gold star mother.

"Thank you, Senator Mathias. Thank you, Senator Warner. Now, ladies and gentlemen, take your shovels in hand," the mike commands.

The wide V comes alive, as participants pick up their shovels. Ambassador Bunker is handed his by a yellow-armbanded assistant. The ambassador refuses further assistance. The loudspeaker drones out something, then, ". . . break ground!"

According to their capabilities, the ranks sink their shovels into the cold winter ground. I watch Bunker as he attempts to dig his shovel tip into the earth. He can't get more than a peck at it. He tries again, a scratch. Arthritis, old age, the burden of the war years weigh on him. He continues to nip away, making his one last impression on the Viet Nam war. As the rest of the diggers scoop their shovelfuls, Bunker continues an attempt to dent the earth. I want to get up and help him. He keeps pecking away. His escort steps to his side. She takes the shovel from his hands. He straightens slowly. She hands the shovel to a military man and turns Bunker away from the line. I am witness to a war story coming to an end.

She escorts him back to the chair next to me. He is visibly shaken from his attempt. Poor Bunker. He sits heavily in his chair, hands shaking. The rest of the rank backs from the line of fresh-turned earth.

Orders are shouted. Flags snap in the wind. Sabers rattle. An honor guard appears. The band strikes up a medley of military tunes. Air Force jets suddenly streak low overhead. I instinctively duck and shudder under the recall of another event . . . never mind, fuck it! Out over the Potomac River, a multitude of choppers fly in formation, flashbacks react to the memories, the guys. Why? Eddie. Why? Kelly. Why? For what? Look at the old man next to me. Bent, broken, a major player. Look at him. Look! Look at the crutches, wheelchairs. Mothers. Widows. Orphans. This group of veterans from the VA.

Turn and stand to the colors. No, don't turn to them. Stand but don't turn, don't recognize the spit, the polish, the veneer. That thin coating of spectacle cannot crowd out the screams for "Doc, Doc, Doc." A trumpet moans taps for the living, as we try to put the dead to rest.

"Thank you all for your participation," the loudspeaker allows, then shuts off. I stand, stunned, as I had many years ago. I turn to see where Bunker is. Got to make sure he's okay.

He's gone. All around me, people are crossing over fresh-turned earth. The band is quiet. The colors, the flags, march off toward the Lincoln Memorial.

"Excuse me."

A woman stands directly in front of me.

"I'm Susan McKenna, of the *Philadelphia Enquirer*. I could not help but note your reaction to the ceremony. You appear to be mildly upset. Were you in Viet Nam?"

Christ! Is there no privacy?

"Yes, I was." I glare.

"Would you care to make a comment?"

"No, I don't have anything to say."

• • •

"I didn't realize how angry I was at the military side of it. The uniformed, saber-rattling, show stuff."

"It was a relief for me. I'm glad to see something in recognition for what we went through."

"I didn't care for it. I don't like the idea of it being a hole in the ground. Being like a wall. And, of all things, black."

"Wha's wrong wid black?"

"Oh, Christ, Point Man! There's nothing wrong with black as a race. There is something wrong with black as a monument."

"Black and gold. The names are to be engraved in gold leaf."

"Mr. Paxton, what are your feelings?"

"I'm proud of my tour of duty in Viet Nam. I am proud of the contributions blacks were able to make in the name of freedom and democracy."

"You crazy, Pax. Nigger's proud o' fuckin' up a bunch o' gooks . . ."

"I told you to watch your lip, Point Man, watch your name-calling."

"Okay. Okay, dude . . . shit, that mo'fucking war din't do nobody no good, 'n that monument is too little, too late."

"Mr. Washington, why are you in hospital pajamas and bathrobe?"

"Ward nurse 'stricted me fur bein' fucked up."

"You smell like a distillery, Point."

"What did you do, Point, raid the terpin hydrate?"

"Mr. Washington, maybe this is not a good time for you to be taking part in the group."

"Says who?"

"Point Man, you were fine after the ground-breaking ceremony. What happened the last week?"

"Wha's it look like happened? I got fucked up. I thought I was celebrating, it got me off guard."

"You're trying to kill the recall," Dr. Smith finally interrupts. "The ceremony may have brought more of the experience to mind than you can handle."

"Ain't nothing I can't handle, Doc, er, man, jes' 'member that."

"Mr. Washington, maybe you'd best excuse yourself from the group until you've settled down."

"I'm settled down, Doctor woman."

"At ease, Point Man," Sergeant Pepper commands, then turns to Dr. Gates. "Dr. Gates, no matter how we act it out, this memorial thing is bringing a lot up in all of us."

"It's got me on edge," Major Berns admits.

"I never lose my edge," Point adds.

"It's just made my edge sharper," I add, "not just this memorial, but being clearheaded has me edgy."

"Gentlemen, when you say you're on edge, I've some idea of what you mean, but I'd be interested to know what your definitions of 'edge' are."

"It's not givin' a fuck," Point adds.

"Taking chances," says Sully.

"It's an attitude," Berns adds.

"The edge is death. Risk. Taking chances like the chances we took in Nam," Sergeant Pepper says.

"It's fear," says Pax. Everyone joins in.

"It's like, you can always look to either side and see nothing but blackness. Bottomless-pit blackness."

"The edge is playing for keeps."

"Like walking a fence that is stuck out in space."

"The edge is walking point."

Everyone looks to each other. It's so true. It wasn't a good experience, but it was our experience.

"Yeah, been through a lot of scrapes, over there, back here. I'm lucky to be alive. I wonder why I'm so depressed with all that experience. I still got my five appendages.'' I grin at the others, hoping they catch the joke. It misses.

"But what we'd like to know," Dr. Smith asks, "is why you men come back and continue to take risks. You know of the danger, yet you continue to . . . live on the edge.''

" 'Cause there's a thrill in it.''

" 'Cause it's exciting.''

" 'Cause it's the only thing I know.''

Everyone looks to me as if I should carry on this round robin. I shrug. "I'd never really given the edge much more thought. I guess I just . . . made it back . . .''

My voice trails off as Pax speaks up. He starts to relate something about celebrating an anniversary. I don't pay much attention. My thoughts are still on the edge . . . living on the edge, is that what it was? I thought it was just living through it, making it back, being invincible. That's what it was, surviving the Nam, running through that hail of bullets, the hand grenades, mortar rounds exploding so close, getting nicked by those booby traps, the diseases. That was living on the edge. I remember—after a while—it was like you had to feel indestructible—or chauvinistic—yeah! I'm suffering from combat chauvinism. It was surviving the whole wild crazy experience. The car wrecks, the motorcycle wrecks, the love wrecks, they're just like the combat operations, firefights, booby traps. More challenges, more thrills, more excitement. I'll keep beating the odds. No one's going to nail Doc Kane. Doc Kane comes from the edge. Doc Kane went to the edge and tinkled over the side.

"I'm afraid our time's up for today, gentlemen.'' Dr. Gates stands, breaking my concentration. The others in the group stand.

"Wait, Dr. Smith!'' I leap to my feet, step to intercept him at the door. "Here's that homework you wanted.''

"Oh.'' He takes it from me, opening the folded sheet. It was an interesting exercise, reflecting on my past. The good doctor wanted me to add up how many places I had lived since returning from Viet Nam. He also wanted to know the number of jobs I'd had. The total was sort of a shock. After giving it some thought, and using all my fingers and toes, the total: thirty-one places lived, twenty-nine jobs. That many jobs and homes works out to a transition every six months. Hmmm! It was such a revelation, I also added up all my auto and motorcycle accidents. I haven't gotten to the love affairs yet.

"What's this, Kane?" he points.

"Sir?" I peer over the note. "Oh! I thought I'd throw those in. Those are the number of traffic accidents I've had since I've been back."

"Nine! Were they all serious?"

"Well, I couldn't drive away from six or seven of them."

"What did your insurance company say?"

"I didn't have insurance. Never had insurance, not even in Viet Nam."

"Sort of a death wish?"

"More like a death want."

I have to admit, it was the right thing to come into the VA Hospital. It sure is nice to have somewhere to go, once you decide to take care of yourself. I step up to the desk.

"Is this the dermatology clinic?"

She looks up at me with shady, nonchalant eyes. "Mondays and Thursdays, 1:00 P.M."

Her gaze returns to the book on the desk.

"Well, that's today, isn't it?" I chance.

She looks up at me. "That's why I'm sittin' here."

"My name is Kane. I have a one o'clock appointment."

"Everyone has a one o'clock appointment. Have a seat, Mr. Kane, you'll be called in turn."

I leave her in the middle of the explanation. I sit and wait.

"Mr. Kane?"

"Yes!" I leap to my feet. A tall, trim black woman approaches, her hand extended.

"I'm Dr. Thompson."

We share a wary handshake.

"Come with me, please." She turns into the nearest examining room. I follow.

"Please be seated." She motions to a chair next to a desk. We sit, and she leafs through a chart with my name on it.

"What brings you to the dermatology clinic today, Mr. Kane?"

I offer the palm of my hand. "I have this skin peeling on my right hand."

She looks over from the chart to my hand.

"How long has it been that way?"

"Off and on, since Viet Nam, but quite a bit lately, and in hot weather. It wasn't anything for a while."

"Let me see the other hand."

I show it. "When I came back from Nam, both hands peeled a couple times, down to the elbow."

She looks intently at my arms, then peers at my face and neck.

"I don't think it's anything bad," I say, to reassure myself.

"Have you ever had athlete's foot?" she asks.

"Ever since I was at Fort Benning."

"Are you a patient in the hospital, Mr. Kane?"

"Yeah. I've been in here trying to get my shit, er, straighten out some war stuff. It's going pretty good . . ."

"How often do you get those pimples on your face?"

"Oh, I've always had those, ever since I was a teenager. They come and go. Some real bad, then they heal up. I use vitamin E capsules on them."

"I need to see your back."

"Sure. Should I take my shirt off?"

"Just pull it up in back. Here, turn."

I do. She helps me lift the shirt.

Silence.

"Okay." She drops the shirttail. I turn back, looking for any kind of expression on her face. She scribbles onto the chart. I tuck my shirt in. Clear my throat.

"What, Mr. Kane?"

"I hope you have something for this stuff on my hand."

"Oh, I'll give you something for that." She continues to write. I withdraw my concern.

She stops, turns to me. "I'll also write you a prescription for the chloracne on your face and back. For the Agent Orange poisoning. That's what those pimples appear to be around your eyes and nose, and on your upper back."

Something screams inside me, No! No! No! Not Agent Orange poisoning, I have no room right now to handle that! I'm trying to get the rest of the war in order.

"Mr. Kane?"

"Yes."

"Are you all right?"

"Sure. Sure."

"I'm going to write you a prescription for the peeling on your hand. I'm also writing one for the chloracne on your face and back."

"It never seemed so bad, I mean, it's always been there."

"It isn't so bad on your face, some scarring from some previous bouts. It's more apparent on your back, the scarring I mean. You've probably not paid attention to it because you've accepted it since adolescence."

"A couple of times, it got real bad, back in the mid-seventies."

"You were probably just getting rid of your teenage acne when you were in Viet Nam."

"I guess."

She returns to her charts. I return to the war. The goddam fucking war that will haunt me, trouble me, poison me, until the day I die. It's so absurd to think I was just getting it all in order. Just when I think it's going to be over, bang!

"Mr. Kane."

"Yes?"

"Lift your shirt again. I need to take a specimen from your back. Dioxin check."

"Sure."

I pull the whole shirt out of its tuck and over my head.

"That's good, Mr. Kane."

It must have been in Ia Drang Valley. It must have been sprayed there. Before the battle, everything was alive and well, the trees in full foliage. After the battle, it was like autumn, leafless trees exposing those bastards who ambushed our people.

"You can drop your shirt, Mr. Kane." I feel a slight sting and the sticky tension of a Band-Aid.

"Keep the Band-Aid on until you shower or bathe."

She hands me a few slips. "This slip on top is your appointment to see Dr. Remmel, our physician investigating Agent Orange referrals. He'll check you again, your back. Screen where you were, over there. How you may have been sprayed. Things like that."

"Oh. Okay." I take the slips, as the shock slips away.

"The other two pieces of paper are prescriptions for medication you apply to your face and back."

"Yes. Okay, okay."

"Mr. Kane."

I look up from the slips of paper.

"Nice to have met you." She offers a hand. I comply.

"Yeah, sure. Likewise."

"The question is whether it is better to die in the kill zone of a well-camouflaged VC ambush in the Ia Drang Valley, or be slowly poisoned by the defoliant, so it haunts you for the rest of your life."

"Not to mention what it does to your kids."

"What it does to your offspring hasn't been proven yet, Pepper," Berns interrupts.

"Tell that to Pax's kids."

"Let Pax speak for himself."

"Where is he?"

"Doc, I also don't appreciate your melodramatic attitude. You know damn well which you would choose. A defoliated ambush site for the lives of our men, no question."

"Right, Berns, right in respect to short terms. But now we're realizing the long-term ramifications."

"Fuck the long-term ramifications, Doc. Defoliants saved lives."

"War never saves lives."

"Gentlemen, this is becoming a vicious circle."

"That's the truth, Dr. Gates. The whole war thing is a vicious circle. It chews itself up. It never ends. I'm just settling myself with one aspect of the war . . ."

Boom! The door bangs open. Pax enters the room.

"Sorry I'm late. I had to go before the supervisor about my job. Me and my boss."

"Did you get fired?" Sergeant Pepper asks.

"No. No," Pax says in lament. "But I'm on a ninety-day probation period. The doctors here gave my employers a good report."

"What was this about?" I ask.

"From last week. Meeting before last, Doc. You were here. Pax was talkin' 'bout how he fired up his boss 'cause the dude came up behind him and got all in his face . . ."

"It wasn't like that, Point," Pax interrupts. "Anyways, it's past now, and they know the problem I have. I have to be careful. I got to remember my anniversaries. I have to take steps to avoid confrontations."

"And keep up with your medications," Dr. Gates adds.

"And not fuck around with the hooch," Sergeant Pepper comments.

"What's all this about anniversaries?" I wonder out loud.

Dr. Gates explains. "Some professionals in the study of traumatic stress disorders believe the experience recurs at certain times of the year, or is initiated by environmental reminders."

"Rains remind me of monsoons. I get real moody, brood, drink, stay by myself," Berns says.

"Like, we lost this dude one time and I had to lead a patrol out to find him," Point says. "When we did, it was ugly. Charley had sliced off his tattoos and really mutilated the poor motherfucker. Anyway, it happened on my birthday. Every year around my birthday, I get squirrelly."

"When's your birthday, Point?" I ask.

"Last week."

"How did you feel?"

"Squirrelly."

"It doesn't necessarily have to be related to the traumatic experience of war," Dr. Gates adds. "It could be a traumatic experience like rape."

"There may be an annual relationship with an occurrence like . . . a natural disaster, a hurricane," Dr. Smith says.

"It happened to me the other night," Pax adds, "during a thunder and lightning storm, a torrential rain. I was in bed, kicked my wife in the stomach while low crawling in my sleep. Flashing real heavy and I nailed her. So I got up, went into Melissa's room, picked her up, carried her in to her mother. Went back to sleep in her little bed. It didn't work, so I sat up in the living room the rest of the night, chain smoking, thinking 'bout it, how it happens every year, with spring thunder, lightning. Happy anniversary, that's how I look at it."

"Yeah, we got our own private little anniversaries," Sully says.

"Our own private little anniversary parties," the Maj confirms.

"Did you hurt your wife, Mr. Paxton?" Dr. Gates asks.

"Not this time. One other time, though, when she just got pregnant, I kicked her in my sleep. She aborted . . ."

"Boy, you got a good woman, to stay with you through all that!"

Pax leans forward, says vacantly, "Yeah. I got a good woman. It's more a question of the woman got a good man."

"Hey, Pax, get off your case." Sully squirms in his chair. "You guys got to accept some of these fates and allow others to do the same."

• • •

Buzz, Hummmm, Gurble, Squawk!

"Cut that speaker, pronto, Booker! And give me that handset."

Booker hands Henderson the handset as he slips the radio off his back, flicks a couple of dials, and slides the radio pack back on.

"Too low, more volume," Henderson states.

Booker slips out of the pack harness. Holding the strap, supporting the radio on one knee, he thumbs a radio dial and looks at Henderson in question.

"Yeah, yeah, that's okay." Henderson holds a hand over one ear, leaning into the handset so as to hear better.

"Here." He abruptly hands the receiver to Booker, who is reharnessed. Henderson turns and picks up his gear. By his manner, I can tell that what is going on isn't good.

"Henderson?"

He comes back from a thought. "Right, Doc. Keep it quiet. We gotta gather up." He slides his pack to his back. "Pass the word, saddle up. We gotta move, maybe fast."

Booker turns one way, I step the other. Don't have to go far. Robert O crouches at the ready by a clump of bamboo. Anyone's been around long enough can feel it in the air.

"Robert O," I whisper.

He steps to.

"Keep it cool, but pass it on, we gotta move, chop chop."

"Right, Doc."

He turns away. I step back to where Henderson stands, staring that vacant stare he wears when he realizes there is trouble.

"Word's out my way, Henderson." He snaps to my attention. Booker steps back from the other side.

"They are ready."

Clang!

"Shhh! Goddammit." Henderson reacts to the equipment commotion back down the trail. The silence is so complete you can hear a snake slither. One of those prehistoric, foot-long centipedes pads over a rock and disappears. Everything and everyone is on the alert. The anticipation hangs heavier than humidity.

"Handset, Booker." Henderson extends his hand in command, as he looks to where the centipede vanished. Booker slaps the set in his palm. Putting the mouthpiece to lips, Henderson mumbles, "Foxtrot, Foxtrot One, over."

The subtle rush of silent air is the answer.

He mumbles our call sign again. Others from the platoon begin to gather in closer. It isn't the right thing to do, to bunch up like this, but it's almost instinctive when the danger signs are so strong. I wave the men back. Grub steps forward instead.

"Kin hear some heavy interdiction back 'round the bend, down in the creek . . ."

"Shhh . . ." Henderson puts up a hand, whispers intently into the handset. "Foxtrot. Foxtrot. This is Foxtrot One. Do you copy. Over."

The hairs start to stand on the back of my neck.

"Come in, Foxtrot. Come in."

"Sarge, the motherfuckers is gettin' louder 'n louder," comes from the other side of the trail. Wonder if I have time to take a dump.

"Fuck it." Henderson hands the set back to Booker, who clips the receiver to hang off his helmet at the ear. Henderson's eyes dart from me, to Robert O, to Booker.

"Everyone here?"

"Present and accounted for."

"Okay, we move out . . ."

"Sarge! Sarge! Foxtrot for you." Booker hands the receiver back to Henderson, who swipes at it.

"Foxtrot One, over."

Standing a couple of yards away, I hear a tone of urgency come from the handset. My asshole tightens. Henderson returns the handset to Booker.

"Move out."

Henderson turns under the weight of his 120 pounds of gear and heads through the jungle brush. Booker follows, then me, as the order spreads along the line.

At the edge of the open area, Henderson stops. I stand to one side. He takes in the whole open space on one slow turn of the head, 180 degrees.

I look out at a clearing, a hedgerow, then who knows what beyond?

"Doc?" Henderson is conferring.

"Whatever, Sarge, it don't feel good wherever we be."

"Let's go." He jumps out of the tree line as a sprinter would out of the starting blocks, lumbering under the weight on his back. Booker and I move right behind him. It always feels so naked to step out from the jungle. I hear the commotion behind me as the others follow suit. Henderson turns and takes quick steps backward, looking at how we are following.

"Move it, Doc. Booker. Get the lead out, double time." Henderson turns back around. We begin a full-fledged open-throttle type of a sprint that brings us to the hedgerow in no time.

"Christ! This is going to be a steeplechase," I mumble. Booker vaults past me with the receiver in his hand as Henderson disappears over the hedge.

"Sarge! Sarge! Battalion says it could be a regiment, heavily armed." Booker vaults the hedge and I stumble along behind him. Regiment! That's just fucking peachy.

"C'mon, goddammit. We gotta get to the far side of this thing and we're home free," Henderson shouts, throwing all caution to the wind. I realize why, as we conquer the rise in the land. We are at one end of this clearing the size of a football field. There sits a military transport at the other end. It's our ticket out of here. A dozen of us spread out along this field. We begin to run with great pride. The plane takes note of this. Its propellers begin to spin. We are caught deep in VC territory. We have one chance to get out. Cong didn't bank on that big ugly prop blaster fitting in this clearing. He will always come out in the open when he has us in his corner. If we run fast enough, we can catch a ride with that beautiful, ugly airplane and fly right out from under Cong's trap.

We run, run, run. Inhale. Exhale, as one big lung, breathing in humid prop wash dust kicked up as the plane begins a slow taxi. The load master screams at us to move ass. Henderson reaches the ramp first and screams toward the cockpit.

"Go. Go. Go."

This spurs the plane to turn. The rest of us scramble up the ramp, helping each other to safety. The plane completes its turn, the propellers reaching full rev. The load master screams into his headset. We plunge back across the field we just sprinted from.

"How's this fucking thing going to get off the fucking ground in such a short clearing?" someone yells above the turbulence.

"She landed, didn't she?"

"Yeah, but she was empty then."

"So, if it's so heavy, we all go down together," Henderson commands.

"No, we all go up on a wing and a prayer," someone grins.

The transport lurches across the bumpy plain, riding blindly back in the direction of the threat we had run from.

Whoa!

The first weightless sense as we take off is an indication that we might . . .

Crack!

The transport's belly hits the hedgerow as we skim skyward, climbing, climbing, climbing. We scrape the jungle tree line as little fireballs follow us from the foliage cover. We climb higher as bigger fireballs trace their way toward the transport's thin skin. Assholes that were tight get tighter. Cong fuckers fire their whole arsenal at us. I look across at Booker. He's put his steel pot underneath him. He recoils as each tracer passes, oh so fucking close underneath us. He bucks and bucks and bucks.

I bolt upright in the dark, sweaty sheets balled up under me in the humid hospital room. The guy in the bed across from me bucks and bucks and bucks.

He's masturbating.

"Dr. Smith?"

He looks up from the papers he's studying on his desk.

"Yes, Kane. Hello. Come in."

"Just a momentary interruption, sir."

"Yes. By the way, I finished that writing of yours. What did you call it? *Veteran's Day*. Very appropriate."

"Yeah, right . . . Dr. Smith, could I get, er, have a weekend pass? It's Memorial Day and all."

"Let's see. Where did I put it?" He rifles through the papers on his desk. "Damn, I'll bet I left it at home. Have to wait." He readjusts his glasses. "Pass. Sure. Have you any plans?"

"Well, sir, sorta, I mean, being on the ward with some of these other patients is starting to give me the heebie-jeebies. I don't mean the guys in the group. I mean some of the others on the ward."

"Well, there aren't enough of you combat veterans to warrant a ward for yourselves, so we have to split you up. Besides, you have to learn to live with others, whether it's in here or out there."

"Yeah, well, do you mind if I go out there this weekend? There's someone I'd like to look up. Someone I used to live with. I think I might find a little comfort there."

"Well, I don't want to keep you from a little comfort, so long as it's not drug- or alcohol-induced."

"She isn't, sir." I smile at the thought of a love affair gone wrong. I would like to make it right.

"Very good, I'll put the weekend pass on your orders; just be careful. It's Memorial Day weekend and you're vulnerable right now."

"I know. By the way, those war group meetings are really the best medication I could ask for, especially that idea about the anniversaries. You know, I seem to have some turbulent times about the same time every year."

"Really? Well, that may be something to think about."

"Yeah." I turn away, whispering to myself, "Or not think about."

"Kane!"

"Sir?" I turn back around.

"Be careful this weekend."

•   •   •

"I have to turn this roast down or take it out of the oven. Hold on," she shouts, thinking I'm still standing inside the entrance to the apartment. I step up behind her.

"You don't have to shout."

"Oh!" she starts.

Using my fingers like a comb, I push her hair to the far shoulder. She shudders at the move. I blow softly at the curve above her collar.

"Oh, baby," she groans.

"Surprised?"

"Always," she says, turning more neck.

I exhale a warm, steady breath at the birthmark she bares. That distraction offers me the chance to sneak a hand inside the blouse and cup a breast.

"Oh, where have you been?"

"Working on the war."

"It doesn't feel like it."

"Does this feel like it?"

I apply a gentle, gnawing kiss to the curve at her neck. She chills at the sensation. I step back.

"I came to one conclusion."

"What's that?" she says, turning to me.

"I'd rather fuck than fight."

"You came to the right place."

She pushes me away, stepping from the stove. I lose my grip on the warm right mound. She unbuttons the blouse. I undo my shirt without taking off the sport jacket, slide out of both.

"We going to do it on the table?"

She slides out of the blouse. I appreciate the pair that stare so strong as to dare. One breast is a little smaller, and turned out. I call that one my working-class breast. The other one could make it on any page of Hefner's magazine.

"I've missed them."

"They've missed you."

I bend to reintroduce myself.

"How about me?" I hear from above.

I come up for air, admitting breathlessly, "You too. I've missed you."

"You lie," she accuses, twisting the romantic bent.

"Why do you say that?"

"I don't know. I only see you when you're horny."

"That's not true. I've been in the hospital. To be honest with you, I'm still an inpatient, but my doctor allowed me a weekend pass."

I turn to find a chair, ready to explain what I couldn't explain to her years ago.

"I tried in the past, you know, to explain how that fucking war dogs me." I slump heavily in a chair.

"No! I don't want to deal with your stupid war. I don't need to hear about any illnesses or any hospitals. Anyway, you don't look sick. You don't act sick."

"It ain't that kind of sick," I react defensively. A rush of fear wraps around my chest and squeezes. The fear streaks right down through my cock.

"Oh, baby, hush up and suck a titty." She reaches for, pulls my head to a breast. What do I do? Suck it? Bite it? Fuck it? Fight it?

She runs a fingernail across my shoulders. I straighten, confused by the issues. Do I want to fuck? Do I need a friend?

"You don't have a boyfriend who is gonna bust in?" I ask, looking for an excuse to get out of this.

"What about that other girlfriend of yours?" she counters.

"I said goodbye to her when I went in the hospital. We broke up. What about you?"

"Never mind me. I'll race you to see who gets undressed first. On your mark, get set, go!"

Anxious to see the rest of that luscious body, I concur.

We step back, unfasten and kick at the legs of our Levis. I get a heel caught, bounce around the kitchen foolishly.

"Beat you, beat you!" she boasts nakedly, as I pull the lagging leg free. "Beat you. Beat you."

Casting my pants aside, I step forward. She stands her ground, taunting. I silence her, mouth to mouth, nibble at the lower lip. There is no resistance. The world is full of cooperation. I place a hand on her lower back, fingerwalk the furrow to her buttocks, so soft and fine. The other hand drops to search below her navel. I nibble to the corner of her mouth.

"Oooh," she groans into me. There it is. A fine, furry

crop of crotch hair. Now, feel around for that spot at the top.

"Oooh," she moans.

"Whoa, so wet we are," I realize aloud, as my hand slides along her slick lip folds.

She steps back. "I'm ovulating."

"Oh?"

"We're going to have to use our fingers and our lips."

"One challenge right after another."

"Shut up. Come." She grabs my hand, leads me out of the kitchen and into the bedroom. I pause at the bed's side. A caution flag flips up inside me. What was beginning to grow, hesitates. Be careful, Doc.

"Maybe we ought to . . ."

"Shut up!" She turns me around, kneels before me, forcing me to sit on the bed's edge. "I'm going to make you glad you came."

She faces into my chest, her lips and tongue working aside the chest hair. She looks for . . . aah! A nipple. Her hands wander below, searching for more of what is known as foreplay. I'd never played this way until this woman showed me her play. That's why I'm back, ready to play her way, so I don't have to work on the war.

"Whoa, baby, whoa!" I let her know she has found me.

"There's my mighty man. Mommy's going to make it big and strong," she whispers up at me, then licks around the tool.

"So-o-o." I start in apprehension. I'm out in the open, a sitting fuck, no defense.

"Are you worried, little one?" she whispers, coming up to face me. "Does it ever hurt?" she wonders. One hand still works below.

"No, no, it doesn't hurt. Just sometimes, I get lost. Something happens too fast."

"It can't be all bad. You keep coming back for more."

"I know . . . I guess."

She hovers over me. I become undaunted down below. Her lips linger at my ear, making those erotic, sucking sounds. I turn to her, throwing caution to the wind. Well . . . at least off the bed. Grabbing hair, I pull her face-to-face, nose-to-nose, breath-on-breath, lips locked, tongue-to-tongue, so fresh, so sweet, wet, soft. Oh, baby! take me away from this fucking war.

"Oh!" she squeals, pressing herself on top of me. Searching for my erection, she slides in that direction.

"Oooh," we moan, as she slides so smoothly onto me.

So much for ovulating.

She pushes herself up to a squat on top. Then bounces lightly while digging her fingers into my chest. She pulls hair as I dare not drop a load in her egg-laden pocket. She teases by tipping back, exposing my root sunk so deep in her . . . Christ!

She swivels off so smoothly my cock slaps . . . crack! flat, splatting semen into my navel as she crawls to an ear and groans, "I didn't want to stay too long."

She leaves, sliding along my side, licking tongue tracks to the hip. I follow the trail. She grasps my swelled situation with one hand. She slips her other hand down between her own legs and buries it in her furrow.

The time is ripe.

She strokes me. She molds herself. I look away. She rubs me. I look down. She rubs herself. She makes me. She takes herself. She loves me. She loves herself. How does she do it? How does it happen? Christ! Could anything feel so goddam great!

Blind with excitement, I grope my way up the stairway to heaven, feeling larger, livelier, riper with every step. It seems so . . . isolated. I look down from afar as she moves her head back, exposing so large. . . . Christ! Is it mine?

She strokes with both hands now, moving the pole to a new position. It gets bigger than it ever was. It changes color . . . colors so very . . . hot!

"Christ!" I shout, as I arch. She strokes, smoother and quicker. I try to see through the ecstasy. She looks up, grinning slyly. I can't hold it any longer. She points this pecker at my face.

Nooo!

She aims.

I fire!

Aieee!

Splat. Splat. Splat.

Twisting and turning my head . . . in a vain attempt . . . to duck the barrage. The fucking bitch shoots me with my own gun.

Goddammit! My loins are warm. My face is wet. I need someone to hold me.

Drive. Drive. Drive, around the beltway. It's the best way to get away from everybody. Jesus! How long have I been driving, three or four hours? Haven't gone anywhere, just kept moving. Keep the radio tuned, the steering wheel turned, and the mind tripping. Now I'll wheel down to see what progress has been made on the Viet Nam memorial.

I remember why I never took up with that bitch. She always covered her ass and waited for me to expose mine. Then she'd take a cheap shot and leave. Shit. She was quicker at leaving than I was. Why did I ever think it would be okay to go back? She was never sympathetic to my war stuff. Where the fuck can I go? Who can I turn to? Where is everyone? Why do I always end up alone? Is there a woman out there who can accept that war?

Be careful, Doc. Be careful, this is when you isolate yourself. This is when you could turn to a drinking binge. I know. I know. Whoops! There's the Lincoln Memorial. Hmmm. Where's the . . . there's some bulldozers. Christ! Look at that fucking hole! It's big enough for a mass grave. Our memorial is a mass grave!

• • •

269

"How did you do on pass last weekend, Mr. Kane?"

"Huh?"

"You were on pass last weekend."

"Right."

"How'd it go, Kane? I think that's what Dr. Gates is getting at," Dr. Smith inserts.

"How'd it go? Well, I stayed up the whole weekend. Did a lot of driving . . . thinking."

"What about that bitch you said you were going to look up, Doc?" Point Man asks.

Thanks, Point, you fucking loudmouth. How in hell am I going to tell this woman I got shot with my own gun?

"Isolation," I blurt.

"Hear, hear!" Berns concurs.

"Isolation, Mr. Kane?"

"Yes. I closed myself off when I got out there. It happens a lot, I guess, not wanting to be alone, but always ending up alone. I just drove and drove and drove."

"Why, Mr. Kane?"

"What happened to that bitch, Doc. The one you said would always give you a free ride?" Point smirks.

"What is Mr. Washington talking about, Mr. Kane?" Dr. Gates asks perceptively.

"Oh, nothing. I stopped by to see a woman first night out, that's all."

"And?"

"I had a run-in with her. After it happened, I just closed up inside myself. Shut everyone out. I guess I realized that's dangerous to do."

"What happened, Mr. Kane?"

"What usually happens. I drive around, listen to the radio, realize how everything is so fucked up. It's best to just be by myself. No one fucks with me. I don't fuck with anyone."

"I think Dr. Gates meant, what happened between you and your woman friend?"

"Used to be, I'd just get loaded. Sometimes go on a

drinking binge, but always by myself. Always shut my-self off from others. Get drunk and drive, all sorts of things.''

"Did you drink this weekend, Mr. Kane?"

"No. No, I didn't, Dr. Gates. And I'm proud of that, but I realized that this isolation brings to mind something you people talk about with this anniversary thing. I think I'm starting to realize that certain times of the year, I am more prone to shutting myself in. Keeping others out. It seems to be about the same time every year. I don't know.''

"Mr. Kane?"

"What?"

"What happened with this run-in with a woman while you were on pass?"

"Ah. Hmmm. Do you really want to know, Dr. Gates?"

"I've not got a personal interest, Mr. Kane, but I'm sure we as a group are very interested."

"Well, you might say I got shot with my own gun."

"You said you didn't own any guns, Kane." Berns remembers everything.

"That isn't exactly how I meant it. It ain't like I got hit so you can see it . . . more like . . . let's just say I got woman troubles.''

"Oh, boy, my favorite subject, bitches!"

"What do you mean by woman troubles, Mr. Kane?"

"Oh, fuck it, I don't know. I guess the trouble is, I drop my guard when I shouldn't. I think she's a friend and she doesn't turn out to be that way."

"Did she fuck you over?"

"No, not really. Like I said, she shot me. I gave her my gun and she shot me with it."

"Well, I'm not going to play any riddle games with you, Mr. Kane."

"I think I know what he means."

"If I want some pussy, I take it."

"Did she jerk you off and hit you with it, Doc?"

"Men, watch your mouths, you're in the presence of a lady."

"Fuck you, Berns, Dr. Gates knows she takes her chances here."

"Thank you for your consideration, Mr. Berns, but I have heard it all before. Mr. Kane, put the cryptics aside if you can, and explain yourself."

"I really haven't . . . I can't explain myself, except to say this isn't the first woman I've had trouble with. I don't mean trouble like with sex, so much as trouble because of the war stuff."

"Are you having sexual troubles, Kane?" Dr. Smith asks.

"Not now, except for being caught off guard. Once I did, some years back. Come to think of it, that was right after I quit drinking the first time. Kept shooting blanks then."

"And this time, you didn't shoot blanks, this time, you . . . ?"

"What happens, it has to do with the war. It gets in the way, I guess. I want to talk about the war. She says she doesn't want to hear it. She gets irritated and says it's my problem."

"It hurt, hearing her say she didn't want to deal with the war, the pain of it. They don't want to understand that it isn't easy, readjusting to back here."

"People back here, women especially, they just know stateside, peace, security. We know peace and war. It separates us."

"Women are jealous of our experience, the camaraderie we share."

"Some of the men who didn't go resent us too."

"Christ! I strip myself down for her, for any of them. It's like being caught out in the open. That's what happens when you get close. They see you out in the open. Pow! They get you."

"Pretty heavy price to pay to get laid, Doc."

"If I want some pussy, I take it."

"I'm getting really tired of hearing that, Point."

"Why the hell do I get attracted to women who won't accept the war?"

"You can't win with women, Doc."

"Be careful of the women who put you down, men. You can't live around contempt and feel good about yourself."

"Find a country woman, Doc. They stick by you. They're not like city girls or chicks from the suburbs."

"Fuck it, guys, it takes a certain type of woman to hang with us. Let's face it, women don't want to fight the war."

"No one back here wants to be reminded of the war."

"Gentlemen, once again, our time is up."

I start for the door.

"Kane, Kane. Don't race out like that." Dr. Smith stops me in my tracks. "Here, here's your writing, your manuscript."

"Oh. Thank you, sir." I turn back and take it from him. Try to leave.

"Wait, Kane. What's your hurry?"

"I'm not settled with this woman thing, Dr. Smith. And I stopped by the memorial construction and that got me going."

"Well, after reading your writing, I came to a realization."

"Sir?"

"When did you read it last?"

"Christ. I don't know. Years, I guess."

"That's what I thought. Read it again."

"Why?"

"To refresh your memory. Let's just say, it's more homework."

"Okay. I will."

• • •

"I read *Veteran's Day*, Dr. Smith," I admit, walking into his office without knocking. He whirls around in his chair, leaving his typewriter humming.

273

"And?"

"And what . . . ? After the first battle, when I lost Eddie, then we were ambushed in the wet creek . . . well . . . "

I slump into a chair next to his desk. "That was when I realized I wasn't going to get out of Viet Nam alive. That is when this futility and despair I carry around with me . . . that is when it set in."

"You've never admitted to futility and despair before."

"Well, I'm admitting to it now." I look at him warily. "C'mon, man, don't challenge me. I need someone to trust. This is strong stuff I'm trying to release."

"I'm not challenging you. I realize how vulnerable . . . rather, the chances you feel you're taking. I hope you can trust me."

"Yeah, well, anyway, after that first battle . . ." I readjust uneasily in the chair. "I couldn't get all that happened down on paper. The rest of the story is the war experience jumbled together."

"Well, you did a very good job of organizing it."

"Yeah, maybe with a story on paper, but not with my life."

"Yes, that's true."

"And the names."

"What about them?"

"The names are slang. They don't go with faces. They seem jumbled together too, like the battles. Maybe that's why this memorial they're putting up has me so uncomfortable. It's not because it's black, or in the ground. It's because it's names. Names I may remember. Names that will mean faces. Maybe that's why we called each other by nicknames, so we wouldn't have to know each other. Now that's in jeopardy."

"I think you have to take one thing at a time here, Kane."

"Huh?"

"First, I think you have to reorganize your war experience. That may help in organizing your life."

"I was really organized over there, you know. Had to be, as a medic."

"I've had some experience in the profession."

"Oh, yeah, right."

"So. What should we do?"

"Well, I think these group meetings are really good for me."

"Yes, they are. What else?"

I pause. What else? What else? "Oh, staying sober seems to be helping. Staying clean. I mean, I'm raw, but really clearheaded."

"Which means it may be a good time for what?"

Good time for what? Good time for what? Get laid! Find a job? Settle down?

"Kane?"

"Huh?"

"Don't you think it would be a good time to review your experience in Viet Nam? You said the battle scenes were confused. Don't you think you could write the experience in another fashion?"

A rush of fear floods over me. Relive it again! Christ! What does he think I am? Crazy?

"What! Again!"

"Why not? You've shown some courage and determination to get this far, why not relate the experience as you realize it now?"

"Well, you know that anniversary theme has really sparked something in me."

"How so?"

"Well, I go through annual phases of uneasiness and erratic behavior that seem to coincide with certain holidays. I realized that Veteran's Day and the massacre at Ia Drang really were on or about the same day. I have a terrible time every year about that time."

"See? There's a point of reference!"

"Yeah, but how can I kick out of the isolation of those experiences? I have no one left who was there with me, at least, no one I can contact."

"That's not true."

"Huh?"

"You have the group."

"Oh?"

"You're not alone. None of you men are alone. You all have the experience of combat. You have no reasons to isolate yourselves."

"Ha!" I exclaim, as if I'd just discovered something. "Right!"

I stand up. "Hey, thanks. I'll give that some thought."

"You're doing quite well, Kane. Now, if you'll excuse me."

"Yeah, right." I turn to exit, pause. "Hey, thanks, man, er, Dr. Smith."

"Sure . . ." He nods, starts to turn back to his work, then pauses. "Oh, Kane, by the way. About the crater scene in *Veteran's Day* . . . ?"

"Yeah?" I turned to him.

"The woman in the bottom of the crater . . . ?"

"It was a goat."

"Christ! Most of the time it was just monotonous."

"No bullshit!"

"Just walking in the heat and humidity, day in and day out. While Cong hid."

"All the rice paddies looked the same."

"Unless it was wet paddies versus dry paddies."

"Leeches in wet paddies!"

"Bitch ants on dry paddies."

"We're aware of the leech problems in rice paddies, but what are bitch ants?"

"They're red ants, about a quarter inch long, that unleash a stinging bite, Dr. Gates," Sully advises. "Their nests were set up in the shrubs that line the paddies. We'd have to pass through the shrubs to get from paddy to paddy. The little fuckers would hitch rides on us as we scraped the bushes, sort of like ticks do back here."

"Fastest strip I ever did," Berns admits. "And not

very dignified for a second lieutenant to be gyrating around, trying to rid himself of those bitching bites.''

''Really!''

''We'd walk all day in that heat. Be exhausted by dusk. Sleep. Do my radio watch. Be up at dawn and do it all over again.''

''Find a clump of bamboo, split one at a joint, soak our kerchiefs in the water sop stored there. It was about the only way to cool off.''

''Heading into the jungle wasn't much better. It got you out of the sun, but it was more humid.''

''You'd have to wrestle with every kind of vine, tree. All sorts of vegetation that snagged your weapon. Hooked your ammo belt. Caught your backpack.''

''It was hotter in the fucking jungle than out in the open.''

''No, it was just more humid.''

''Never did like walking out in the open.''

''But the jungle, the ambushes were always on the trails.''

''Or at the LZs.''

''We'd scrap our way to the top of a hill, sometimes it took all day. Then we'd be met by those little land leeches.''

''Were they different than the leeches found in the rice paddies?''

''Much. They looked like inchworms, very small. They'd not feel as obvious when they started sucking blood.''

''They'd get in the waistbands of our pants, down in our socks.''

''Under arms.''

''The crotch.''

''Had a dude have one crawl into the head of his dick!''

''Oh, bullshit, Point Man.''

''Fuck you, man, I saw it.''

"Yeah, right. I can just see you eyeballing some guy's pecker for a land leech, Point."

"Fuck you guys."

"We used the mosquito repellent on the land leeches. First, spray it on them, or spray a stream of the stuff in a circle around where we'd sleep. The little fuckers wouldn't cross the stuff."

"They'd fall out of the trees."

"At least the repellent was good for something. It didn't do any good for the mosquitoes."

"Really! The mosquitoes would suck you dry overnight."

"Malaria," I blurt. "Sickest I've ever been. Fucking mosquitoes kicked our asses. The central highlands were notorious for mosquitoes, and wait-a-minute bushes."

"Wait-a-minute bushes! I almost forgot about them."

"I did more hand-to-hand with the wait-a-minutes than the Congs. Those bad boys stopped me in my tracks."

"What were wait-a-minute bushes, Mr. Washington?"

"Dr. Gates, they're these bushes with tiny little thorns all on their vines and stems. You'd brush them, push them with your hand or arms, those thorns come off in your skin, prick through your clothes. Almost jump on you!"

"Point Man's not exaggerating, Dr. Gates. They were bastard bushes to move through," Sergeant Pepper adds.

"You had to tell everyone to wait a minute, so you could get the fucking vines off you."

"The little thorns would still tear the skin enough so the salt from your sweat would make the sting more like a burn," I recall, then flash on Kelly, our point man, leading us through the monotonous days of October and November 1965. If it wasn't wait-a-minute bushes it was the mosquitoes. It was the leeches. It was malaria. It was tedious. Walk. Walk. Walk. Day in, day out. Hot. Hot. Hot. Week in, week out—110 degrees, 112 degrees, 115 degrees. Never seeing Cong. Walked all the way to Cambodia and back. Up mountains, through empty Montagnards' villages. Then there were the . . .

"Punji stakes," I belch out, almost burping up stomach bile at the recall of the punji spike that strikes chest high. The trap set to pierce the skull. The point tearing at fatigue pants, groin high.

"Really, punji stakes were always ready," Sergeant Pepper admits.

The stake that stuck me in the crotch. The ankle stakes that so easily pierced my leather jump boots.

"Mr. Kane."

"Yeah?" I turn to Dr. Gates.

"Where are you?"

"Ia Drang Valley, October, no, November 1965."

"You said 'punji' stake?"

"Yes. Along with everything else, punji stakes were ever present. Sticking up out of the grass. Whipping out over the trails. Anywhere you moved. There they were.

"Holes dug so you'd drop on them."

"Montagnards used them for snares too, for animals. We'd just happen to run into them."

"Ia Drang Valley was the first big battle of Viet Nam. Were you there, Doc?"

"For about five weeks, then the Seventh Cav relieved us. They were massacred. We went back to save what was left of them. It was hard to understand. We walked that valley from October right through to November. We looked all over the place for Cong. We crisscrossed the valleys and mountains so often, the place was ours. After a while, the powers that be stopped the chopper resupply because they thought it was giving away our position. We lived off the land. Raided Montagnard vegetable gardens."

"Those little red peppers were the hottest fucking things I've ever eaten."

"The Spanish brothers loved them raw."

"We collected water by funneling the leaves of bushes so the night dew would drip into our open canteens."

"That was some sweet water."

"Just was never enough of it."

"Folks back here don't know what it's like to go thirsty."

"Or hungry. We ate the roots of plants, wild pineapple, mangoes."

"Coconut."

"Everyone ate coconuts."

"Water buffalo," it dawns on me, "Two-Tone shot a water buffalo. She was pregnant. We ate it raw, even the embryo."

"Oh, Doc, no!"

I whirl to Pax, who sits there grimacing. I flush, not like embarrassed, more like defensive. I turn back to Dr. Smith. "I guess I have to write it out, don't I, Dr. Smith?"

He nods.

"Gentlemen, time's up."

•   •   •

VETERAN'S DAY, 1965
IA DRANG VALLEY

"Drop your cocks and grab your socks. On your feet and into the heat. The Seventh Cav has been ambushed by the 325th People's Army of North Viet Nam in the Ia Drang Valley. We got to go bail them out."

It's hot, 110 degrees in the shade, but that doesn't matter, except that it hastens the smell of decaying bodies. We start sweeping the valley we've swept so many times before. This time, it's different. The B-52s have swept it. It doesn't need sweeping anymore. The valley floor is pockmarked with bomb craters and leafless plant life. The jungle hills are twisted and split from the shrapnel of Air Force and artillery bombardments. This is not the same place we'd lived in for six weeks. It's not livable anymore.

"We need water, Doc!"

"Don't tell me, tell Henderson."

"We're headed that way," Henderson says, without prompting.

We come up on a creek bed. A couple of guys rush to its edge to fill their canteens.

"Remember to use your iodine tablets, gentlemen," I remind everyone.

"You heard Doc, men, put those tablets in your canteens, fill them, and wait five minutes for the iodine to dissolve."

"Right, Sarge."

"Hey, Doc, how's this?" Grub shows me a tablet, pops it into his mouth, then takes a swig of water.

"Almost, Grub."

"Ah, I'll get it right one of these times, Doc."

"No hurry, we got all the time in the world," I say, looking about for some privacy to take a leak. I don't know why. I follow the creek as it makes a turn and step out of sight of the others. I unbutton, and tinkle, sizing up the desolation as my bladder empties. I spy a pile of enemy lying in the creek upstream. There are about six of them, soaked, bloated. They make for an interesting mix as they decompose. Buttoning up, I step back down the creek and around the bend. The guys are feasting on the water as if it were wine. I don't say anything. I don't know why. Henderson orders us to saddle up. We move away from the scene, none of them any wiser.

We begin to sweep across a rubber plantation. That's a place where they grow condoms. Bad joke, you're right. I don't know what's come over me. It just isn't civilized out here. We kick through dead vegetation with no idea what killed it. Dead leaves cover dead bodies that we stumble over in hot pursuit of what's left of the 325th People's Army of

North Viet Nam. Our helicopter gunships skim the treetops above. Air Force P-40s streak in the same direction. We come up on some of our men from C Company.

"Hey, Farmer, is that you?" I call out, close enough to see a medic friend ministering to one of the enemy troops. I step over the VC. Note he's closer to dying than living. Farmer's giving it his best shot, anyway. He looks up momentarily.

"Hey, Kanie," he says, tying off a compress. "There, that ought to do ya, Mr. VC," he says, standing, stuffing gauze and compresses back into his aid bag.

"Not a bad job of lifesaving, Farmer," I judge.

"Thank you, Kane."

One of the group steps up to the wounded enemy. Puts his rifle to his shoulder, aims down.

Blam! Blam! Blam!

The body bounces in repercussion.

"Well, fuck almighty," Farmer says, jutting out his jaw.

No one is the least bit affected by the event. I look to the victim. He's for sure dead. I look to the rest of the men and comment, "If you guys plan on shooting these fuckers, please let us know. We can do a lot more with our compresses and tourniquets than wrap them around dead people."

We traverse a slow rise, stepping among the leafless rubber trees. Crunch. Crunch. Crunch. Viet Nam exported such products as rubber, tea, and lumber, until Western civilization started importing war. Shuffling through the autumnlike scene, we arrive at a small band of American troops sitting around a burner of coffee. They are not of our battalion. They are not of anyone's army for that matter. They are of the survivors' army.

"These must be the boys from the Seventh Cav,"

Henderson comments. "Hold here. Don't bunch up. Spread out. Spread out."

He steps to their man in command. We fan out through the trees. I take in the sickly scene. There are about a dozen VC hanging dead in the trees. They had tied themselves to the trunks and tree limbs so they wouldn't fall out. Their weapons sling lifeless below them. They are burnt and bloated. Napalm.

The smell of true death is in the air. Decay has set in like a fog. There are no life signs. There are no life sounds. Henderson returns. Stops alongside me. Comments, "They got caught in a horseshoe-shaped ambush. Gooks in the trees did most of the damage, killing off ninety percent of the company. The Air Force dropped napalm to get them off the hook. Nothing left for us to do but sit and wait for our next orders."

I look out at the battlefield scene. "Mind if I step out there and take a look?"

"Don't let me lose sight of you."

I step out among the scorched trees. Their burnt limbs hold men and weapons in a macabre embrace. A still life of death masks filling a death scene in Death Valley. I walk beneath the remnants of human beings dressed in black PJs. I keep an ear open for a whisper, a moan, a rifle bolt to cock, anything to signify life. Not a sound. I come upon one who has been burned out of his perch. He lies on his back, swollen and bloated from fire and time. One leg is shattered to above the knee, exposing the bone. I pause, wonder, bend down, and tear off a piece . . .

•   •   •

"Mr. Kane?"

"Ummh."

"Mr. Kane, where are you?" Dr. Gates asks, bringing me back to the group.

283

"Oh, nothing, just been thinking about some things I'm writing. Dr. Smith suggested I try to settle the confusion I have about my tour. I'm concentrating on writing around the anniversary theme."

"I'd like to read your writing, Doc," Sergeant Pepper says.

"Yeah, maybe," I mutter.

The door swings open. Dr. Smith enters. "Sorry I'm late fellas . . . Dr. Gates."

All eyes follow him as he sits.

"Dr. Smith. Dr. Smith. I got a question. We bin talkin', some of us, 'bout this readjustin' to society after living over there in Nam, living like animals."

"Not animals, Point."

"Dr. Smith, we come back feeling like we're on the outside looking in."

"Not all of us, Dr. Smith, some of us come back and go right into police work."

"What Point is trying to say is contrary to what Berns commented on. Some of us have the sense of living outside the law."

"Outlaws."

"We were raised as Christians, to live by God's law, then we went over there and killed. That made us feel outside the law. We killed. We broke God's Fourth Commandment. We are outlaws."

"But it was a situation, as soldiers representing our government, we can be excused from. We had to kill or be killed."

"I don't need to be excused from nothing. I didn't mind killing."

"It was the wild west over there, lawless, untamed, shoot 'em up."

"Really, we were the law over there."

"Whoever had the gun was the law."

"Whoever has the superior firepower is the law. It's true, even to this day, in all the world."

"We weren't always the law. That's what the ambush

was all about. One side catching the other side off guard and killing them. Running them out of town, so to speak."

"Where we patrolled was called Dodge City. There was always something happening there."

"We had a firefight that was like the gunfight at OK Corral. We accidentally met these gooks outside this village. Five of them, five of us. Shot it out. We got 'em, killed three, two ran. They zapped Beans, wounded the Greek and Stevens. Me and Magic made it through without a scratch."

"There was a certain thrill to it."

"Life back here is pretty boring, that's for sure!"

"It was instant hysteria. Insanity at its highest level. The ambush, the kill zone, were total terror."

"Killing someone is the most powerful thing in the world."

"It's the best way to control."

"It's the ultimate control."

"The air assault is so insane. Fly into a landing zone at a hundred miles an hour below the treetops, gunships blazing away. The speed, wind, noise . . ."

"Yeah, and if Charlie was waiting for you, guys were hit and falling out of the choppers. Choppers were blowing up in midair. On the ground. Flipping over."

"I'd get a hard-on."

"We were crazy to do that shit."

"It was the most terrifying, insane experience anyone who wasn't there could realize. Movies don't even do it justice. It leaves you with a touch of hysteria, madness. It stays with you forever."

"Flashbacks."

"How 'bout on-line ground assault? Stepping out into the open? Deathly silence. Spread out and sweep across the paddy or up the hill, exposed like a bare ass. Charlie waits till you're so far out in the open you can't get back to cover. Blam! Mowed us down."

"When the shit hit the fan, the seconds were minutes, the minutes were lifetimes. People falling, clutching at throats, stomachs, legs, faces. Terror, pain, screaming. Firing at everything that moves. So much fucking violence!''

"The sounds of fear."

"The smell of fear."

"A few ran from it. Most stopped in their tracks. Whoever was left would lead. That's what it was all about. Those that could. Those that did. Those that wouldn't.''

"It was so confusing. Such terror."

"It didn't matter who you were, or even what rank. The test was the first fight you were in.''

"Marines had it worst, with Khe San.''

"Oh, bullshit, Point. Everyone had it worst.''

"The army had Ia Drang Valley, Hamburger Hill.''

"It didn't matter in the long run. If you had better training, you could avoid something a lot of the regular grunts couldn't.''

"It's such hype, who was the baddest. That's where the rivalry was confusing. Thinking you were bad because you had more guys die in battle. Bullshit, that's not the sign of being tough. The best are the ones with the most kills and the least casualties.''

"The Koreans over there were ruthless.''

"They killed everyone and everything in a village before we could get there to stop them.''

"That's the only way to wage war!''

"I'm saying the uniform doesn't make the difference. Look at the Jews in World War II, they walked to the gas chambers like so many thousands of sheep. Now they are the most ruthless aggressors in the world.''

"It depends on the background of the people.''

"Your superior firepower.''

"How civilized your society is.''

"We feel guilty when we come back because we killed, and in killing, we broke our Christian code. We broke the Commandments. We stepped over the civilized line. We will never be the same again.''

"Mr. Kane, you haven't said much throughout this whole conversation."

"Can't seem to get rid of this bad taste in my mouth."

• • •

Henderson hands me the smoke grenade.

"We called the chopper, Doc. Better head over to the high ground and pop the smoke. Med evac should be along directly."

"Yeah, right, see ya." I turn. Try to figure out where I'm going.

"And get your ass back out here when you're feeling better."

I stumble away without answering. I'm burning up with a fever that leaves me speechless. Three times in the last twenty-four hours, I flush, shake and chatter. The first signs of malaria. I finally take my temperature. One hundred and one. Tell Henderson, "Mosquito finally got me."

Whup. Whup. Whup.

"Better move your ass, Doc. Chopper's only going to make one pass."

Whup. Whup. Whup.

I try to tear through the wait-a-minute bushes. Struggle toward the clearing, yanking at the pin on the smoke grenade. Christ! No strength. Whup! Whup! Whup! I feel so fucking sick. Whup! Whup! Whup! Wait, you bastards. Whup! Whup! Whup! I'm gonna die. Whup! Whup! Whup! I'm gonna fucking die . . .

I turn the corner of the Quonset hut. The aid bag slips off my shoulder, catches in the crook of my arm. I grasp at my pants as they fall. I didn't button them after taking a dump in the middle of the med evac LZ. The shit feels like it's still running down the back of my leg. I wish I hadn't unbuttoned my shirt. What was once too hot is now too cold. I'm so fucking thirsty, I'm enjoying the taste of the sweat trickling off my lip.

"Well, hello there! Are you coming to see us?"

I turn to a voice I would love to hear in a dream. It's a woman. A real, round-eyed, white woman. No, the malaria has caused delirium. I'm seeing things.

"What have you got, honey? Malaria? Where's your tag? Didn't the medic tag you before he sent you in?"

She has auburn hair that lies in a languid turn under a chin of ivory white skin. She has round blue eyes. She looks like all my lovers. If I'd ever had any round-eyed lovers.

"Did you come in all by your lonesome, soldier, or did the chopper cowboys bring you in?"

The auburn hair, so red. The round eyes, so blue. The white skin, so ivory white. She's in the wrong place. She wears a green fatigue shirt with captain's bars on it. The shirt is half-unbuttoned, exposing an ivory-white cleavage. That warms my imagination. She'll get rid of the chill.

"Did the medics send you in, honey, or did you come in all by your lonesome?"

"I am a medic," I admit, breathlessly. "Mosquitoes finally got me. No strength to write a tag, but I'd fuck you in the middle of a firefight."

"Well, now, that's real sweet of you, dearie. I'll bet you didn't realize you could get it up until your first firefight. Come on over here and let me take your temp. You look a little disorganized there."

I let the aid bag fall. So do my pants. I grab for them, weakly. Waddle to the cot. Sit.

"I could help back here. I'm Doc Kane. I got experience. We could get married, settle down, raise a family."

"You are delirious, babycakes. Now hush up and hold this thermometer under your tongue . . . that's

288

it. For god sakes, you couldn't be much older than my baby brother. Give me a wrist so I can check your pulse. What'd you do? Shit your pants too? You must be a sick puppy. Pulse isn't very good. Let me feel that forehead. God! You're burning up. Let's see that temp, 102 already. Come here, baby boy. Lie down."

That's right, mama, let's you and me lie down alongside each other. I got a temp so strong, you'll never be cold. I'm a boss medic. I'll take care of you. I can help with everything but math . . . I flunked math, you know. That's why I didn't graduate from high school. Oh, God! That feels good. It's so nice to lie down. Come down here beside me, Captain. God! I'm tired. Maybe I'll sleep a little before we get married, then I'll take that math test.

"Here, honey. I have a little something for you, for your fever. Take these APCs. I'm going to put this towel on you."

Jesus Christ! That towel is cold. I need water for these fucking pills. Why give me cold towels when I'm shivering already?

"Here's some water, sweetie."

Christ! It's so hot, so cold, so dark. If you're not going to marry me, then kill me. If you're not going to marry me, round-eyed, red-haired white woman, then kill me. . . . Love me or kill me.

"Kane. Kane. Can you hear me? This is Dr. Iverson. You keep fading on us. We're going to med evac you, son. Out of the country. We're going to send you to Okinawa. You have malaria pretty bad. You'll get better treatment there."

Just as long as you send a round-eyed woman with me. Not that I have anything against slant eyes. My first piece of ass was a slant eye. I'm just used to living with round eyes. Okinawa, where's that? If the round eye doesn't go with me, I'd just as soon die. Die and get it over with. This is too much to take. First hot, then cold. Joints ache so bad. I can't bend them. So stiff. Too many blankets. Not enough blankets. Thirsty. Always thirsty. Too dark. Get that flashlight out of my face. I don't care where I go. Okinawa, Ia Drang, Happy Valley. Hell! Get me out of this limbo. Kill me. Quit all the indecision.

"Private Kane. Private Kane. Can you hear me? Hospital policy warrants that when a temperature gets above 104, we have to use ice. You're over 105, so we have to pack you in ice."

Goddam! Send me back to Viet Nam. Okinawa ain't no better. Christ! It's so fucking cold, then hot. I ache. I thirst. Exhausted. When will it be over? When will it be over? When will it be . . . ?

". . . O, little town of Bethlehem, how still we see thee lie . . ."

Where is that coming from?

". . . above thy deep and dreamless sleep . . ."

Angels singing. I got my wish. I'm in heaven. No, I couldn't be, those are casement windows over there, like they have in hospitals. There's a nightstand.

". . . the silent stars go by."

Angels are singing. They really are, outside the window. It's got to be angels; it sounds like them. Is this a hospital in heaven?

"Hark, the herald angels sing. Glory to the new-born King."

Christ, it's Christmas. I forgot there was such a thing as Christmas. I thought life was ice baths and firefights. I'm so tired. Oh, it hurts. Oh, God, the ice is so cold. Would someone please hold me? Warm me? So I don't sh . . . sh . . . shiver s-s-so.

Tears start to roll off my cheeks. They sizzle as

they hit the ice water. The hot and cold mix up a lukewarm sadness as I lie in this cruel situation. It doesn't look like I'm going to get to go to heaven. I guess that's a good reason to cry. . . .

"Okay, Mr. Kane. We're going on a little adventure. We're going to start by seeing if you can get out of bed and into this wheelchair."

"Sure, no problem," I say to the nurse, sitting up slowly. The sheets pull at me a bit with dampness. They trail as I slide out of bed. Whoa! Little dizzy. Take three slow steps. Turn. Sit down, slowly.

"You did that like a pro, Mr. Kane."

"Fuckin' paratrooper, ma'am." I turn and look up at her. She's a round eye, dressed in a starched nurse's uniform. She wears captain's bars. She has freckles.

"First, we're going to weigh you, Mr. Kane. Then a shower. Do you feel up to taking a shower, Mr. Kane?"

"I sure could use one. It's been since . . . since . . . What time is it now?"

"About ten-thirty in the morning."

"No, I mean, is it still December?"

"January, Mr. Kane. January 12, 1966."

"Good time for a shower."

We wheel into the bath area. She stops.

"I put a chair in the shower stall for you to sit on if you get tired. No, don't go in there yet, Mr. Kane. Step over here first. Here. I want you on the scale. I want to weigh you."

A bit dizzy from standing so quickly, I turn slowly from the shower to the scale. Step up. She pushes the little weights across the notched bars.

"Goodness! You weigh less than you look. My God!"

"What?"

291

"Seventy . . . seventy-eight pounds. You weigh seventy-eight pounds, Mr. Kane!"

• • •

"Mr. Kane, you've been very quiet these last couple of meetings," Dr. Gates comments.

"I'm listening, thinking, realizing, Dr. Gates. I'm doing work outside the group also. Writing."

"Well, are you getting anything out of these meetings, this hospital stay, Mr. Kane?"

"Of course I am, Dr. Gates. I mean, it's pretty uncomfortable going through some of this recall, but I think it should do me some good."

"It ought to get easier to handle as time goes on, Kane," Dr. Smith adds.

"Do you have anything you want to share with the group, Mr. Kane?"

"Ah. No. No. I'm writing it down, maybe in due time. . . . Wait, there is something I'd like to get off my chest. The guys could understand, relate to this."

"Shoot, Doc."

"Yeah. It bugged me when people would ask me about Nam, after they found out I was there. I'd tell them I was a medic. The first thing they always asked was if I'd killed anyone, or if any of my friends died."

"Or if we saw anyone die."

"Whatever . . . even after I'd remind them I was a medic, they still were concerned with killing and dying."

"So, Doc? That's what we did."

"No one ever asked me how many lives I saved."

"Ohhh, that's heavy shit, Doc."

"Heavy, shit! It hurts. It's like all these morbid fuckers back here want to know about is the rotten stuff."

"Well, Kane, death does have an aura of mystery to it. People find that killing . . . people who have had something to do with killing are different."

"When you do it, you realize it's easier to kill people than to save people."

"Especially under fire. You're right, Doc. Our Doc was something. He got killed trying to save the lieutenant."

"That's what you learn in war, that it's easy to kill."

"There's another thing that's bothered me since I've been back. About how people react to my experience."

"What's that, Mr. Kane?"

"No one ever asked me if I learned anything in Viet Nam. All that time and experience under the most strenuous conditions, and no one thinks you learn anything from it."

"Hey, yeah, Doc. What did we learn over there?"

"It's easier to kill than to save lives."

"There's got to be more than that to it. All these wars, after all these years . . . centuries. If we didn't learn something from them, then why do we keep getting into them?"

"Something to think about for our next meeting, gentlemen. Time's up."

• • •

BONG SONG—FEBRUARY 1966

I drop from the chopper. A couple of men heave bodies aboard for the return trip. I help, pushing in dangling arms and legs. It may seem callous to treat our dead this way, but we have to fit as many on as possible. Cong ain't gone, and he likes to collect ears, fingers and peckers as much as some of our guys do. The chopper lifts off without warning. The door gunner is hanging over his M-60, holding his nose and puking his guts out. Must be a fucking new guy.

The narrow valley settles into a dusky, deathly quiet. There never is a sound right before or right after an ambush. I readjust the shoulder straps of my gear, straining under the weight. I'm out of shape.

Heading toward the strongest smells and thickest smoke, I'm not sure of what I'm walking into. Are the guns resting? Whoever is left must be stunned. A whiff of fresh-turned dirt allows me one assumption. Mother Earth has had the wind knocked out of her.

I come upon a huge bomb crater. Slowing, I shiver at the sight of its destruction. I missed another one.

"Halt!"

Christ! I drop to a squat, reaching for a weapon, as I realize I don't have one.

"Don't shoot! Don't shoot! Doc Kane. Doc Kane," I whisper loudly at the falling darkness.

"Doc! It's you!" A dark figure stands up out of nowhere, ten feet from me. "It's me, Doc, Two-Tone!"

"Christ, Tone! You almost got me to shit on myself."

"We heard they evacked you to Okinawa, Doc," he drawls, approaching me casually, M-79 hooked in his arm.

"I was. They just sent me back. What happened there?" I gesture to the large hole.

"Compliments of our Air Force. Someone gave someone the wrong coordinates. One of our fly boys dropped a five-hundred-pound concussion bomb on Doc Alvarez and a bunch of his wounded."

"Oh." I looked down into the hole, realize a mutilated form at the bottom. "Is that Alvarez?"

"Naw! Alvarez lived through it. They poked him up on some of his own morphine. He's lying around here somewhere, stoned out of his mind."

"What happened to the wounded?"

"Dead, I guess."

"Who's that down there?"

Two-Tone pauses, looking into the hole. His tongue wets a cracked lip. "It's a goat."

We stand and stare. I'm lost in thought. Why the hell didn't I figure a way to find a ghost job while I was in the hospital? Why didn't that captain nurse take me up on my offer? We could be making love down at the bottom of the crater, instead of me standing up here at the top . . .

"C'mon, Doc." Two-Tone pulls at my sleeve. "I got a front-row seat for us at the all-night show." He pushes me to a crouch. We move through the falling darkness.

"Comin' through. Comin' through," he whispers hoarsely. "Doc Kane's with me. Doc's back."

Tone drops abruptly and rolls up against a three-foot levee. I just slam into it.

"Ooofff!"

"Welcome back, Doc," I hear from the left.

"That Robert O?"

"Shhh!"

"That's Henderson."

"No, Henderson is further down."

"How many of us are out here?"

"As the main line of resistance, we number eight."

"Eight?" I shriek.

"Shhh." That sounds like Henderson.

"Goddam, Doc," Tone whispers hoarsely. "There's about thirty dead or dying Congs 'bout thirty feet in front of us. You want them heading this way?"

"All right. All right. But Christ, Two-Tone, the truth of the matter is, I came out here without a weapon."

"What?" he says loudly.

"Shhh!"

I reach to hush him up. He clasps a hand over his own mouth. We listen for a reaction. The jungle sleeps.

"You ain't got a weapon!" he finally whispers. "Not even a .45?"

"Nope." I feel like a fucking new guy.

"Did you lose it?"

"No. They didn't have any at battalion. All three companies got hit at the same time. Weapons were supposedly sent up on the chopper ahead of me." I pause, and feel foolish. "Besides, I figured there would be a few weapons lying around out here. Always have been in the past."

"Christ, no, Doc, unless there are some out front. We picked everything up and shipped it out." He pauses. "Hey, wait!" He turns, cupping his mouth with his hands.

"Hey, Little Mike."

We're going to get shot yet.

"Yo!" comes a muffled response.

"Crazy Doc Kane's back. Came up without a weapon. You got something?"

"I think so."

"Bring it over."

"Okeydoke."

Two-Tone turns back, slaps me on the knee. "Gonna fix you up, Doc."

"Sure. Sure."

"Though you ought to have your head examined, coming out here without a weapon!"

"There's usually something lying around."

"I know, I know. But this ambush is different. We got our own dead still lying out on that hill to your right. Cong's lying to our left and front. The shit's still deep. No one knows who's going to come crawling out of the woodwork."

"Who bought it?"

"Anderson's platoon. I'm going out there soon as we fix you up with a weapon. Take a look-see. Maybe get a few scalps. Want to make sure you're all right, first."

"I've made it this far. I'll be all right. You won't be needing your M-79 if you're going to be crawling out there."

"M-79 ain't going to do you no good, Doc."

"Yo! Two-Tone, comin' over," a whisper comes from the right.

"C'mon over, over."

"On the way, wait."

There's the sounds of scraping and scampering. Then the appearance of a very young white face.

"Here you go, Tone. That crazy Doc Kane?"

"It's him. Doc, this is Little Mike. He was a FNG until today."

"Howdy, Little Mike."

"Hope you come for me if I'm hit, Doc. Here, here's a weapon for you. It's a Russian SKS, like our M-14. Got three rounds of ammo to go with it. Two for Cong, one for you. Sorry. That's all we could find."

"That's okay, it'll do fine."

"What the fuck is Doc going to do with a Russian rifle and three rounds of ammo?"

"Want me to take it back to Moscow and trade it in for an AK?"

"Get back to your hole, kid."

"Thanks, Mike, it will do fine."

"Sure, Doc. Good luck staying with Two-Tone. He's crazy." He disappears into the darkness.

"You gonna be squared away here, Doc?" Tone asks, not wasting any time.

I don't answer. I readjust my pack against the levee wall. Put my aid bag above it, turn, and lean on it. Pull the rifle against my chest, put the three rounds of ammo in my pocket.

"Doc, you just sit tight. I'm going out to have a look-see. Put this M-79 next to you."

"Right, get a couple of scalps for me, Tone. I'll send them home to my mom."

"You gonna be all right, aren't you, Doc?"

"Piece of cake. Piece of cake. Get your ass out there, Tone, 'fore you miss something."

"Okay, see you later, Doc."

He rolls over the ledge and crawls into the darkness. I readjust myself on the packs. Got to get settled. Goddam, I'm exhausted. I'm the only medic out here. Damn, where did they put Alvarez? Hope he's all right. Anderson's platoon gone. Dino gone. Goddammit! Dino couldn't wait to come out in the bush and be a Doc. Now he's dead. Christ! When will it be my turn? If something goes wrong in the middle of the night, what the fuck do I do? Crawl around until I bump into Two-Tone and he takes my scalp?

My mind starts to fog. Do I dare fall asleep? Ha! How the hell can I stay awake? Why the fuck am I back out here? Am I the last medic in the world? Christ! I don't even weigh 110 fucking pounds. I know. I know how I'll stay awake. I'll just think about that nice round-eyed, red-haired captain nurse with the blue eyes.

My groin begins to warm.

Luscious breasts, milky white, with tight, light red nipples. I'll lick them. Flick them. They'll get tighter under my tongue.

What if a Cong cuts my throat while I'm in mid-stroke? I won't hear him coming but he'll hear me coming!

She'll turn over on her back. Hiking hips, she'll slide out of fatigue pants. With my fingers, I'll trace little loops down so smooth a stomach. Circle, circle, circling my way around the subtle indent of her navel. I'll bend to it, licking at the little belly button hiding from my lips. My fingers'll get caught in the crop of reddish hair that guards the pussy fold . . .

Stop! No fucking way I can start whipping myself into a lather out here. Christ! Get those fucking hands away from there. Listen. Listen to the jungle night. It moans and gasps. The dying wish they were dead. The rest of us wish for our women. Fuck it, I'm gonna just lie here. I hope that if I fall asleep, I'll wake up before the bastard cuts my throat. Or I'll never wake up at all. Goodbye, Mom.

Goodbye, Dad. Goodbye, Gene, Greg, Chris, Marie
. . . Jane. Goodbye, Jane. I wish we had done it
before I left . . .

"Medic! Medic!"

"Doc Alvarez! Doc Kane!"

"Someone. We found someone of ours."

"It's Two-Tone. It's Two-Tone."

I struggled out of my dead man's sleep. Roll off
my pack. Grabbing the aid bag, I crawl over the
levee wall. Scrambling to my feet, I try to figure out
where the shouting is coming from. Why isn't there
any gunfire?

Is Cong gone? It's light enough to be dawn. Some
of the guys must already be up and noseying around.

"Doc, get your ass over here!" I turn in the
direction of the familiar sound of Henderson's order. Gone six weeks and this is how he welcomes
me back. I run toward a group of guys standing at
the tree line. Others come rushing from the left.

"Welcome back, Doc." Henderson scowls as I
reach the group.

"Yeah, right," I nod to him breathlessly. The
group parts. I drop alongside a body. It's Two-Tone.

"What happened?"

"Nothing, Doc. Cong's gone, left his dead behind. Don't know how Two-Tone got here."

I look him over, no life signs. There is a cord
wrapped around his neck, a portion of his scalp
missing.

"What about the others we couldn't get to last
night?"

"All of Lieutenant Anderson's platoon is dead."

Shit! Dino bought it, too. Fucking war. I search
around Tone's torso. Something in his breast pocket
. . . a playing card. I pull it out . . . the ace of
spades. Someone above me speaks.

"Get a close-up of that card, Adams. Soldier,

could you hold that playing card up by the man's face, so we can get a shot of it?''

I look up at a film crew taking pictures.

"Turn the card more this way, soldier. To the left. To the left."

* * *

I step into the room as quietly as possible.

". . . and it looks like it will be ready on schedule, so they are going ahead with the rest of the plans. A parade, then the dedication, with reunions at local hotels of all the armed forces units that served over there. It's something I've been waiting for since 1970 . . . welcome home! Did you catch all that, Doc?"

"Sorry I'm so late, you guys. I had to go through more interviews on this Agent Orange study. What is this about a reunion?"

"Veteran's Day. Mark that on your calendar, Doc. The memorial is going to be ready for dedication on Veteran's Day. The Viet Nam memorial committee has organized a parade and reunion, a 'welcome home.' We're finally going to be welcomed home."

"If it hadn't been for a few Nam vets putting up with a lot of bureaucratic bullshit, the memorial would still be a wet dream."

"Well, it's happening."

"I still can't get used to the idea of confronting all those names."

" 'Confronting,' Kane? Why 'confronting'?"

"It's going to instigate a lot of tough memories. I've tried to forget names."

"I'm not all that excited about recalling all those names either."

"Gentlemen, I'm sorry, but I must be excused. That doesn't mean you have to stop." Dr. Gates rises and bows apologetically.

"Yes, men, carry on if you please, but I too have to keep to the hospital schedule." Dr. Smith also rises.

They both head toward the door. The rest of the fellas lean back, relaxing, taking out cigarettes.

"Dr. Smith, wait!" I leap from my chair and follow him into the hallway.

"What, Kane?"

"I wanted to tell you . . . since I've been reviewing my tour, I realized how much I romanticized the war."

"What do you mean, Kane?"

"I don't know how else to say it."

"Dramaticized."

"Yes, that's another word for it."

"Kane, in all the years that I've been working with veterans, and that goes back to World War II, I have yet to encounter a war story that didn't have some sort of dramatics or romantics attached."

"But Dr. Smith, when I recall my war experiences, I realize it wasn't romantic. There is no need for dramatics."

He gives me a very inquisitive look. "So you're writing with that caution in mind?"

"No, sir, more like I'm reliving and rewriting the experience with a clear mind. I'm trying to set the record straight on what was depicted in *Veteran's Day*."

He begins to portray a sense of impatience. "Kane, really now . . ."

I cut his comment short, pulling out the bundle of letters from my back pocket. "Here."

He looks at my offer but does not take it. "What are these?"

"Letters. Letters to Two-Tone, a couple from Two-Tone. One from his grams."

"I was wondering what happened between you and him."

"He's dead. He was killed in Nam."

"Oh? That's not the impression you give in your writing."

"That's what I'm trying to say, sir. You see, there were two guys I became close friends with in Nam. One white guy, Eddie, one black guy, Two-Tone. We shared hopes, dreams, plans with each other. You know, for what we would do when we made it back from Nam."

I pause and choke something back that wells up inside me.

"Excuse me . . . er, well. Eddie got it on our first operation, that was the wet creek ambush, Happy Valley, October '65. That changed my perspective on life and everything. That's where *Veteran's Day* became confusing, er, not to you, but to me. Things became even more desolate by February of '66, when Two-Tone was killed. I didn't want to accept that. I remembered all the hopes and dreams we had talked about, so I put the way his future could have been on paper, in these letters. I didn't have anyone to talk with when I got to the States. I kept Two-Tone alive so I could express what was going on with me. I didn't want any of the guys, any of us, to lose out on the future. I tried to keep hope alive with these letters."

Dr. Smith takes what I offer.

"This last year, everything just got to be too much. After all these years of holding the experiences in. Drinking, ramming around, everything just became a disappointment. I became so depressed with my own loss of hopes, dreams, a future, I killed Two-Tone. I guess I was finally admitting I was killing myself."

"Well, I surely will look through them."

"If you would, please, it puts some things to rest, giving those letters to you. It brings things out in the open. It was a pretty rough thing to do, keeping him alive for so long. It's a pretty hard thing to do, keeping all those guys alive. I guess that's one good thing that the memorial will bring about. I'll have to accept their deaths."

I shiver involuntarily.

He looks at the letters, then at me. "Yes, I guess so."

I smile broadly. A huge load has been lifted from my

shoulders. "Maybe this will help me get on with my life."

He smiles. "It won't hurt. Er, clear something up for me, Kane."

"Sir?"

"What was this deal with Two-Tone and 'woman-slaughter'?"

"Oh, that happened for sure. I wasn't there though, I was in Okinawa with malaria, but Two-Tone got into a fight with some white dude over some whore down in Sin City. There was a bar there we hung out at, called the Sugar Shack. Anyway, Tone and this dude went at each other and this whore got caught in the middle of it. She paid the full price. There were charges pending when he was killed."

"Oh? And what, pray tell, was Sin City?"

"Oh, that was a government-sponsored town of bars and whorehouses where we could go. It was secure from the VC and VD."

"Government sponsored?"

"Sure. If the government can sponsor fighting, they can sponsor fucking."

● ● ●

MEMORIAL DAY—1966

OPERATION CRAZY HORSE

We leap from the chopper. It slides sideways off the makeshift log platform. The whirling blades flail at the humid air in a desperate attempt to gain altitude. We stumble under the prop blast, tearing ourselves up on the fresh-cut tree stumps. The chopper makes enough headway without our weight and escapes a crash into the mountainous jungle. As the noise of the machine subsides, we melt into the tree line. We'll wait for Henderson and the last load to come in.

This is LZ Hereford, fresh built by the boys from

recon. We were up on this ridge earlier today on another search and destroy mission. When we finished our sweep, we met C Company's mortar platoon at the other end of this ridge. I hooked up with their medic, Crocker. We chatted about stateside stuff. Henderson bickered with Shep, their platoon sergeant, off on the side.

"Saddle up, Doc," Henderson erupted, heading my way. "Saddle up. Shep just bet me we couldn't get back to fire base before his mortar platoon."

"But they're flying back!"

"Exactly. That's why we gotta saddle up and move it out. I got a case of Kool-Aid packets says we beat them back to base."

"Hey, Kane, you want to give me any gear so you won't have to carry it down?" Crocker asks.

"No thanks, man." I slide my pack up on my shoulders. When Henderson makes a bet, he intends to win.

"Move it out," he says, disappearing into the jungle.

No sooner said than done. We are down off the ridge and tramping across the valley floor, a rice cache burning behind us. We discovered it on the way down and fired it up. Now we're sliding our packs off our backs at fire base.

"Kool-Aid packets for everyone," Henderson announces. Everyone chuckles at the sight of the mortar platoon, visible up on the ridge, still waiting for the choppers.

Clouds begin rolling in. The humidity increases. The daily afternoon storm begins brewing a bit early. That's what Cong was waiting for. The approaching storm grounds the choppers. That leaves the platoon on the hill like sitting ducks. The rains start over the ridge. Little black-dot bastards dart out of the jungle, surrounding our guys. The assault, initially visible to us on the valley floor, is quickly covered by the storm. Pleas for help from the hill are monitored on the radio. The monsoon rain keeps any support from going to their aid. Then the radio pleas stop. Dead. The choppers that were supposed to pick them up come to pick us up.

The last chopper load balances perilously on the log landing zone. Henderson and the others leap off, lightening the machine's load. It slides, fighting for altitude, skimming the treetops, reaching for the sky. Then it's going, going, gone. When is it all going to end?

"All present and accounted for?" Henderson whispers, hoarsely. The inquiry passes quietly up and down the line.

"Affirmative," is the answer.

"Move out."

We spread out under the jungle canopy, stepping cautiously down the trail. It's so soaked with rain the silence is oppressive. We move toward another massacre.

Blam!

Christ!

Dive to survive.

Chunk! Yeeouch!

I see stars as I hit the dirt. Rolling in the jungle cover, I listen for more gunfire. I wonder if I'm hit.

"Hold your fire! Hold your fire! Hold your fire!"

I put the M-16 to my shoulder, flick the safety over to rock and roll, then freeze my finger on the trigger.

That's right, folks, Doc Kane is finally armed and dangerous. I ain't fucking around, even though my bell has just been rung. I'm seeing double from whatever hit me. It may mean twice as many to kill. It may mean I'm hit bad. It may mean . . .

"Doc! Doc! Doc, up!"

Wait a minute. I'm not calling for me yet. Let me find out how badly I'm hurt.

"They're calling you, Doc. Hey, Doc, they're . . . hey, Doc, you're bleeding!"

I roll to the side where Little Mike squats. I feel the warm flow of something down my neck. Blood drips on the stock of my weapon. Holy shit!

"Is it bad?"

"I don't know. Let me see." He noses around my neck and chin.

"Doc! Get up here!"

"Looks like you gashed your chin, Doc. Probably on the handle of the '16 when you hit the ground. Don't look bad."

"Oh." I turn the tip of my fatigue collar up against my chin.

"Ouch!"

It ain't bad. I get up slowly, a little dizzy.

"Doc!"

"Tell 'em you're hurt, Doc."

"Naw. I'm okay." I take a step, a bit unsteady, then another. My focus returns from double vision. I trod down the trail as the others step aside. They offer me various observations and explanations for my blood-soaked front.

"Go get 'em, Doc."

"Doc! Look at you, you're bleeding."

"You're bleeding like a pussy, Doc."

"You need a doc, Doc."

I come up on Henderson and Robert O standing alongside Horn. I join the view. A dead Cong with his chest blown wide open. Sticking out of his black PJs is one of the biggest hard-ons a man could hope for.

"What? Did you catch him fuckin'?"

"By himself, Doc?"

"Jerking off, then?"

"I surprised him, no?"

"Yeah, Horn, you surprised him all right. Doc, what do you think?"

"He died with a hard-on."

"We should all be so lucky," Robert O says, wistfully.

"Okay, roll him off the trail. Let's move out. Doc, you're bleeding!"

"Happened when the shot rang out. I hit the dirt. Hit my chin on the handle of my '16."

"I surprised him, no?"

"You sure did, Horn, now roll him off the trail and get back on point!"

"Okay, Sarge, but first . . ." He draws a knife from his belt, bends over, and slits the Cong's dick string. I fish through my aid bag for a compress. Pull one out. Prep it, and press it against my chin. I step over the body. Head on down the trail.

The jungle hangs in the heavy humidity. We walk in and out of the fog banks shrouding the mountain ridge. Everyone settles down and spreads out. I discard the compress, unsticking the scab. It starts to bleed, slowly.

Fuck it! It'll stop or I'll drop. I'm fed up with all this shit anyway. What the hell is that up ahead? Fresh-turned mounds of dirt? Nobody seems to be taking any notice. Looks like ant hills, now that I'm closer. Two ant hills of fresh dirt rippled with the rain's run-off. No, it ain't that either. Dirt from a bunker, or a foxhole.

No! It's a body! Everyone's walking right by him. He lies there on his back, knees bent up, leaning against a pile of dirt. His clothing is covered with a thin layer of dirt. I step off the trail. His face is uncovered. It's awfully pale, lost a lot of blo . . . he's alive! I fumble for my aid bag.

They left him for dead. He grins at me. I search through my bag. What am I doing? I don't know what's wrong, except that he lost blood. Look him over. Check his arms and legs. No blood spurts. No way of telling what's wrong. He's weak from exposure as much as anything. But still alive. I check under his chin, as someone checked under mine not long ago. His throat moves as he swallows. I look back at his face. His eyes widen. His nostrils flare. He works his mouth as if trying to say something. The smile turns to a frown. I check the eyes again. They glimmer. Black holes. Nose, flaring black holes. Mouth, black hole. What is that on his lips? They try to move. Get real close, lend an ear to what he's trying to say.

Maggots!

Christ!

His face and neck are crawling with hundreds of lily-white, wormy, fucking maggots. His whole face is contorting with their movements, smile to frown, comedy to tragedy. The worms turn. He's for sure dead and getting a final scouring. In another week, he won't even be here.

Goddam, I'm losing it. I get up in a daze. Realize the last man in line is standing there.

"C'mon, Doc, they're getting ahead of us."

"Goddam, I thought he was alive."

"You been working too hard, Doc."

"Yeah, maybe I ought to ask Henderson for the rest of the day off." I move ahead, quicken my pace to catch up with the rest of the crew.

"Doc, up!"

"Yeah. Yeah, I'm coming. I'm coming." The trail is harder to see as darkness sets in. The guys seem to blend in with the jungle. I pass them. Don't really know any of the names anymore. Not even sure of the faces.

"Still bleedin', Doc?" comes from somewhere off the path.

"No, I'm cool, I'm cool. Ho!"

I run right into Henderson standing at a bend in the trail.

"Doc, we're going to set up here for the night.

We're close enough to the massacre. I can smell the dead. Cong got some holes and bunkers set up here. We just sit down in them, maybe they'll come back. Got one special for you.''

"That's nice. Where?"

"Over here." He steps past me, just off the trail. "This is a good one. You can sight right down the trail where we came from. You said you wanted a body count of your own, right?"

"Damn straight."

"Good. Here's as good a place as any to greet them if they come trotting down the trail. Can you handle it?"

"I don't need any more motivation." I peer down at the foxhole. Covered with sturdy logs, camouflaged in dirt, leaves and shrubs, it has a step down into it.

"Okay, Doc, you're set. C'mon, the rest of you, follow me."

Henderson and the others turn and disappear into the darkness. I drop my gear into the hole. Turn, and sit on the roof. I cradle the '16. Strike a cigarette, giving my position. What the fuck am I doing? I cup the smoke, Nam style. No sense giving it all away. Got to watch my attitude, it's slipping. I'm getting careless. I slide from the roof, down into the hole. Sit on the step.

I peer out into the darkness at ground level. My stomach growls. Haven't eaten since I had a snack with Crocker. Poor Crocker, dead and gone. None of those guys made it, I'll bet. I'm getting fed up with losing all these good people.

I flick the cigarette out of the hole.

"Hey!" comes a cry from one of the bunkers behind me. "Douse the smokes, goddammit!"

Shit! I'm fucking up. Better get down deeper into the hole. I prop up the pack. Lie back on the bottom of the hole. I stretch my legs up on the step.

Set the '16 nose-out. C'mon, VC, come back to your holes. You got your dibs in this afternoon. You're feeling real cocky. C'mon back to your hole. I'm not leaving. As a matter of fact, I don't figure on getting out of this hole alive. I'm going to join Crocker and Eddie and Nevin and Two-Tone and Dino and I forgot how many. So come on, Mister VC, come back to your hole. We'll die together . . . in your homeland. . . .

Blam!

My eyes open wide. I struggle to turn around in the foxhole. I kneel on the step, placing myself and the '16 at the lip of the hole. Face down the trail, peering into the early daylight.

"C'mon, motherfucker, come back to your hole."

No more shots ring out. I hear a faint cry behind me.

"Shit!" I realize. Duck into the hole to retrieve my aid bag, then scramble back out onto the trail.

Horn sits on the roof of the foxhole behind me. He sees me.

"Doc," he says weakly.

I climb to my feet, pace back to him as I unfold the aid bag. His M-16 lies on his lap. The faint hint of heat curls from the barrel.

"Doc?"

"What did you do, man?" I step in front of him, look at the damage.

"Doc." The strain of pain shows plainly on his face. His good arm cradles a shattered forearm. He offers it to me.

"Doc." I turn a surly cheek to avoid looking at the mess. Remind myself of my job, bend to look. It's not so bad. He held the barrel at the fleshy underside of the forearm, just above the elbow. It's a neat little hole, no heavy blood flow.

"Lemme see the other side, man."

He tries to turn the arm over.

"Can't."

"You did a nice job, Horn."

"It was an accident, Doc. Honest."

"Right. Turn your arm over."

"I can't."

"Want me to turn it?"

"No! No! Aaaah."

He turns the forearm to expose a hole just below the wrist. The round burrowed between the bones, tearing muscle, fat, and tendon, then exited out this hole, very neat.

"Nice shot, man."

"It was an accident, Doc. Honest."

I go into my aid bag, pull out two compresses and a sling. He's not bleeding bad, no need for a tourniquet. Morphine? Naw, fuck it, save it for something heavy. He's tried this before and failed. Let him have the presence of mind to think it over, like for the rest of his fucking life. What makes guys like him do it? They don't believe? They don't trust us for support, to overcome the fear. They won't take the chance. They make their own chance. Isolate themselves. "I'll shoot myself," they decide, then the anticipation is over. The anxiety is gone. Choose your own wound. Name the day you go home.

I turn back to him. "Where's your canteen?"

"Right here."

"Take a couple swigs of water."

"This is it for me, ain't it, Doc? Looks like I'll be heading home, huh?"

$$\bullet \quad \bullet \quad \bullet$$

"If you are to defeat a man and you must do it at the risk of your own life, then you must destroy him totally. No rules. No laws. If you can't get at him. If he won't confront you but continues to harass you. You must destroy what he lives for. That's how the war is won. That is how you rule. That is how you control."

311

"And you live to tell about it," Berns says.

"Wipe out everything and everyone he lives for. If there is anything left standing, it will only be the man. He won't stand tall. He won't rebel. You've taken everyone and everything he'd rebel for. The women are gone. They won't love, nurture, or procreate. The children are gone. They won't grow up to be a threat. You won't have the responsibility of supporting the widows and orphans."

"Destroy his land," Point Man concurs.

"Then put him to work trying to make it productive again. Kill the spirit of the man. Kill what he lives for. Then make him do your shit work for you."

"Mr. Kane, when did you all of a sudden arrive at these assumptions?"

"You're talking pretty heavy stuff, Doc. Pretty deranged," Pax says.

"I didn't all of a sudden arrive at those assumptions. That's how I felt toward the end of my tour."

"Oh?"

"I just finished writing down the recollection of my last operation. My last anniversary date. Now I realize why I've been so troubled all these years. I've been living with those feelings."

"But it's what got you through the Nam, Doc."

"Can't be civilized. Go to war. Come back to be civilized."

"Yeah, that's the truth. When I looked back at how my tour started. And I took stock at the end of my tour. Then I realized how one makes it."

"You got to be lucky and tough."

"You don't have to be ruthless, necessarily."

"Bullshit. How many guys were killed or fucked up so bad because they didn't play the hard line?"

"Quite a few."

"Let me finish this, please," I ask. "I want to get this war off my back. It rules me. I don't want that. In writing *Veteran's Day*, I romanticized war. In writing

312

these anniversary recollections, I realized the ruthless person I had become. I was tough, all right, callous, hard, as much a product of war as anything else. Now I realize surviving, coming home, isn't all it's cracked up to be."

"War is a man-made disaster."

"Every battle, every ambush, booby trap, artillery barrage, bombing run, is a man-made disaster."

"Nuclear war is the ultimate man-made disaster."

"What I realize from my recollection is that the worst threat came at the beginning of my tour. My worst day in Viet Nam was the day before we walked down into that wet creek ambush in Happy Valley. I couldn't even put it all into words. That's when I realized I'd never get out of Viet Nam alive. The whole rest of my tour was spent just missing getting hit, or we would just miss getting ambushed, or the booby traps would spare me. I became a survivor by fate. Living through one man-made disaster after another. I developed an attitude toward man, and society."

"And that attitude is, Mr. Kane?"

"That man is cruel, malicious, insensitive. To his own as well as to others. Civilized as we are, we can revert so quickly to being animals."

"It's not easy to forget how to be an animal, once you've lived like one."

"Mr. Kane, I'm quite amazed at how you've seemed to open up more at these meetings. Could you share with us how it developed?"

"Well, first, I'm not finished." I turn to Dr. Smith. "I think I've had a hidden anniversary that lands around the time of the wet creek ambush. It has to do with baseball, ironically enough. I'm going to try to work that out before I hand you the whole recollection."

"Whatever you wish, Kane."

"How has this all developed, Mr. Kane?"

"Well, I'll tell you, Dr. Gates. My tour in Viet Nam,

and my behavior patterns back here, revolve around some pretty interesting dates."

"Let's hear them, Doc."

"Well, okay. I don't know if I'll be able to get this right, but so far, I know that I have a very hard time celebrating Veteran's Day, because every year, it brings back the memory of the carnage and massacre of Ia Drang Valley. I never dream of a white Christmas, I recall instead the nightmare of malaria and ice baths. Valentine's Day doesn't motivate me. I lost my heart in Bong Song as I struggled so futilely to save the life of a man I really cared about. Like so many men I really cared for, I wouldn't let him die until just recently. And every year for I don't know how many years, I've spent Memorial Day weekend crashing cars or bashing heads. It's as if I'm still waiting in the bottom of a VC foxhole, waiting to die in hand-to-hand combat so I can join my men in the vengeance that is death."

"I got in a fight last Memorial Day. We almost killed a dude."

"So did I, Point. Closest I've come to dying since Nam. First time I'd been ambushed since Happy Valley." I turn to him, tears brimming in my eyes. I haven't been this close to feelings in years.

"This white dude was beating up on a brother in the hallway of this building. We was downstairs and heard it. Me and another brother came up on them. I grabbed the dude from behind. We proceeded to whip the shit out of that motherfucker."

My tears subside. My eyes quickly dry. I recall a similar scene. "Point Man, was that last year, in an apartment building downtown?"

"Yeah, in D.C., on Columbia Road."

"Was the name of the building Beverly Court?"

"Yeah. Yeah. That's the place."

"Point, the white motherfucker you beat the shit out of was me!"

"Oh."

• • •

"Have you settled your differences with Mr. Washington . . . with Point Man, Kane?"

"Is that why you called me in here, Dr. Smith, to ask me that?" I wonder, sitting down in the chair across from his desk.

"That, and a few other things."

"Well, the answer is, there is nothing to settle between me and Point Man. I got beat. He happened to be one of three men who beat me. I was caught off guard, drunk. It was foolish to be caught that way in the first place. So, I got what I got. You know, Dr. Smith, it's a shame blacks and whites and browns and reds can't maintain the same kind of camaraderie back here in the States we did over there."

"Yes, I know. It is a sad testimony. There is a certain unity amongst you men, sitting in the group, but once you all step outside, it seems to go the many separate ways you all go."

"It's the difference between civilization and survivalization."

"Speaking of which, Dr. Gates and I have conferred with the nurses on your ward, and we think you're ready for civilization."

"Great! It's no fun being locked in every night with a bunch of crazies."

"How are you doing with the AA meetings?"

"Good. I've put together the prescribed ninety days and then some. I have meetings I can go to on the outside. I feel very comfortable not drinking. I think the best thing the hospitalization did for me was break me of the routine of drinking. It helped me to socialize myself away from that lifestyle."

"Yes, well, we think you've done very well with it. You ought to give yourself some credit."

"We'll see. It ain't over yet."

"Do you have somewhere to go when we release you?"

"I have somewhere to stay. I think that's one of the first things I have to do when I get out, stay in one place, not go anywhere."

"I didn't mean 'go' as in 'moving around.' "

"I know. I know. I'm just being real narrow-minded about how I think about things. By the way, I have the recollections of my battle anniversaries finished. Do you want to see them?"

"In due time, I haven't gotten to Two-Tone's letters yet."

"Oh, no hurry. One other thing. I wanted to expand on the first battle I was involved in, Happy Valley. I could never figure out what it tied in with until I realized the World Series is coming up. I am always drunk for every World Series. The wet creek ambush happened while the Dodgers played the Twins in '65."

"Don't write about it, bring this one up in the group."

"Ah . . . I don't know if I should. There's some anger in this battle I've never been able to express. I thought putting it on paper would be the best . . ."

"No. Present it to the other men. You'll be a good example for them to follow."

"You think so?"

"Sure."

"Well, okay. Is this all we have to cover?"

"Yes. Look for a discharge in the very near future."

"Sure. That means I can still come to group, doesn't it?"

"You'd better!"

I smile and rise, extend a hand. "Thanks a lot, Dr. Smith."

He bows his head shyly, but extends a hand. We shake.

"My pleasure, Kane."

"So I'm going to be discharged. I really feel good about what has happened with my stay here."

"You know, Mr. Kane, we never did follow up on what you said you learned in Viet Nam."

"Yes. I know. I've something to cover today that may satisfy that. I also plan on continuing these group meetings, even though I'm not in the hospital."

"We're family, Doc," Sergeant Pepper says.

"Yeah. I think you guys are a good replacement for my platoon, although I have some reservations about how involved I want to get with that again."

"I believe we all are wary of getting close after all the losses we suffered in Nam."

"There is something I want to get off my chest, you guys. I wanted to write it out, but Dr. Smith suggested I talk it out, so if everyone doesn't mind . . ."

"You always have interesting things to say, Doc. Speak."

"Thanks, Pepper, you've been a good support for me." I pause, wring my hands as a way of getting the anxiety cornered. "After reliving these anniversary recollections of my battles, I realized that the worst for me was the first operation we went on, Happy Valley. My baptism of fire turned out to be the most traumatic of the war for me. It was no Ia Drang massacre, but then, if we'd been caught like the Seventh Cav, I wouldn't be sitting here talking today. Anyway, I wrote about a big air assault into Happy Valley. It was hot! Humid. First casualty was our machine gunner. Heat stroke. I took him off the gun, put my best friend, Malewicz, in his place."

I pause, start to replay the scene that I've lived with constantly for years and years and years.

"Mr. Kane."

Dr. Gates brings me about.

"Yes, ma'am, sorry, just going into that Memorex thing again."

"The old instant replay."

"Right, Bernsy. So we're into the tip of the valley,

sweeping across the open rice paddies. Brandt's squad is on point, then the rest of us. Eddie shouldering the gun alongside me.''

"Shouldn't have the medic and machine gunner next to each other.''

"Like I said, Pax, we were green. So, all of a sudden, some gunfire from the tree line. We hit the paddy muck. It's third platoon. They're doing recon by fire. It shakes everyone up. Firing stops. Lots of shouts of 'Okay here. Okay there.' We get up. Move forward, wary. Pop. Pop. Pop, from up ahead. It's gunfire and it isn't M-16s. We take cover at a high dike wall. There are screams and more gunfire. Someone yells, 'Medic!' Henderson yells over at me, 'Doc, it's your turn.' 'Right,' I say. Eddie sets the machine gun next to me, bolts it loaded. There's more gunfire from our right and front. 'Cover me, Eddie,' I say. 'Right, Doc. See you later.' Those are his last words. I jump out in the open, run ahead through the rice paddy muck. These big raindrops start hitting all around me.''

"I bet the sun was still out, right, Doc?''

"I see Brandt's squad laid out in the open, pinned down. I race to them, singing, 'It's my party and I'll cry if I want to.' Weird, huh? Well, I'm happy as a pig in shit, because I'm getting to do my job, you know. Save lives.''

I look about at the group—rapt attention.

"That changes abruptly as I get to them and Cousins yanks me down. It isn't raindrops falling at my feet. I ignore the initial predicament by taking care of the wounded guy. He has a pretty bad shot in the arm. He's begging me not to leave. I square him away. Then I turn to Sergeant Brandt. He's shaking like a leaf, stammering and stuttering. He can't even give orders. I realize the predicament. Piss my pants. Henderson yells from behind us. 'Malewicz is dead. We're pulling back.' Christ! I wonder. How could Malewicz be dead? I just left him! Rocket gunships fly up behind us. Fire into the tree line.

Fly off. The wounded guy grabs me. The other guys around me start squawking. Cousins and I size things up. We decide to sprint, one by one, across the open area to a tree line behind us. The wounded kid, then each of the other guys, gets up, goes zigzag to better cover. The whole time, I'm saying prayers and goodbye to all my family and friends. This is like movie shit, except it's for keeps, with live ammunition and no time-outs."

"Tell it, Doc. Tell it."

"Shhh, Mr. Washington."

"It's down to three. Brandt finally gets the nerve to move. Then Cousins. It's just me. I look at what I have to sprint across. The guys are waving to me at the tree line. I jump up, start running my ass off. The gunfire kicks up water like huge raindrops around my feet, in front of me. I try to get my legs to go faster. They can't. I run right out from under them, sprawling headfirst in the water. Go down so hard, I knock the wind out of myself, gasping, choking, crawling. I look up to the tree line . . . they're gone. I'm flat out in the open, struggling away from death's door, and the guys in the tree line are gone. The fucking guys left me . . . my fucking people split . . ."

I stop, and look around at the group. The guys drop their eyes. Dr. Smith does, too. Dr. Gates looks me square in the eye.

"That's what I learned in Viet Nam, Dr. Gates."

"What's that, Mr. Kane?"

"Just because you risk your life to save someone else's life doesn't mean that others will do the same for you."

• • •

What time is it? Goddam, I better get my ass moving.

I throw the note pad and pen on the table, push out of the chair, search for my motorcycle keys. Since leaving the routine of the hospital I've been behind schedule on everything. Where are those damn keys. Wait, pat the pockets. Idiot, they're in your pocket.

Okay. Remember we aren't going to put ourself down. Right. Right. You're not an idiot, Doc. And you're not a Doc anymore either. Yes, I am. I'll always be Doc. It was the best job I ever had. Hey! it's time for war group. Get your ass moving, Doc-idiot.

I swing the door open, step down the hall. Wonder where the others are? Work, probably. Pass through the living room, open the front door. Keys, where are the keys to lock the front door. Charge back to my room, poke around the desk. There. Don't see why I should lock the door. I'd love to catch someone breaking in the house.

One more check at the door for everything. Keys. Wallet. Head. Belt so your pants don't fall down. Check.

Swing the door open to a pleasant September day. Beautiful, I can enjoy beautiful days.

I shut the door, key the lock, turn, race off the porch.

"Bang!"

"Yee hah." I drop to a crouch, heart pounding in breathless reaction.

"Bang! You're dead, mister. I shot you."

I stand slowly. My initial fear turns to embarrassment. I'm confronted by a five-year-old pointing an M-16 at me. He's dressed in camouflage fatigue gear, ammo belt and all. My embarrassment turns to anger.

"Kid, don't you point that thing at me."

Surprised at my comment, he drops the stock from his shoulder. The resolve melts from his expression.

"Don't you ever point a gun at someone unless you're ready to take the responsibility for killing them."

The eye he used to train the sights on me turns from a squint to a glint of fear. I've returned fire and it's hit its mark. His fear at my reprimand turns to tears. He drops the weapon to his side, turns and runs, scraping sparks from dragging the plastic barrel on the sidewalk. Frustrated at what I just did, I say aloud to the neighborhood, "What the hell was I supposed to do, clutch my chest, fall over and play dead?"

"I guess the best way to describe it is to say I have a short fuse. It is more obvious now that I'm back out in the big world where I have to deal with frustration, incompetence and anxiety everyday."

"That's a good way to put it, Doc, short fuse."

"What happened, Mr. Kane?"

"Little neighbor kid was playing war. Ambushed me. Scared the fuck out of me. I got all over his case for it. Scared him pretty bad."

"Can't take it out on the kids, Doc. It ain't their fault."

"I know. His momma probably dressed him up in the G.I. outfit to begin with. It also reminded me of a little kid we had to blow away in Nam. That kid threw real grenades."

"How come we got short fuses, everyone?"

"The stress of combat and living on the edge can burn a fuse down pretty quick."

"Fuses don't grow back."

"You shouldn't have jumped all over the kid, Doc. I don't know the whole story but it sounds like you were a little rough."

"The children must learn what it's like to be rough. They have to be ready."

"Bullshit, it will happen soon enough. Let them learn other things besides killing and survival."

"Doc, do you mean by short fuse, short-tempered?"

"Yes."

"I got a long fuse, want to see it, Pepper?"

"You're a sick man, Point."

"Gentlemen, our meeting doesn't seem to be going anywhere today."

"I haven't been going anywhere for years."

"What do you mean by that, Mr. Kane?"

"Oh, nothing, just capitalizing on your comment about the meeting not going anywhere."

"Are you adjusting to your new schedule? How is your housing situation?" Dr. Gates wonders.

"It's okay. It's me and four other people in a good-sized house. I get to be alone but I'm not isolated."

"Who do you live with, Doc?"

"Three women, one other guy."

"Wahoo, Doc, do you get something different every night?"

"No, Point, I don't. Did you ever hear of the saying, 'Don't play in the pool you piss in'?"

"No."

"Well, food for thought. Dr. Gates, I'm doing okay. I'm glad to be out, but you know, I don't seem to have the same enthusiasm for getting into the system like everyone else."

"We don't get the equal opportunities veterans used to get."

"It's not just that, Berns. It's more like . . . you know, I wish I could go on TV and say something like: 'I don't know if your skin cream or his racing machine or that condominium overlooking the eighteenth green is worth my nightmare screams.' "

"That's pretty good, Doc."

"People back here are cutting their Thanksgiving turkeys with electric knives and I can't find a can opener for my pork and beans."

"Should have saved your P-38 opener from Nam, Pax. See, I still got mine." Point displays a small can opener.

"I don't think that's what Mr. Paxton meant, Mr. Washington."

"It seems like the system passed us over."

"Folks back here, the ones my age and younger especially, they've not seen sacrifice, the loss, suffering that takes place for the freedom of personal independence."

"You mean personal indulgence."

"Shit. I'm seeing Vietnamese here get better jobs than I got."

"You'd help yourself if you'd learn to read better, Point."

"Fuck you, Pepper."

"Folks just sit in front of TVs, slurp beer, eat potato chips."

"Who?"

"Everyone, they just sit in front of TVs and consume. They watched us in Nam. They criticized us for going or for not doing enough. But so many of them could not stand up to the same challenges."

"Yeah, but war is such a fatal challenge."

"I didn't know anything about the system when I was eighteen. I just knew that where I came from there was nowhere to go after high school unless I wanted to get into trouble."

"Where are you from, Doc?"

"Upstate New York was where I was raised, a little town. It's a depressed area, no jobs. Like so many kids, I got out of the area by joining the Army. It was going to be fun, travel and adventure. I could jump out of planes and the draft board wouldn't be on my back. Next thing I knew, the shit was hitting the fan in the central highlands of Vietnam.

"So much for fun, travel and adventure."

"A lot of adventure, travel as far as your feet could carry you, not much fun."

"I mean, I'm glad to have survived and be living in this great country but I'm having trouble living with the other people who live here. They are enjoying the comforts of the system I can't seem to enjoy. I feel like I was sucked dry at nineteen years of age so everyone back here could be comfortable. I was not allowed any readjustment time when I came back. For years I don't really think I knew where I was."

"You were still in Nam."

"It's a shame you men can't give yourselves credit for how responsible you were over there. As a medic, Kane, you were very responsible. Why didn't that carry over back here?"

"I don't know, Dr. Price. Dazed. Confused. Drunk. Disorderly. You tell me."

"Short fuses. Burned out."

"Our responsibility now is to overcome our limitations and negativity. Temper our resentments and take advantage of the system."

"That's heavy shit to be saying, Berns. Mind explaining it so I can understand it?"

"Learn to read, Point Man."

"I'll say this. My hospital stay helped me to clear my head. Being sober and all that. Now I have to focus on releasing the negative feelings and experiences I have so I can make room for some peace, some comfort. The bad experience seems to perpetuate itself. Maybe good experience will do the same."

• • •

I've found her. I've started on the road to recovery. Yes, sir, we've been having a good time for about three weeks now. She's just like me. She sleeps as lightly as I do. It *must* be love. At least it's a nice secure feeling to wake up in the middle of the night for radio watch and not be alone.

I roll out of her bed as stealthfully as a VC suicide sapper. Slowly straightening, I look back at her then step silently to the foot of the bed. She mumbles. I freeze. She scratches her chin then rolls flat on her back. The nightshirt lies open, exposing a very tight nipple atop a firm breast. She must be dreaming about me.

I start to move. She gropes for herself. I freeze. She grabs a bunch of the nightshirt down by her Y. Drawing legs up around her hands, she rolls slowly to her other side. She has to be exhausted. She works seventy hours a week. The only time I really get to look at her is in the dark.

I move noiselessly along the bed, turn, step quietly by her side. She lets go a throaty groan. I freeze. If she were awake, she'd apologize for sounding "so unladylike."

I move out into the hallway, making sure not to step on the center boards where the wood is worn and squeaks. I tiptoe along the left wall, turning in at the bathroom door. The cold tiles of the floor make me suck air. I freeze. Did that wake her?

No noise is good noise.

I pull a towel from the rack, fold it on the floor in front of the toilet. She says it wakes her when tinkle hits the toilet water. I kneel on the towel, coming hip high with the bowl. I lift the seat.

Squeak!

Dammit!

I freeze, the seat halfway up. I better soap those hinges tomorrow. I listen. A subtle snore comes from the other room. I cautiously push the seat back against its cover. It would be a damn shame if that woke her after all this work.

I lean up against the toilet bowl, placing my most private part on the porcelain lip. The tinkle can just trickle in . . . if I can . . . come on tinkle, trickle. I know. I'll straighten, get the bladder above the bowl. Come on, gravity, take over.

It does. The toilet seat falls.

•　•　•

"I realize what it did."

"What what did, Mr. Kane?"

"The Nam. The war. The experience and how I relate to women."

"You can't blame everything that happens between you and women on the war, Kane."

"Maybe not, Dr. Smith, but I can't seem to maintain a permanent relationship with a woman for very long without it fucking up."

"Why do you think the war is responsible, Mr. Kane."

"The war isn't totally responsible, Dr. Gates, but I've been able to review some things, and I realize I had intimate contact with war, death and fear before I had real intimate contact with love, life and security. That affected how I behave in relationships."

"What happened," Sergeant Pepper wonders, "this latest love of your life bottom out, Doc?"

"Yeah."

"What about the group you live with, Doc. Why don't you jes dick around with the bitches there?"

"I told you, Point, I don't mess with what's too close to home. It would be too much like being married . . . I've got a good enough thing going where I have my own privacy and quiet."

"What, do you rent a room, Doc?"

"Yeah, a room and kitchen privileges in a big house. Share a bath."

"Let's not get too far off the subject, gentlemen."

"Yes, thanks, Dr. Gates. I was reminded when I read some of my earlier writings, I reread a Dear John letter I got over there."

"Who didn't get a Dear John over there?"

"Why save the letter, Doc?"

"Oh, it wasn't that bad, for Christ's sake. She was still in high school while I was trying to figure out how many casualties I had. We were worlds apart. I guess the only thing it did was make me feel more . . . alone. It was just another set of plans that died. Dreams dissolved with every death of everyone you dared share a future with."

"It always seemed like someone didn't return from a patrol."

"Really."

"I did two things to live with the rest of my tour. After Happy Valley, I got into this hope thing. I dreamed if I ever made it out of Nam alive I was going to come home, find me a woman, get married, settle down on a parcel of land in a cozy bungalow. I'd be a Doc, have little ones, grow some veggies, chickens for eggs. Things like that, be in love and raise a family."

"Sounds quite normal, Mr. Kane."

"It is."

"Could be boring, Doc."

"Let me finish. So even though I didn't know the worst had happened to me as far as fighting was concerned, it was only October and already guys were dropping like flies. Then there was Ia Drang valley, booby traps, other guys getting massacred and why wasn't it us. Goddam, that stinking smell of death that we got so used to, like animals . . ."

"Don't lose track, Mr. Kane."

"Right. Right. Then malaria and wishing I was dead."

"Malaria was a killer."

"Mr. Pepper, please let him speak."

"Sorry, Dr. Gates."

"Then the Valentine's Day massacre in Bong Song. I have to recover more dead friends. I become like a zombie. I forget just about everything that happens except that Two-Tone gets it. Kelly gets it. Grub gets it. Dino gets it. I'm losing grip on just about everything I'm living for. I think it's right after Valentine's Day I started to lose the dream of surviving so I could come back to that woman, a family. I started to sink into something like futility and despair. Then operation Crazy Horse on Memorial Day snapped me out of the self-pity. New guys who replaced replacements who replaced the people I started the tour with, they started dropping. That's when my initial hopes were dashed, losing Crocker and all C Company's motor platoon. There I came onto my second resolve. I remember at some moment saying if I ever got out of this war alive, I was going to touch as many women, travel to as many places, try as many things as I could. I was going to live what's left of my life to the fucking hilt, if I didn't fall to the VC first.''

I pause to see the group's reaction. The guys nod. The doctors wait.

"It was almost a semihysterical commitment. I went from living for one purpose to living for another purpose, without knowing if I was going to live.

"Then all of a sudden, I'm back in the States. It's like I got a reprieve from death row. No visible scars but I'm not old enough to buy a beer. I'm thankful to be back, but I'm confused over what I should do. I try to re-adapt what had been my initial inspiration for living, which was to settle down and raise a family. But I had let that purpose go. Do I move around and raise hell? I have a conflict, settle down, move around. Raise a family, raise hell. It settles into all areas of my life. I went from being responsible for everyone and everything in Nam to being responsible for no one and nothing back here. From always taking orders to refusing any suggestions. What I lived for in wartime, I'll die without in peacetime. I get close to no one and I always sleep alone. What a disappointment. How sad.''

"Combat bachelor.''

"What?''

"Sounds to me lik1you're a combat bachelor, Doc,'' Sergeant Pepper says.

"Sounds to me like we're all combat bachelors,'' Berns admits.

The door swings open, abruptly.

"Sorry I'm late, everyone.'' Sully paces in and sits at the nearest available chair.

"I hope I didn't miss anything. Our memorial is ready. I just came from the site. They even have it freshly sodded, looks like it's been there for months. Christ, you guys should see it. Hey, did I miss anything?''

"How's your love life, Sully?''

"I'm going through my second divorce, why?"
"I bet you didn't know you were a combat bachelor."
"Who?"

• • •

I step up on the curb, stop, and gaze around. There's a grove of young trees, open ground, what looks like fresh sod, then more young trees. Hmmm. Where is it?

I step cautiously through the grove, stopping at the edge of the clearing. I try to pick up on the feel of the place, using all my senses. Take a chance? Doesn't feel right, move off to the left. Make a wide berth. Step over the freshly laid cobblestone path. I'm not going to get caught; being out in the open is bad enough. I move to the left, while looking to the right.

Christ, will you look at that! I step along the curve of the land as it descends, revealing a black edge. It cuts into the green grass, interrupting the natural contour. I stand taller to get a better look, craning my neck, on tiptoes, stepping cautiously forward . . .

Goddammit! It's fucking huge!

I am drawn in the direction of descent, drawn to the massive black block. I take in the width, breadth, and magnitude of the huge, black stone wedge. The edges of the monument vibrate as I feel it drawing me in. No! I turn away. Step back to the tree line, the first row of saplings. I lean against a slim tree trunk, pull out a cigarette, fire it up, and draw. Goddam, goddam, goddam.

So fucking many . . . I turn back around slowly, taking in an experience depicted in stone. I gaze at what interrupted my life, loves, pursuit of happiness. I guess this means I don't have to go out to those cemeteries in Chicago, Scotia, Fayetteville, Lone Pine, Lubbock, Billingham, Fremont, Portland, Puerto Rico. Jesus Christ, it's as big as the United States of America.

A dazed gaze turns into realization. I know how the names are set up. I know where Eddie is. I know where

Kane is. They're down at the bottom, on the right, at the beginning. That's where they are. That's where I am. Fuck it. I've seen enough. I better get out of here.

Throwing the lit cigarette aside, I look about. Okay, step out into the open, but move it, Doc. No. Don't run, just willfully move away from it. Why did they have to make the fucking thing so huge? Don't they know that those of us who were alongside those names realized how they died? Gave them absolution? Have been grieving for years? It only confronts us again, a reminder.

Just move, Doc. Look straight ahead. Remember your objective. Get the hell out of here. Get to the car. Stay intent on getting to where the car is parked, no one will get in the way. Don't pay attention to the enemy fire from the tree line. Don't be intimidated by the rounds of ammunition kicking up at your feet. Remember, you made it through the kill zone before, when others didn't. Not so fast, you'll fall. You have time, time others don't have. Keep going, there's the car. Get away. "Keep on keepin' on," that's what Two-Tone always said. You've seen enough. You know enough. Get the hell out.

• • •

"So don't be surprised if you don't see me for the next couple of meetings, guys. I have to square things away with my ex-wife and kid. It's gotten out of hand."

"You're going to march in the parade, aren't you, Pepper? Go to the dedication and reunion?"

"Sure, I wouldn't miss it for the world, but in the meantime I have to take care of this rowdy kid of mine."

"Would you like to share some of the situation with the group, Mr. Pepper?"

"No thanks, Dr. Gates, it's a family affair. What's come over you, Doc? You look . . . different."

"Oh, nothing, sometimes I wonder how the hell you guys with families, with more responsibility than me, I admire how you are making it. God, I would have fucked up a whole bunch of offspring."

"That wasn't a look of admiration on your face, Mr. Kane."

"No, Dr. Gates, it wasn't. I took a look-see at the memorial the other day."

"What did you think, Doc?"

"It's awesome."

"It's a disgrace."

"No, it isn't, Berns. It's unsettling, but it isn't a disgrace. I think it is good, not necessarily good for us because of the memories it will bring back but ... I guess the more memorials we have to Viet Nam the better. Anyway, I've just been reviewing a lot of things after I went down to check it out.

"It got me really thinking about this whole process, I wish my brothers could be in on all this."

"We are, Doc. We are your brothers."

"No, Point. I mean, yes, you are my brothers but I mean my own family of brothers. They were all in Nam."

"You never talk about them."

"I know."

"How many, Doc."

"Two, my father also. We were over there from 1965 to 1970."

"Jesus, Doc," Sully exclaims, "they might as well rename the country Viet Kane."

The group chuckles.

"So what about your brothers, Mr. Kane?"

"Oh, I guess I feel bad that they had to go through that mess. That my being there first didn't keep them out of it."

"They made it back, didn't they?"

"Yes, but they're as troubled as me, erratic, disturbed, roaming around the country."

"You can't blame all that on the war, Doc."

"I know, Bernsy, I don't. Our family wasn't that squared away before the war. We would have had to deal with problems like alcohol and violence, but the war confused things even more. It split us as a family, that's what hurts.''

"Did your brothers join?"

"No, they were drafted."

"Draft got my ass," Point says.

"Yeah, the draft caught me changing colleges," Sully admits.

"The draft was just another form of prison," Pax says. "Get caught in it. Go in. Do your time. Get out alive, so be it. After a while, it didn't matter who you were. They just wanted to fill in the ranks."

"The war dragged on so long, when my second brother made it home I spoke out against the war."

"The anti-war mobilization was a primary reason we lost the war," Berns says bitterly.

"I wouldn't say that, Berns. My family was involved in the war mobilization for five years, it kept on. Six, seven years, that's a long time to get a war won."

"Those anti-war people didn't help any."

"They turned on us."

"Spit on me when I came back."

"Anti-war people should have been tried as traitors, Jane Fonda included."

"Didn't have enough courtrooms for that."

"Hey, you guys. I was anti-war," I defend. "A lot of people were anti-war who weren't as abusive as Jane Fonda. They had that right. You all spend too much time dumping on her."

"You were different from her and the others, Doc." Sergeant Pepper finally speaks up. "You did as you were ordered. You went first, even if you didn't like it."

"Yeah, not like deserters and draft dodgers."

"Everyone paid the price in that war. The guys who went to Canada left homes and futures here."

"How 'bout conscientious objectors."

"They caught a rash of shit for what they believed."

"They weren't shot at."

"It fucked everyone up throughout the country."

"Not like us."

"That whole time, the sixties and early seventies, was turmoil. Black power. Drugs. The love generation."

"Yeah, the love generation, my ass. That whole make love, not war, bullshit we came home to was a farce. I don't think people realize, even today, how much harder it is to make peace than war."

"Really, like making love, not war, is so fucking easy."

"Hey, the kids on campuses, all the people we've been talking about, were demonstrating, reacting because they didn't want to die."

"Whose side are you on, Doc?"

"There are no sides, Point. The world is a circle. We're all in it."

"What goes around, comes around."

"Yeah, but you're with it or you ain't."

"Will you guys let me finish something here?"

"Go ahead, Pepper."

"You only need one person to start a war. Only one person has to be the belligerent for things to happen."

"What's 'belligerent.' "

"Someone who's nasty."

"One person attacks another, that person has to defend himself."

"We were the belligerents."

"North Viet Nam went into South Viet Nam first."

"What about the Gulf of Tonkin?"

"They damn sure weren't the same type of belligerents."

"Mr. Washington, Mr. Paxton, would you please back off each other."

"Sorry, Dr. Gates."

"I'm not sorry."

"So, to fight, all you need is one person. Then everyone else has to defend themselves. Which makes a mockery out of the love generation. That's why the peace thing isn't as everyone makes it out to be. I mean love is just that. People don't make love in public. People do fight in public. Loving is private."

"Yeah, how many people get wrestled to the ground because they are making peace."

"People who want to fight will start a fight."

"That's what I mean. That's what's so . . . naïve about the peace thing. If someone goes berserk you got to fight. We have to be ready for that."

"What's 'naïve' mean."

"Stupid, stupid."

"Fuck you."

"Yeah, but did we have to go halfway around the world to Viet Nam to stop a fight?"

"The farther a society is from its wars, the less likely the war is a threat to the society."

"Where did that come from, Pepper?"

"I just thought it up."

"It's a rather obvious assumption. Better to start a war over there than be confronted on our own shores."

"I still contend the peace movement was as shallow as the war movement."

"Listening to all this reminds me I got to take a bowel movement."

"No one ever questioned the cost. I don't mean just human lives. We are still paying for it. I'll bet Jane Fonda's paying for it."

"I'll bet big business isn't paying for it."

"How does anyone know who's paying for it?"

"We're the only ones paying for it."

"That's not completely true. Folk back here who lost people over there paid a heavy price. Anyone who has to put up with the likes of us is paying for it."

"War is too easy to start."

"We have to keep trying to get along so things don't get so bad there are more wars."

"You don't quit, do you, Doc."

"Hey, Bernsy, who had to tie off the bleeders? Who had to offer the last rites? I can't quit. It's real easy to go off to war. It's just so damn hard to come back from one."

• • •

It's the noise. A nightmare that starts with noise. It is the worst-sounding noise in the world. It sounds like an animal crying, dying. It's the noise like the wounded, pleading, bleeding. The sound comes from deep below the belly, in the bowels. A bellowing, haunting noise that comes from someone who is trapped alive but would rather be dead.

As the sound softens to a whimper, a picture takes hold. I look up at the lip of the creek bed. I reach for it, pulling myself out of the rocky water. I lie on the edge of lush jungle foliage. This must be Happy Valley.

Whap. Whap. Whap.

Moaah, woaah, waaay!

The bellowing begins again, close by. I lie low as the sound reaches a painful pitch. I crawl toward it. I want to silence it. The wail subsides as I elbow the edge of a well-camouflaged bunker. I trace its outline under the jungle shrubbery. It is a large, deep bunker, with reinforced sides and a roof of logs.

Whap. Whap. Whap.

Moaah, woaah, waaay!

The sound comes from inside the bunker. I peek warily inside. Noise or no noise, these bunkers are the home of Mr. VC.

Whap. Whap. Whap.

I feel the concussion of the blows . . .

Moaah, woaah, waaay!

. . . as I note a man, his back to me, standing in the

far corner of the bunker, delivering overhead blows into the corner.

Whap. Whap. Whap.

He changes his position. I recognize my father.

Moaah, woaah, waaay!

I clench my teeth, tightening down memories of another place, another time. The sounds are coming from my mother, crouched down in the corner of the bunker. She can go no farther to avoid the blows. She covers her head with her hands in vain protection. The pummeling shakes dirt from the ceilings and the walls. He starts to kick her.

Moaah, woaah, oooh!

I roll over the edge of the bunker. My father realizes my movements and turns to attack me. Arm cocked, he throws a punch.

Smash!

Crash!

I sit up in the middle of concussive stars on the hardwood floor. The side of my face is numb. I look up at the edge of the bed I just rolled out of. I am never going to go to sleep, ever again.

•   •   •

I push through the door and into the meeting, breathless.

"Why learn to read, Dr. Gates, when the only thing I gets to understand is the charges bein' brought against me?" Point Man turns from her to me. "Hey, Doc man, where you been?"

"Sorry, everyone. I had another one of those nightmare nights. Then I had to wait in that fucking parking lot for a parking spot. Christ, I hate to wait on fucking lines. As a matter of fact, if it weren't for coming to this group, you guys, I wouldn't wait in that fucking line, I'd shine the fucker on."

"Mr. Kane, you always portray your agitation in your language. What was the nightmare about?"

"You don't lighten up for one fucking minute, do you, Dr. Gates?" I pause, then smile. "But that's all right, I'd miss you if you weren't here."

"Why, thank you, Mr. Kane. I'll take that as a compliment."

"You're welcome, but let's not get sidetracked here," I taunt with one of her own comments, readjust in the seat. "I hope no one is into anything?"

"Go ahead, Doc, I'm finished."

"What'd I miss?"

"Social commentary. Speak."

"Okay, thanks. I had a bitch of a nightmare last night. It was like a war nightmare, but it happened before the war, at least before Viet Nam. I mean, what it boils down to is this. What's the sense in going off to war when it deranges you so much you come home and intimidate everyone around you. My dad did that with us kids and my mom. My first introduction to ambushes was my father all of a sudden beating the fuck out of me 'cause he had a hair up his ass. We got real good at hiding from him. My mother, she couldn't hide so well under the bed or in the closets. He'd really beat the fuck out of her. That's what my nightmare was. It got me thinking of a bunch of things. Do you all mind hearing them?"

"Go to it, Doc."

"My first thing was this booby-trap thing I get into. About being impaled in the face or chest or nuts, or dropping on one like we almost did in Ia Drang."

"You haven't talked about that one, Mr. Kane."

"No, but I've dreamt it. It was an operation where we were supposed to make a combat jump into Ia Drang. At the last minute, they changed their minds and we walked into the area. We found the whole area we were supposed to jump into set with these six-, seven-, and eight-foot stakes. They would have impaled us if we'd jumped. They were booby-trapped so that when one of the guys from A Company pulled a stake out, he blew up. It was hairy. Anyway, that's not the point, no pun intended. The point is, my grandmother got me all squirrelly about being impaled when she told me stories about Ireland's fight for freedom. That story went back three centuries to when Oliver Cromwell impaled Catholics on stakes. Christ, now I remember how I visualized that as she told the story. It totally freaked me out. Ten, twelve years later, I land in Nam and there are those punji-stake traps that get me. Three or four years later, I go to Ireland to find my roots. I watch a parade in the North, where they wear buttons saying, "Cromwell was right," and "Remember 1690." Christ, I mean, I realize this war thing perpetuates itself. We're raised to be soldiers of Christ in the Catholic church. My father was in World War II. My uncle in Korea. Me and my brothers in Nam. We feel righteous in protecting our system from communism, but our women are afraid to walk the streets at night. They're raped and beaten. Our children are molested, beaten, and abused. Our old folks get ripped off by embezzlers and break-ins. They have three or four locks on the doors and bars on the windows. They live in jaillike conditions because they are afraid. I wonder. I mean, I'm proud to defend my shores from the communist aggressors and so on, but if wives are still getting the shit beat out of them by their husbands, if little boys and girls are being harassed by pedophiles, if grandma and grandpa are getting hoodwinked by fast-talking con men, then our job ain't over, and we ain't free."

• • •

"You know, if we hadn't lost that war, we wouldn't be sitting here wasting our time."

"We aren't wasting our time."

"Guys who came back from World War II had these groups."

"Did they? Did they, Dr. Smith?"

"Yes."

"But they won, they were accepted. We lost. We weren't accepted."

"We won every battle."

"Tet fucked us up."

"How can people in this country say we lost that war? How many homes, how many villages, cities here were scorched, or burnt to the ground? How many people back here were displaced from their neighborhoods, moved from the country to the city? How many mothers and sisters back here turned to whoring? How much farmland was destroyed by saturation bombing? This country has never felt war. How can folks here say they lost the war if it wasn't here?"

"There never has been an outside aggressor to occupy this country."

"The Civil War."

"The War of 1812."

"Who has sat in this group and described the Battle of New Orleans, man? C'mon, you know what I'm getting at!"

"We really left Viet Nam in a mess."

"Our leaders, and the people back here, lost the war. They paid for it but refused to pay attention to it."

"The war was kept low-key by President Johnson, President Nixon, and the Pentagon, because it caused such dissension. On the other hand, the TV network news broadcasts kept it alive every night."

"One side hushes it, the other side flushes it."

"That's why there was no fanfare or parades when we rotated back, because there were still people going over there and dying, and the Administration didn't want no celebrating while it was on."

"They wanted to keep a low profile."

"There was no glory to this war."

"Inertia, man. Some people realize once you get a war going, it's going to be hell to stop."

"There's a tactic, like the Gulf of Tonkin. LBJ and those kinds of folks knew if they could get one act of aggression to show to Congress, say, 'Hey, these little yellow fuckers are asking for it.' Once he got everyone to believe there was aggressive intent."

"Yeah, like PT boats going after frigates and cruisers."

"David versus Goliath."

"It worked, didn't it? It got everyone believing there was aggressive intent."

"Where is the Gulf of Tonkin?"

"You were in Viet Nam, and you don't know where the Gulf of Tonkin is?"

"I was in the Marines, not the Navy."

"If only they had let us win the war, we could have done it."

"But it wasn't a war we planned to win. It was like the Korea thing. It was supposed to be a war of occupation. We just wanted to sit on China's doorstep."

"We were going to scruff up Chairman Mao's boots."

"What were we going to do? Wait until all of the Vietnamese were registered Republicans and Democrats, then leave, saying we had won the war?"

"The scary thing to me about the war, win or lose, as soon as a close friend dies, or a brother, father, uncle is killed, then it becomes a personal war."

"And a lost war because you lost somebody."

"It becomes a war that will never be over, because they killed someone close."

"That reminds me, you guys. Dedication, parade, and reunion is next week. I hope everyone's ready, 'cause we're finally going to be welcomed home!"

• • •

"How 'bout this guy?" The camera stops in front of me.

"Sir?" The question appears as a microphone in my face. I turn my head aside and step back.

"Better not," says the voice behind the camera.

"How 'bout this guy? Sir?" The microphone moves to my left. The camera follows to another vet. He's black, dressed in tiger fatigues, a headband. Medals hang from his shirt pocket. He stares at the intrusion.

"This guy, too." The camera backs up to get a wider viewing range. I look, spy a heavyset black man sitting in a wheelchair. The vet in the fatigues drops to a knee. I step back, giving the scene more room.

"You, sir," the microphone extends to the man in the wheelchair, "why are . . . ?"

"Don't ask me why I'm here. My son wanted me to come. I wouldn't be here otherwise."

"Oh." The mike turns to the other fellow. "You, sir. When were you in Viet Nam?"

"In '67, '68, '69."

The mike switches to the wheelchair. "What happened to you, sir?"

"I got shot."

"In Viet Nam?"

The man in the wheelchair looks at the camera disdainfully, then looks over the group of us forming up.

The interview switches back to the other veteran. "What do you think of this dedication, sir? This Welcome Home? The parade?"

"It ain't gonna change nothin'."

It has become obvious these guys are no more willing to share their feelings than I am. What do you expect? This is a very apprehensive day for so many of us. Welcome home? After all these years, we are welcoming ourselves home by parading down the streets of Washington, D.C. We will dedicate a memorial to ourselves, which was paid for by money that Viet Nam veterans raised from private sources. Then there will be a reunion of the units from Army, Navy, Air Force, Marines, at local hotels. Welcome Home!

Whether you agreed with the war or disagreed with the war; love the memorial or hate the memorial; march in the parade or stand in the tree line. This is the day, November 11, 1982. Welcome Home. Today! Our day, finally. The experience can come to rest. It will not be hidden away any longer. It won't be brooded over privately. It does not have to be shamefully rejected. Viet Nam veterans can come out of their closets.

"Okay, you guys, listen up, listen up," a parade marshal shouts, as a band, then bands, start to blare up ahead. He shouts over the din. "D.C. is up soon, line up seven abreast, you'll be moving out. Who has the state . . . er, what do you call D.C. anyway? Who has the flag?"

"Right here, I have it," a familiar voice triumphantly claims. Pax steps out of the group.

"Good. Keep your place at the head of the delegation. The rest of you men guide by him. Your band will be coming momentarily." The marshal disappears.

"Hey, Pax," I call out.

"Hey, Doc, glad to see you marching with us."

"Hey, Doc." Point Man steps out of a group of black vets.

"Yo, Point Man. Glad to see you." I flush with the recognition. It's almost like they are the guys I served with in Nam. I'm missing someone, but I'm not. "Where are the others?"

"Sergeant Pepper is over with the state of Maryland. Major Berns is with the state of Virginia," Point volunteers. "I ain't seen Sully or anyone else from the group."

"Hey, Rod."

I whirl at the salutation. Mike, from V.V.A.W. and the 4130 house, stands before me, grinning.

"Mikey! Great, 4130 is represented."

I haven't seen him five times since the V.V.A.W. house broke up, truly another partner from the war. "Is anyone else from the house here?"

"Jack is around somewhere. The others I lost track of years ago."

"How 'bout Pietranowicz, is he here?"

"Oh, I'm sure he's part of the police parade coverage, crowd control, or something."

"How 'bout Ray Grodecki, or Allen Glick?"

"Oh, I saw Ray, yeah. He's marching with New Jersey or Pennsylvania. I don't know where Allen Glick is."

Our conversation is drowned out as a small band, with the tiniest member banging the biggest drum, steps alongside. They are accompanied by a parade marshal carrying a brown paper bag. He shouts over the din, "Here's your band, D.C. These kids are from Roosevelt High School. Some of you guys went to school there. Where's our guide-on?"

"Here. Here I am," Pax claims, hoisting the D.C. flag. "Come here, Roosevelt, over here."

The band steps to Pax as they test their instruments.

"Here." The parade marshal steps to me, pulls something out of his bag, drops it in my hand. "Welcome home."

The comment shocks me. It's the first time I've heard it. Live, in English. WELCOME HOME. I look at what he gave me; a small facsimile ribbon, the same color as the Viet Nam campaign ribbon. Everyone who served in Viet Nam received one. This one is a bit different; along its top and bottom borders is the statement: "Marching along, together again."

Shit! I'm starting to get excited, emotional, or something. Another marshal shouts, "Okay, D.C., get ready to come back home."

The delegation ahead of us, Delaware, I presume, begins to move. Damn, I have to tinkle.

"Get ready, little brothers and sisters," Pax cautions the school band. "Some of us veterans have been waiting on this for seventeen years. Play your little hearts out!"

The band nods at his direction. I fidget with anticipation, turning to Michael. He stands there as cool as a cucumber, grinning.

"I never thought I'd see this day, Mike."

"Nor I, Rod."

Above the din comes the call, "All right, D.C., it's your turn to come home. Stand tall, stand tall."

The way before us opens to the street. Pax raises the District of Columbia flag. Our band strikes up some sort of tune. We step out and off the grassy mall, then turn onto the street. Stop. Step in place. Start up again. Trumpets blare, drums sound, as we adjust our steps in some sort of order. There are spectators on both sides of the street. We turn onto Constitution Avenue and the crowd actually fills the sidewalks. Christ. I never thought I'd be marching down the streets of Washington, D.C.

"I'm back," I hear behind me. I turn to that announcement. A well-dressed black man with a Marine fatigue cap perched on his head looks at me in wonderment. "I'm back," he says. I nod, smile, and turn back to the parade's advance. Our military training keeps everyone in step, though at a more relaxed pace than rigid gait. Years of isolation and rejection parade down the avenue together. We pass people who wave, clap, laugh, cry. Are we crying? I turn to look at Mike, then over the group, at Point, Pax and others.

"I'm back," announces the black Marine behind me.

It's like an enormous weight being lifted from our shoulders with every step. This is like taking care of one hope, one dream we all shared when talking of coming home. It doesn't make the war worth it, but it puts the period at the end of the sentence of surviving it.

"I'm really back."

"Welcome home, brother."

I'm confronted by a big, hairy guy, dressed in black leather, a biker. He offers a hand. "Welcome home, brother." He keeps pace alongside me.

I grasp his hand. "Thanks, man." My voice cracks.

He pats my shoulder, steps to greet the black vet behind me.

"I'm back."

I look over my shoulder to see these two men reach out and hug each other. "Welcome home, brother."

"Yes, yes. Thanks, brother. I'm back."

"You're home."

We parade under a huge American flag draped between two ladders extended above fire trucks set on either side of Constitution Avenue.

"Hey, Rod, look," Mike calls out. "It's Westmoreland."

I look to the right. Sure enough, a small reviewing stand has been erected on the edge of the Ellipse. Every seat is full, and Westy sits quite obviously in an upper tier, bareheaded. I ought to step over there, shake his hand, and say, "Welcome back, Westy. All's forgiven, sir, if you know what I mean." I am making peace with my war.

The crowd at both curbs whistles and applauds as we pass by.

They shout, "Welcome home, son."

"Glad you made it."

"Welcome home, boys."

We step closer to the newly built memorial. It's really happening! Veterans from the states that have finished the parade line the avenue. They wave. We wave. We welcome each other home.

"I'm back!"

I wish all of us had made it.

"Welcome home, fellas."

"Welcome back, you guys."

"You're back, men. You can get on with your lives now."

"We love you guys! We love you guys! We love you guys!"

Jesus! I can hardly see in front of me because of the tears welling up in my eyes. I grope in a pocket, pull out the trusty sunglasses. Put them on. A parade marshal

comes trotting alongside. He shouts, "All right, gentlemen, you'll have to disband once past Eighteenth Street.
Then you can return to the parade route or go over to
the memorial. Welcome home."

Our band strikes up one more rousing march. We
renew our step with intent. It wasn't long enough. It
wasn't far enough. Who wants to stop?

"Let's march to the memorial," Pax shouts, as some
of the vets step out of line.

"I'm really home."

"Don't disband, kids. Keep playing," Pax says to the
band as a marshal steps forward and funnels them up
Eighteenth Street. All but the littlest drummer follow.
The avenue becomes disorganized with marchers, pac-
ers, watchers, and a small group of D.C. vets who won't
stop marching.

"C'mon, Rod. Let's go watch the rest of the parade."
Mike pulls at my arm. I look to him, look toward the
crowd surrounding the memorial area. I step out of the
group as the District of Columbia continues behind their
little drummer.

I follow Mike back along the crowded sidewalk, stepping a little lighter and quite a bit higher. There are quite
a few smiling faces.

We push through a thin space in the crowd and stand
at the curb. Hawaii marches by. Two vets. One vet
carries the flag, the other a placard stating the state's
name.

"Yay, Hawaii," comes the call from the crowd.

"I got thrown in jail in Hawaii, on a stopover when
we sailed over," I admit. Mike turns at my confession.
"I didn't know you went over on the boat. Most of the
first units went by boat."

"Yep. I was with one of the first units. What did you
do? Fly?"

"Of course, most everyone did."

"I guess we didn't share much about Viet Nam when
we were together at 4130."

"Everyone was too drunk, drugged, or high on their own egos."

"Yeah, that's true. We sure didn't support each other, emotionally, I mean."

"Rod, the only support you needed was under each arm as we carried you into the house, or up to your room!"

"Yeah, I was pretty well fucked up. The war never really did end for me."

"I know you took it harder than most."

"I was in the VA hospital earlier this year, Mike. I'm trying to put it to rest. I haven't had a drink in almost nine months."

"Really? Well, good for you!"

"No, good for everybody. I'd love to have a drink right now. I'm wary of going to this reunion. By the way, Mike, who were you with in Nam? What did you do?"

"Nothing important, wasted my time. I was stationed north of a town called Qui Nhon."

"Christ! We landed in Qui Nhon. I know that area. Who were you with?"

"I was attached to the White Horse Division of the Korean Army. I was in procurement for the senior staff of the Korean command."

"Koreans were motherfuckers out in the field."

"That's what I hear. I didn't see any action, Rod. Viet Nam was a waste of time for me. A lot of us over there just wasted our time."

I gaze down the avenue as I try to reason that war past all the waste. There has to be more worth to it. It can't just be a waste of time. Texas marches by, then Virginia, Virgin Islands, the W's. After the states, service unit organizations pass by with bands blasting away at intervals. The crowds on either side of the avenue become deeper as more vets circle back from their march. A contingent of vets in wheelchairs rolls by. The 173rd Airborne, 101st Airborne.

"Hey, the First Cavalry. Look, Mike."

"I see."

The horse platoon and huge cavalry banner march by. I flush emotion again. A lot of feelings are going to come up for air this weekend. For a lot of us.

"Rod, look."

"What?"

The parade has thinned as the end is in sight. Here comes Captain Jack, carrying one side of a banner: Viet Nam Veterans Against the War. He's dressed in his jungle fatigues and boonie hat, cigar clenched in his teeth.

"Who's that, carrying the banner with him?"

"A woman. He got a woman to carry the banner with him, Mike."

"Hey, Captain Jack!" we shout in unison as he stomps down the middle of Constitution Avenue. "Hey Jack!"

He looks over at us, smiles, and raises a clenched fist.

She ducks under as some push closer to the board to scrutinize the computer list she's tacked up. I wait for the crowd to thin, then step close enough for a look-see.

Where's the First Cavalry? Where's the Airborne units? The infantry? Transportation. Artillery. Aviation. Field hospitals. Special Services. Where's the fucking infantry units? There, at the bottom, of course. No Airborne? What did they do, change things after we left? Whoa! Look at the dates when those guys served:

WILLIAMS, A. D.   B Company '67–'68
RYAN, E. D.   D Company '70–'71
MCCLAIN, R. D.   C Company '70–'71
MATUZZI, L. N.   A Company '69
LINKS, P. R.   A Company '66–'67
LINCOLN, A. R.   H & H Company '68–'69

No one there from '65 to '66. Over a thousand guys boarded the boat in Georgia in August '65 and there's no one on the list. Christ! I am alone.

I turn away from the board, feeling the "sole survivor" pangs of isolation. Dammit! I expected to find someone who knew what we went through. Someone I could ask, "Hey, did it really happen?" Someone whose hand I could shake.

From the crowded room comes a shout. "Any of you gentlemen who are wondering how to get your name on that Welcome Home list, you have to fill out a registration form and take it to the computer operators for entry. They're located to the right of the escalators as you come in. That's your military right."

I come out of my consternation as vets sweep by me. Christ! After all these years, I wonder if Henderson and Alvarez are still alive. Al's probably still on the West Coast. He probably wouldn't be able to get back here. Henderson, though . . . he might . . . ?

Having put my name into the computer, I step out of the crowded banquet room and step on the "up" escalator. It empties me onto the lobby foyer. A big placard rests against a pillar:

FIRST CAVALRY DIVISION—HOSPITALITY ROOM 712

Shit! I don't know. I look around the lobby at the handclasping and backslapping. Vets greet, meet, appear to join again, in reunion. Laughs and grasps, it almost hurts to see it happening. So many of us made plans, then the plans lay in pools of blood, or flew off in med evac choppers. Fuck it! I'm going up to check out the Hospitality Room. I just don't see how they'll fit a whole division reunion in one room.

I get off the elevator and turn in the direction of the arrow to "702–728." God, I hate hotel hallways. Why the hell did they decide to hold the reunion in a high-class hotel anyway? Remember, Doc, no booze. No beer. Grab some tonic water, add a slice of lime, and look like a gin or vodka man. Coffee even, but no booze, even if there's a toast.

What about reefer? What about it? No one will be smoking reefer in this hotel. Besides, everyone you smoked reefer with in Nam was killed. Hell, everyone I was with in Viet Nam was killed or wounded. Fuck the reefer! I turn down the hallway. Slow down. Be wary. A boisterous noise filters out into the hallway. I step to a doorway, see the big First Cav patch hanging on the door. I peer in. Too many men in too small a room. One grenade, one frag, and it's all over. Go in, Doc, if someone throws a frag, you can fall on it and request one last drink as you lie in your death throes.

I step into the room. A couple of men turn to look at me. I look at them. Know them? Know me? Nope. We nod, then ignore each other. It won't be that easy. Christ! Look at all the beer bellies and gray hair. Has it been that long? Do so many of us look like old men? A tall man passes through the crowd. Hey! Was that . . . ? Was he that tall? What'd we call him?

I whisper what I think his name was. Should I shout it out? What the hell!

"Bananas?"

His head turns in recognition.

"Bananas?"

Spying me, he shouts, "Kane?" then bowls a group of guys over to greet me. Still that big, broad-shouldered man with the wonderfully foolish grin.

"Bananas! How the fuck are you?"

"Great! How are you?"

We half hug, slapping each other on the shoulders.

"I almost didn't recognize you with all that gray hair. It's the foolish grin though."

"You haven't changed at all, Kane."

"God, Bananas, when I left, you had a good part of your tour to serve. You're so fucking big, Cong couldn't have missed you!"

He laughs that laugh that gave credence to his name.

"Well, they missed, and I made it through to December '66, when I rotated back. I got out soon after that."

"Where're you living?"

"New York."

"Really? That close!"

"How 'bout you?"

"Right here in D.C. Hey, what happened to the other medics? Did any of the other medics come back?"

"Nope, just me."

"Really?"

"Linley got hit in Pleiku. Quigley bought it in Kontum City."

"Oh, no!"

"Hey, guess who's here? Lieutenant Litton."

"Litton, Litton. From A Company?"

"Yeah, let me go get him. He'll be glad to see you. Stay right there."

He leaves me to reflect. Christ! Bananas! What was his real name? It was something that sounded like that. He and Quigley and Linley were our first replacement medics. Goddam, Quigley replaced me when I was med evaced for malaria. Linley was a Canadian.

"Kane!"

"Bananas!"

"Boot to Boot," he shouts, pushing the crowd aside. *Boot to Boot* was our war cry from the 185th airborne infantry. He grins as he slaps my back.

"You were Special Forces before you came to us, right, Bananas?"

"Yeah, but remember, you taught me 'Boot to Boot.' "

"Yeah, yeah, I guess I did."

"Here, Kane, look! Here's Lieutenant Litton."

An older man limps badly toward me.

"Doc Kane. Doc Kane. How are you? How are you?"

As he extends a hand, I remember the resemblance to a much younger man. Someone who didn't have so much pain etched in his face. I grab his hand.

"Howdy, sir. I remember you. A Company. You were with Weapons Platoon."

"I had my own platoon, after a fashion."

I feel the sweaty palm.

"The fuckers got you."

"Yep. Could have used you, Doc. December '66, Pleiku. On patrol, we ambushed a couple NVA, one of them played dead, got me as we were leaving the scene. AK-47 rounds took out my right butt and leg."

"So sorry, sir."

"The high price of war."

His face attests to that fact. As I recall, he was a career man, real military, by the book, but a real good man. How many real good men did the military lose over there?

"How are you doing, Doc?"

"Oh, not bad, sir. Better than I was. Got out of the VA hospital not long ago. War shit caught up with me."

"Oh." His smile fades.

"Hey, you want a drink, Kane?" Bananas interjects. "How 'bout you, sir? What are you guys drinking? They got a free bar."

The room starts to close in on me. Litton's pain. Quigley dead. Too crowded in here. Don't drink, Doc.

"No, thanks, Bananas. Not right now. Hey, could you guys excuse me for a minute?" I vaguely feel like I want to throw up. Goddam, so much, all at once.

"Sure, sure. Don't go too far though, Kane. We got to catch up on things. Boot to Boot," Bananas chuckles.

"Excuse me, sir."

"Right, Doc. Nice to see you."

"I'll be back."

I exit as quickly as possible from the crowded, smoke-filled room. Walk past two men in business suits sharing a joint. "Hey, would you guys mind?" I ask.

"No." One of them hands me the joint. I take a draw.

"Thanks."

"Sure. Welcome home."

"You, too."

My head starts to clear as I get to the elevator. Doors slide open. Hotel security people rush off and head down the hall. I bet they don't catch anyone.

Christ, Quigley and I never did get along. As a matter of fact, I can't imagine him risking his neck for anyone. He must have, though, if he's dead. How come so many of these guys are dressed in camouflage fatigues? We didn't even have plain old green jungle fatigues in the beginning. Is that what they wore in the end? Maybe long-range recon wore camouflage, but that couldn't include all these guys. I bet it's just John Wayne troopers.

"Hey, Doc Kane."

I start, turn to face a black man. I think I recognize him. Then again, I doubt it.

"It's me, Doc. Dwight Williams. You were my medic in recon at Fort Benning. We went to Nam together on the boat . . ."

"Williams?"

I reach for him, throw an arm over his shoulder, grab his hand. He does likewise.

"Williams. Williams. Goddam, goddam."

"How ya doin', Doc?"

"Great! Great to see you, man. I thought I'd never see you again."

"Same here, Doc. When I rotated back to the States, you were still in a line unit."

"That's right, you ETSed out of Nam."

"Served my two years, got out in June of '66."

"Christ, when did I start med coverage with you guys? March of '65."

"About then, Doc. Still don't know why they took you from us. We sure could have used you on that hill!"

"Yeah, that's right. You guys, Onana and the others . . ." I pause, remembering the skirmish where he and his men were wiped out. "Did anyone else make it after that assault?"

He bows his head. "Sears, McClain, I don't know if any others did. I was the first to get out of Nam."

"I guess we could find out easy enough who made it and who didn't by going down to the memorial. Hey, where are you living, Williams?"

"Philadelphia. You were from New York, right, Doc?"

"Yeah, but I live here in D.C. now."

There is a short pause. What to say now?

"You know, Doc, when I came back, I was real strange. My grams said she didn't even know me. My moms was scared of me. It took me quite a few years to get my shit together."

"Me too, man. I was wild in the streets, on and off, until about nine months ago. Heavy boozin', movin' around, lots of jobs, car wrecks, women wrecks. I got out of the VA hospital not long ago. They said I had chronic post-traumatic stress disorder, PTSD. I still attend a therapy group for combat vets."

"I'm here with a staff of doctors from the Coatesville VA. That's in Pennsylvania. We do PTSD work there. We have a little clinic set up here for any guys who go off. I was in one of the first programs for readjustment, Doc. Now I'm a counselor."

"Really, Williams?"

"Yeah. Since I've been through it, I've tried to help others."

"You're a better man than I am, man. I admire you for that. I'm proud of you."

"I'm proud of you, too, Doc. You did some great stuff over there. Even greater to go through the PTSD program."

A commotion distracts us as two vets carry a third one, who appears quite inebriated, into the room Williams pointed out as a clinic.

"Looks like we got a customer."

"Should you go in?"

"There's a doctor in there. I'll head in in a minute.

You know what I think it is, Doc? What's below our self-destruction, the rage, anger?"

"Guilt for sure."

"Yeah, guilt, but more than that, beyond guilt. You know what it is?"

"What?"

"Grief."

"Huh? Grief. Hmmm. Well, we sure did want everyone to survive."

"Yeah, and we got close to each other and lost the friends and plans and hopes. We come back here. No one here knows to what extent those dreams are shattered. It's a grieving process. Hey! I got to get in there. You got an address or phone?"

I'm still trying to realize what he said. "Oh, yeah, sure. We'll have to keep in touch more. Here."

We both take out scraps of paper, jot down information, and trade.

"Williams, it's damn sure good to see you."

"There's something good going to come of this, Doc. For sure."

"Hey, First Cav has a hospitality room upstairs. When you're finished, check it out. Remember Doc Bananas?"

"No."

"Good man. He and Lieutenant Litton are up there. It's sort of a zoo, a lot of boozin'. I don't drink anymore, do you?"

"No."

"Well, welcome back, Williams."

"Welcome back, Doc."

We grasp hands.

"Christ, I don't want to leave you, Williams. You're one of the few people who know it all. There was no one on the list downstairs from '65–'66."

"Got to accept that, Doc. Not many of us originals made it back. Hey, I got to get in there. Nice to see you, Doc."

"Good to see you, Williams, really."

We hug quickly, then turn our separate ways. I walk through the lobby, past reunions just like the ones I've had. Glasses clink, laughter, sobs, a war whoop. The atmosphere is warm but wary. I don't think any of us can believe it. I never thought this would happen. I never thought there would be a parade, a memorial, a reunion. And Williams. And Bananas. Better go back and check on Bananas.

I step in the elevator. It ascends, stops, ascends, vets exit and enter, traveling to different unit reunions on different floors. At one, Bananas gets on.

"Yo, Bananas," I shout in the crowded elevator.

"Kane! Rakkasan! Whoo! Whoo! Whoo!" He rocks the elevator with his cheer. Everyone starts moaning. The elevator stops at 7. I push through. He steps off.

"Going back to the reunion?"

"Coming back up here to see you. I don't care for the crowded room. Where you been?"

"I just walked Litton back to his room. He ain't feeling so hot. He's got a lot of pain with that leg of his. I went down to see if there were any new names on the computer list. Saw yours. Got your address and phone number."

"Is yours in there?"

"Yeah."

"Well, what is it?"

"What's what?"

"Your name. I know your name isn't Bananas!"

"Oh. No. Banaitis, my name is Banaitis. Say, speaking of names, what was the name of that buck sergeant you wanted to fuck with? He left you out on that ambush. Put you on K.P. and burning shitters in base camp. What was his name?

"Christ, Bananas, don't remind me. I had forgot all about him."

He starts that great laugh of his. I change the subject.

"So that's why we called you Bananas. What's Banaitis, Polish?"

"No, Lithuanian. I was born in Lithuania. My parents
. . . we had to split when Stalin, the communists, in-
vaded us, back in the beginning of World War II. I was
just a baby, so I don't remember a whole lot, but we lost
everything to the communists."

"Oh."

"My father is dead. My mother still plans to go back.
We have hope to run Brezhnev out of Lithuania, Latvia,
Estonia. Down south, too, in Armenia. Lots of us lost
out. Hey! You remember Estevez, I think he was in B
Company?"

"Yeah, he was."

"He was from Cuba. He fought with Castro till Castro
turned commie. Remember Erdos? He was killed in
December '66. He had to leave after the Russian invasion of Hungary in '56."

"Christ, it ain't never gonna end, is it, Bananas?"

"Not unless the commies give back what they took."

• • • •

"Relieved."

"At last, it feels like I'm home."

"I feel better."

"I met a fella I had gone through basic training with.
He lost his right leg, arm, and eye over there. He's
married, has three kids, owns his own business. He's
hanging in there. Made me feel better about us. The
whole weekend was an inspiration."

"It was so damn crowded, I couldn't have gotten near
the memorial if I'd wanted to."

"What do you think, Mr. Berns?"

"I still don't like it, Dr. Gates. I believe we shouldn't
rest until the Vietnamese release the rest of our POWs,
and make accountable the MIAs."

"I think the weekend was great."

"It was beautiful."

"People were clapping and cheering for us in the
parade."

"The parade was great."

"I met a couple of guys at the First Cav reunion who were in Nam when I was there. I don't feel so alone."

"Well, that's a change, Mr. Kane."

"Yes, ma'am, it is."

"Did you all see who the majority of vets were? A lot of the vets were young, young kids."

"Of course, man, Nam was still going on eight or ten years ago. Some of the guys don't have to be more than twenty-six or twenty-eight."

"In less than three years I'll be celebrating my twentieth anniversary since Nam."

"The responsibility for that war fell on the shoulders of the young ones, the foot soldiers, privates."

"Boy, did we ever get fucked up at that hotel reunion."

"D.C. was our town last weekend, wasn't it, you guys?"

"Still is."

"The military will never recover the loss of some of its best leaders in Viet Nam."

"And the country will never recover its volunteers and draftees. Dope addicts and drunks. Baby killers and crybabies. I learned this weekend that all kinds served in Nam."

"I learned how important this group of ours is. A lot of guys are really alone and isolated out there."

"We got our own platoon here. We got a Doc, an officer, Sergeant Pepper, a point man."

"I don't know if I'll ever feel comfortable with Point Man on point."

"Fuck you, Bernsy."

"What I realized this weekend was that what we went to war for played second fiddle when we were in the bush. This may be true for other wars also. You live for each other in combat, you don't think about the rhetoric that got you into the war. In the Viet Nam war we fought for each other. We lived and died for each other. We were a close-knit group out there in the bush."

"We couldn't have made it out without the help of each other."

"That's the truth."

"We got to go back and get those we left behind."

"We were duped into that war."

"What I learned about the war comes from these group meetings. Some came from the welcome-home activities this weekend and some of it comes from writing out the experience, but what I learned can be contradictory. I am proud of my service to my boys. It was important to save lives. It was exciting. It was devastating. I didn't realize this, sitting on a barstool. I never realized it, watching a war movie. I never realized it from the six o'clock news. I was successful at the most destructive practice we humans can force on each other. I realize what I accomplished. I'm proud. I realize what I lost, the friends, dreams, sleep, and I'm hurt. The war left me full of pride and honor. It left me full of grief and despair. I perpetuate it. I despise it. Do we have to live with it? Can we live without it?"

"You're always so fucking heavy, Doc. Why do you have to put a damper on things?"

"He's right though, Point. Was the celebration this weekend worth all the hell that breaks loose in an ambush? Is it worth all the lives?"

"A bunch of us were sitting around, sipping beer on Sunday at the hotel, reminiscing about how it was for us when we came back. Now, mind you, it was me and three guys from my platoon. We hadn't seen each other since Nam, but we all admitted that we came back with a chip on our shoulder. It was such an all-sacrificing, demanding experience that we resented society for a while for committing us to it."

"What do you mean, 'resented for a while'? I still got a chip!"

"Unless we talk this stuff out, we'll always act out of the resentment, the anger. We'll lash out at each other, those around us."

"We hurt ourselves."

"Well, I feel like I've been grieving for years. Grieving for those I had hoped to know. Grieving for those I knew and lost. Lost so many."

"Got to let go of it, Doc."

"I don't know if I can let go of it, Pepper, but I know I can put all the grief, resentment, pain, anger, in one place. I can put it in an imaginary file called 'the war experience,' so it isn't going to spread out all over the rest of my life. I'm to the point where I rule my war. The war doesn't rule me."

"Hey, yeah. If you see that the file starts to fall out, you can push it back in again."

"Or take it out, sort through it, then put it away."

"Let's face it, guys, it's rough to hear that being in that war was our responsibility, our problem, especially when these people back here paid for it. The truth of the matter is, Viet Nam, combat, is ours to deal with. No one else back here has that experience. Our wives and girlfriends weren't in it. Taxpayers weren't in it. Guys with college deferments weren't in it. We, who have the problems because of it, are the ones who can solve it."

"But it ain't our fault."

"I'm not talking fault. It's past fault. We can't be caught up in being victims of the war. We have to assimilate for our own best interests."

"What's 'assimilate'?"

"To adjust, Point."

"The only way to solve our problem is no more war."

"All that's ever discussed about it, Pepper, whether it's pro-war or anti-war, is blame and fault. That doesn't take care of my sleepless nights. That doesn't take care of the emptiness I realize in my life. That kind of discussion just alleviates some of the frustration."

"It helps to fault others. It relieves some of the responsibility."

"Okay. We deal with that a lot in this group. Why don't we deal with solutions to our part of the experience? How do we handle constant recall? The errors? Surviving? There is no one outside of us who has the expertise to deal with the experience. Even you doctors are learning from us.''

"More so than you think, Kane.''

"And who has the right to pass judgment on who should carry the brunt of the responsibility for the war? Everyone in the country was, is, affected by the war. We're just affected the worst. The only thing we can do, for ourselves and for those we outlived, is to carry our load as best as possible, whether we were drafted, joined up, or are twenty-year military. Me, Sergeant Pepper, Point Man, Major Berns. What say we shut those people up who say it's our problem? Let's deal with our problem and leave the rest alone. We have a lot of work to do.''

"Yeah, Doc, maybe you're right. But we don't have to stand for those accusations about being baby killers.''

"Yeah, atrocities over there weren't anywhere near the atrocities back here!''

"That's why women, peace freaks, those type folks are afraid of us. Atrocities over there is a hint of atrocities back here!''

"I'd fuck up a child molester if I ever caught one messing with my kids.''

"People back here are afraid of us 'cause we've killed. They paid for us to do it. They sponsored it. Veterans have provided security down through these last decades, since World War II.''

"I'm afraid of these people back here. They scare me.''

"I don't see where you have any grounds for being afraid of the people back here in the States, Mr. Pepper,'' Dr. Gates says. "Why do you express such anxiety?''

"Dr. Gates, any country, system, that drafts its youngsters into a war six thousand to nine thousand miles from home . . . wasn't it that far, you guys?''

"Close enough, Pepper."

". . . sends its kids to jungles and rice paddies to be ambushed, booby-trapped, diseased, then doesn't say anything to us when we make it back. All the while watching the damn war on TV every night. Arguing whether it's right or wrong while tax dollars pay for it, fueling it on and on for five, six, seven years . . . tearing families apart. Then not giving us any consideration when we try to fit back into civilian life . . ."

"Spit on us!"

"Scorn!"

"For years, men and women go over and return, every day, ignored, overlooked by the system, and you tell me I shouldn't be scared of these people, this society. They sponsored having me killed. When I survived that, they didn't seem to care, or it was scorn for going. I'm scared of people like that, Dr. Gates. I'm scared of my own people!"

There's a pause in the group.

"Maybe that's why we isolate ourselves. Not just because of grief or pain, but fear."

"We can help each other out of this war thing. Others will see it. They'll help us, or leave us alone. We have to help ourselves."

"Gentlemen, as usual, our time is up."

"Men, hold it. We've had a couple of new admissions spawned by the welcome-home activities. They are combat veterans. I believe they could use our advice and experience. How about it? Can we take in a couple of new members?"

"Yes."

"Absolutely."

"For sure."

"Bring them on, Dr. Smith. What do you think, Dr. Gates?"

"Yes, I think so."

"Wait a minute. They're not Marines, I hope. We may not be able to help them if they're Marines."

"You got it wrong, Pepper. Army boys are hopeless. Look at you and Doc."

"Hey, Doc, you got a cigarette?"

I hand Point Man a smoke.

"Kane, come to my office and pick up the last of your writing."

"Do I have to do it today, Dr. Smith? As it is, I'm late for a dental appointment."

"Whenever . . . it's ready."

"Hey, Doc. When are you gonna let us read your stuff, man?"

•   •   •

I follow the cobblestone path, down. Its slope pushes me. This is the closest I've come. I pass the tips of black marble. Is that one name or two? I don't look. Why? Why names? Names I have forgotten. Names I hoped I'd never remember. Names that bring back faces. Faces that lived. Faces that dreamed. Faces that hoped. Faces that shared plans together.

Go down to the memorial, Kane, it's good therapy.

I'll step to the bottom of this crowded pit to find the spot where my name could be. Where Eddie took it instead of me. Where two Kanes went into Happy Valley but only one Kane came out alive.

I try to move slowly down the path. My reflection ripples across golden names etched in the black glossy marble. Maybe I shouldn't have come here alone. Fuck it. Here I come, Eddie, Two-Tone, Kane, Dino, Nevin, Baylor, Sherman, Crocker and all you guys whose names I've forgotten. It's Doc Kane. I'm alive. I made it. I'm here to tell you, surviving hasn't been all we hoped it would be. One reason is because you're not here.

Stop!

As the depth of this memorial cuts out the street noise, the silence becomes deadly. It is the same silence that wraps around that moment right before the ambush is sprung. It is the moment when everyone wants to be somewhere else, like home making love. The gunfire starts. We live and die through it. The gunfire stops.

This is the deadly silence right after the ambush. I am afraid to be here. I am afraid I'll see names. That will remind me. I had so many casualties, so many dead, so many dying that I ran out of resources. I had so little time to devote to so many in need. There was sniper fire coming from the tree line. More casualties were dragged out of the creek bed. The man with the hole in his chest, gasping and grabbing. The big fella with the sliver of shrapnel that sliced through his spinal cord leaving him motionless and helpless. Here comes Coins, cradling intestines in his arms.

"Doc, I'm hit."

"Doc, over here."

"Doc, how 'bout this guy?"

"Doc, help me, help me."

Who gets attention? Who gets absolution? Who is too far gone? Who is right on the edge? Who lives? Who dies?

At the bottom of this wall, where the beginning of the war meets the end, the panels tower over me. My war begins at the bottom of panel two. It continues at the top of panel three. If I want to be reminded of who died, I have to get down on my knees. If I want to review my whole tour, I'll need a ladder to climb to the top of panel three.

I turn away, step briskly up the cobblestone walk, pushing through the crowd of wall watchers. I'm not ready for this wall. It's for you people back here. It's for Veteran's Day. It's for Memorial Day. It's even for Valentine's Day. Take your turn, America. Cast your reflection. Reach out and grieve. Pass your hands across the names of loved ones. Be thankful you weren't the nineteen-year-old who has to live with the experience of choosing who should live and who should die.

•   •   •

"Dr. Smith."

He looks up from his desk. "Come in, Kane, come in."

"Sorry I couldn't get by sooner to pick up the rest of my writing. This last week has been really hectic."

He pokes through the papers on his desk, pulls out a familiar binder. "Here are your anniversary recollections and . . ." He pauses, sliding a desk drawer open then pulling out a bundle of letters, ". . . Two-Tone's letters."

"Thank you." I pick all of it up.

"Quite dramatic, Kane."

"Dramatic like how, Dr. Smith?"

"Dramatic like whether it's romanticized or hard-core fact, the feeling is there. That's what's important. You've expressed it very well. It's something that must be shared. The question is what do you do now?"

"Wait a minute, you're leading up to something, I've been around you long enough. What do you have up your sleeve, Dr. Smith?"

"I don't have anything up my sleeve, Kane. Why must you men always be so suspect of motivation?"

"Well, because . . ."

"I know, I know, because you feel you were misled about the war . . . Kane, have I turned on you?"

"Never mind, I'm sorry, man, er, Doctor. What is it you have in mind?"

"Just that I think you are ready to step beyond your role in the war. You've been so successful with your writing, why don't you try to find some way to express putting the war to rest."

I wonder at that thought. Put the war to rest? It's been so much a part of my life, how could I put it to rest?

"Kane?"

"Sir?"

"Give it a try. Write something with the purpose of putting the war aside."

"Okay, I'll try."

"Good, that's all we can ask, eh, try. Now, what's this about you having had a hectic week?"

"Oh. Dental work. I'm having crowns put in the back of my mouth. The dentist says I've been clenching my teeth for so many years I've lost some of my back teeth. We're going to cover what's left."

"Good, see if he'll make you a bite guard also."

"She."

"See if she'll make you a bite guard. Wear it to bed, it may help you to sleep."

"I'll ask her next time. I went down to the memorial finally."

"You did! How did that go?"

"Oh . . . not so cool. I didn't stay long enough to find any names. I don't think it was a good idea to go down alone."

"Well, I'm glad to hear you say that."

"I'll ask one of the guys from the group to go with me next time."

"Good idea."

"By the way, I didn't mean to doubt your intentions a moment ago, man. You really saved my ass by taking me into the group."

"You saved your ass, Kane. Do you realize how much better you look and act?"

"I feel better. I'm out of that self-destructive routine. Being sober makes a big difference for me. Alcohol really robbed me of my confidence."

"That's true. How 'bout drugs?"

"I never really had an affection for drugs, Dr. Smith, except for reefer. I took a toke from some guys at the reunion. That's about all I've done."

"Watch out, Kane, you're not out of the woods yet."

"I know. But something I have now I didn't have for quite some time is the memory of the hopes and dreams us guys had in Nam. I mean, I don't have to harbor the horror of that war. I can remember to live with those plans we shared over there. I feel like I can turn the grief around."

"Wise move."

"Thank you. I have this feeling of vulnerability though, I mean I'm not living as a begrudging survivor or victim anymore, but I feel vulnerable enough to keep my warrior guard up. I'm still offensive and intimidating to those around me. What do I put in its place?"

"You haven't found the peace and comfort yet to replace the neurotic strength of intimidation. Give yourself credit for getting this far. Give yourself credit for getting further on. It will happen."

"Okay."

"You men don't give yourselves enough credit."

"We hang around people who don't give us enough credit."

"You have control over that. Find a woman who will appreciate you for who you are."

"I guess I'll have to do something with the warrior in me."

"You can do that."

"Yeah, I always have the group as reference. The warrior will never be far away."

"Do something different, set another goal. Do something for your emotional stability, for the soul."

"Yeah, I've been thinking about that. You know what I think I need to do, something that I've tried but I've been blocked up with all this war and fear and anger."

"What, Kane?"

"I need some peace. I want to love."

Epilogue

Combat Bachelor
by DOC KANE

H E COVERS THE CHEST WOUND WITH THE CELLOPHANE of a cigarette pack, then a battle dressing. It results in blood bubbles forming over the mouth. Taking the compress away, the bubbles burst from the chest wound.

"Is it bad, Doc? Is it bad?" the wounded man pants.

"Shhh. You should just worry about breathing. Slow down, relax."

He covers the hole, to trap oxygen in the chest cavity. This shuts the man up. The blood bubbles form around the lips again. It starts to choke the man. He takes the compress away.

"Cough! Are the choppers coming? They can't get in here, can they, Doc? Cough! Can they?" he wheezes.

"Don't talk. Shut up and breathe. Don't talk. Shut up and breathe."

He returns the compress to the hole, but can't hold it too long—the man will drown. He must get someone to watch him. He has to check the others.

"My kids, Doc. My son. Oh, God, my wife, my daughter. What about my family?"

He must leave the man. He's done all he can. He must check the others.

"Watch out for my family, Doc. Please. Please."

He wakes in the usual manner, trying to remember if he has slept. It has been a routine, down through the years—to go to bed alone, curled up with eyes clamped shut against the darkness. Then, all of a sudden, to blurt awake, exhausted from the experience of another night patrol.

Rolling out of bed, he limps to the shower, wounded by the burden of experience. Picture one who suffers, but he knows not from what. A blast of cold shower water changes the mood. His temperature drops. His heart pounds like a bass drum. The echo sounds like artillery salvos off in the distance. Stepping back in the stall, he lathers down then steps under the staccato of the pulsating shower head.

"Aaaah!" The tension ebbs away under the steady stream. "What a convenience the shower is!" he says out loud, then regrets the comment. His guilt recalls that some never made it back to the convenience.

"Fuck it!"

He twists the fixtures to off. In the sudden silence, the water rolling down the shower curtain becomes a humid jungle sound. Drip. Drip. Drip. The bamboo drinks.

"Airborne!" he shouts, ripping open the curtain. He leaps out of the stall as if from a C-130 troop carrier. He lands on the wet tile floor without slipping. A drop zone it ain't, but he still passes the test, another jump, another safe landing. Everything is okay. Without drying off, he slides into Levis, a jungle fatigue shirt, and Frye boots—his uniform—well fit, well worn.

"Ain't worn no underwear since '65," he brags to the mattress and poncho liner on the floor. "What a feat."

The toaster pops up Irish muffins. Butter melts into all the nooks and crannies. A steaming kettle whistles to freeze-dried coffee.

He moves the breakfast to a crate in the sparsely furnished living room. Sitting on cushions salvaged from a dead sofa, he rolls a taste of Uncle Ho's choice home-grown. It is a spur to the appetite. Firing up the appetizer, he puffs himself back from the edge into a second state of mind. He sits, contemplates, without eating, then gets up and retrieves the morning paper from the porch. He sits back in front of the food and discards all the news but the classified ads. This is the usual routine.

I'M LOOKING FOR YOU, WAR WIDOW. I'LL BE THE FATHER TO YOUR SON. WE WILL JOIN OUR HOPES TOGETHER, THEN THE WAR'LL BE WON.

Jobs, cars, and merchandise of every description. Dogs, homes and transplants of any size; he passes them all by going straight to the personal notices. To the bankruptcies, runaway pleas, and late birthday greetings, it's the same every day. He frowns, disappointed. His mind wanders, losing interest in the search for a salutation, a phrase, some signal to spark . . .

COMBAT BACHELOR, THE ETERNAL FLAME HAS DROWNED, I'M READY TO BE FOUND!

He crushes the newspaper in disbelief. It's her! He drops his head. His heart pounds itself to bruises.

Read it again!

He opens the newspaper in belief. Where was it? It's not here! Under personals . . . third column . . . on the right, not the left . . . above the fold . . . there!

. . . flame . . . drowned

. . . ready . . . found!

He recrushes the newspaper in relief. It *is* her! Leaping to his feet, he shouts, "It's paid off! War widow, I have found you!" Surprised by the echo that reverberates through the rooms, he quiets. Thoughts race through his psyche, the praying must have helped. He drops to one knee, head bowed in supplication.

"Thank you, man, thank you."

Looking for the war widow, as with any goal he wishes to attain, is like bobbing for apples. The event finds him on his knees, hands tied behind his back, at the edge of a washtub full of frothy water. The water leaps at the sides of the tub as apples bob and roll on its turbulent crest.

He bends over the tub, staring at the apples as a challenge. There is nothing else going on in the world but for this confrontation. There is nothing else to live for. Without thinking, he takes a gulp of air and plunges headfirst at what he believes he needs. Once under water, he opens his eyes. In the murky distortion, he nips at the vague blobs, breaking the skins. The apples slide off the offense. No sooner than he has tasted of the flesh, he swallows water, taking some into his lungs. With an underwater gasp, more water enters through the nose.

Cough!

An apple, any goal, quickly loses its appeal.

He bursts to the surface, gasping for air. Dizzy, burping water, he reels back from the challenge. Sitting on his heels, hands arrested in twine, water runs down a soaked head, wetting his chest and back. He coughs, retching from the waist, throwing stomach bile back into the tub. Eventually, he settles. The blear clears from his eyes, as does the fog covering his mind. He refocuses on the washtub. The apples bob complacently in the water. His heart sinks. The apples roll as a tease. Despair sets in. The apples spin as in a tempest. Hope ebbs away. Futility sets in. There is a strong urge to kill.

Damn! She really put an ad in the paper. I knew she would. I knew I'd find you, war widow. I knew we'd be together. There have been so many longing, lonely nights for both of us. He stands and claps his hands. Smack!

Releasing a curt, emotional fit. Then he makes two very tight fists.

"What if it's a hoax? Relax, slow down!"

He runs his hands through his hair, trying to soften the pounding thoughts and fears.

"Did she say 'drenched' or 'drowned'?"

He spins back to the paper, snares it, and peers . . . "drowned?" Crushing the news shut, he closes his eyes and sinks slowly into serenity. In the quiet, the peace, comes an affirmation, a culmination of patience and waiting. He rises and slowly paces across the creaking floor.

"I'll bring them here. They'll fill the empty closets with belongings, throw full carpets over the longing, cover the walls with family. She'll make this space smile sweetly."

He looks to one of the smoky, opaque windows. Her presence takes form before it. She steps to him, reaches out. "Let us share something more than grief. Come hold me."

He hesitates. "What about the boy?"

"I sent him on some errands. He's off on the bike you gave him. Now come." He follows her to their bedroom. Her shadow is elusive, but it is his. . . .

Replacing the scissors in the medicine cabinet, he pats the trim of the moustache and sideburns. He realizes the song he is humming . . . "Time goes by so slowly and time can do so much, my love, my darling . . ."

"God, I haven't heard that song in a long time," he says to the cabinet mirror. "Wonder why that all of a sudden popped up?" Without waiting for an answer, he rinses the sink of hair, shakes water from his hands, and wipes them on hip pockets. He tramps through the living space. The echo, as he crosses the floor, sounds like a battalion of paratroopers marching through the streets of victory. It's too bad no one else hears it.

Patting all pockets for keys, money, cigarettes, lighter, he affirms that everything is in order. He is ready to find her. What if she's not there?

"Shape up, little house, we are going to turn into a big home," he says as he exits. It doesn't echo, like so much he has said. Slam! He shuts the front door without locking it, leaps off the porch, and crosses the yard, walking under the drape of a willow tree. Amidst the willow's womb, he halts, puts hands to face to choke back the fear.

"Oh, God! What if she's not there?"

He charges out from the shroud; nothing can stop him, not even doubt or fear. He walks up to the motorcycle leaning at the curb.

"Look out, war widow! Here we come!" He inserts the key, turning on the only friend he's had since he lost his dog. He steps on the starter arm and kicks the machine to life. It coughs combustion. He throttles the engine up to a warm rev, leaps on, and scrunches his testicles.

"Goddam fucking nuts!"

He straddles the motor, adjusting his privates publicly. "Maybe I ought to start wearing underwear again. Gonna have to clean up my act with the war widow around, not to mention the kid."

A passerby, an elderly man dressed in a respectable fashion, turns at his comment.

"Have a nice day," he says to the elder. He sits back on the spine of the machine, whispers to himself, "Relax, G.I.," and pulls out into the street.

Moving through the city, waiting patiently at stoplights, obeying every stop sign, he's in no hurry when it's happening. There is a sense of freedom after all these years. Passing into the suburbs, he happens onto more open road. Looking to either side, he picks up speed. The motorcycle ride is reminiscent of those helicopter air assaults in the Nam time—the speed, the excitement, the wind, the openness. Hair flies free, the jungle fatigue jacket grips his chest.

Passing through the 1980s symmetry of living, these suburbs, he adjusts uncomfortably in his seat. He's never felt comfortable with his progress in America, yet it goes on all around him.

"Goddam, I forgot to pay the rent!" He mentally kicks himself. "Wake up, Doc. This ain't no fairy tale." He affirms his commitment to responsibility. Tightening his grip on the handlebars, he peers into the rearview mirrors at the disappearing suburbs. It confirms his decision.

"That's all right," he exclaims to the wind, to anyone listening. "Fairy tale or not, war widow, if you want to live in the suburbs, I'll live in the suburbs. I'll live anywhere with you."

The road opens up as he moves into a more rural area. He picks up the pace, a smooth, steady speed.

She had pulled the station wagon out from behind the stone wall, an exit from the lawn of monuments. She would tell the police that she comes here with her son and daughter every month to place flowers and a flag by his grave.

"The lantern's flame was out this time," she mumbles vacantly. "The flame had died out this time, hadn't it, Suzie?"

"Yes, Mommy."

The tears flow amongst the family.

"Excuse our tears, officer," she says, wiping them aside. "Even after all these years, the loss . . . the loneliness . . ."

The police officer nods understanding that the grief had kept her from seeing any distance. She hadn't meant to pull out in front of the motorcycle.

"I'm so sorry. I didn't see him coming."

His heart was ahead of himself. He was not paying

attention to the road ahead, a fatal lapse in the survival instinct. At the last, he reacted to avoid hitting the station wagon. Accelerating, he swerved into the oncoming lane. There was just enough time to lay the machine on its side, in mock protection, before he slid neatly under the front wheels of the tractor trailer.

Without a word, and who knows how many last thoughts, it's all over.